S0-BBC-118

Voices of the Country

Voices of the Country

Interviews with Classic Country Performers

Michael Streissguth

Routledge
New York and London

Published in 2004 by
Routledge
29 West 35th Street
New York, NY 10001

Published in Great Britain by
Routledge
11 New Fetter Lane
London EC4P 4EE

Copyright © 2004 by Michael Streissguth

Routledge is an imprint of the Taylor & Francis Group.
Printed in the United States of America on acid free paper.
Design and typesetting: Jack Donner, BookType

All rights reserved. No part of this book may be reprinted or reproduced or utilized
in any form or by any electronic, mechanical or other means, now known or here-
after invented, including photocopying and recording or in any information storage
or retrieval system, without permission in writing from the publisher.

Library of Congress Cataloging-in-Publication Data.

Streissguth, Michael.
   Voices of the country : interviews with classic country performers /
by Michael Streissguth
      p.   cm.
   Includes bibliographical references.
   ISBN 0–415–97041–5 (hb : alk. paper) — ISBN 0–415–97042–3
(pb : alk. paper)
   I. Country musicians—Interviews. I. Title.
ML394 .S87 2004
781.642'092'2—dc22
                                                    2003024530

To my Big Three Trio:
Emily, Cate, and Willie

CONTENTS

ACKNOWLEDGMENTS

So many individuals helped me as I researched, wrote, and edited *Voices of the Country*. I am particularly indebted to those who allowed me to interview them: Eddy Arnold, the late Chet Atkins, Anita Kerr, the late Red Kirk, Ginny Wright, Hank Locklin, Loretta Lynn, Charley Pride, the late Sheb Wooley, and Billy Walker. Thanks also to those who helped me arrange the interviews: Robert Edging, Fred Kewley, Jack Gale, Hank Adam Locklin, Schatzi Hagemen, John Daines, Linda Dotson, and Bettie Crook Walker.

When I first began interviewing blues singers many years ago, an endeavor that ultimately led me to country singers, my friend Johnny Sprague of Damascus, Maryland, almost always accompanied me to their shows and waited while I conversed with performers. Johnny and I met in the early 1980s when he was managing the bakery where I worked after school. I immediately learned about his fabulously large record collection, which spanned Americana and beyond, from the Johnson Mountain Boys to Muddy Waters to Washington D.C.'s sultan of insanity, the late Root Boy Slim. Together, sometimes with my brother David, we logged hours sifting through racks of used vinyl in shops such as the Music Trader in Frederick, Maryland, the Record Exchange in College Park, Maryland, and Orpheus Records in Washington, D.C.

The records stowed at home, we often drove his '76 Monte Carlo—with its impossibly long hood—to the Wax Museum, the Carter Barron Amphitheatre, Friendship Station, the Bayou, the Roxy, and other music venues in and around D.C. The best spot, though, was Twist and Shout in Bethesda, Maryland (later immortalized by Mary Chapin-Carpenter in her "Down at the Twist and Shout"). Although housed in a small VFW hall, giants trod on its linoleum floor: we saw Carey Bell, A. C. Reed, Hank Ballard, Sleepy LaBeef, and others whom we considered gigantic.

On Sunday nights, Johnny religiously taped Steve Hoffman's *Blues Experience* on WDCU-FM. Hoffman's playlist sliced through Washington's radio pap, unleashing blues new and old and necessitating more visits to the record stores.

Sadly, the *Blues Experience* and Twist and Shout have shuttered their doors. But Johnny is still around, and we still comb the record stores, although not as frequently since I've moved to New York. I am thankful for his friendship and for helping me discover new music.

I must also thank two editors who have supported me in recent years: Michael McCall, formerly of *Country Music* magazine (which is now, sadly, defunct) and Greg Loescher of *Goldmine*. Over the years, they have patiently listened to my story ideas and even bought a few. Portions of five interviews in this book first appeared in their magazines: Hank Locklin, Sheb Wooley, and Billy Walker in *Country Music*, and Charley Pride and Loretta Lynn in *Goldmine*.

I cannot forget two additional champions: Alanna Nash, author of *The Colonel: The Extraordinary Story of Colonel Tom Parker and Elvis Presley*, whose encouragement, tips, and observations keep me going, and Chrissie Dickinson, a wonderful writer who kindly published my work during her editorship at the *Journal of Country Music*.

My first editor is always Leslie Bailey Streissguth, my wife. She attacks lame prose and dubious observations, saving me enormous embarrassment. Thank you, Leslie. My friend and neighbor Ed Brown carefully edited the manuscript, probing various points and bringing elegance to more phrases and passages than I'd care to admit.

I am also grateful to Bob Ogles, Robbie Witkowski, Richard Weize, Gene Allan Carr, Mark James, and Steve Andreassi of the IUP Lodge and Convocation Center in Hoboken, New Jersey.

Finally, I thank Richard Carlin at Routledge, who agreed that the voices of the country deserve an unfiltered forum. Richard bought my first book at Schirmer Books. I'm happy that we have reconnected.

Introduction

On the cover of Studs Terkel's *Division Street: America*, small people, dwarfed by the steel and wooden El station, sauntered down the sidewalk of a Chicago neighborhood. Did the rattling trains on the entangled tracks above drown their conversation? What did they think about the Chicago world around them, torn in the 1960s by ethnic strife and political hurricanes? Intrigued, I bought Terkel's oral history of Chicago from the used bookstore, carried it to my college dorm room, and pored over the interviews with the city's homemakers, activists, laborers, and immigrants. It had been twenty years since the book was first published, but almost immediately *Division Street* enlivened my romance with the Windy City, a romance recently stirred to life by British writers Giles Oakley and Mike Rowe, who foraged through the city in the 1950s searching for the voices of blues music.

Terkel, in his foraging through Chicago, yielded Chicagoans who defined the city, who told its stories. They and their interviewer painted for me an alluring, ever-young place. But Terkel's cigar-stained hands had done more than capture a vision of Chicago: he had pulled open curtains to reveal the rewards of sitting down with somebody, rolling tape, and inviting conversation.

The urge to try it myself—to interview people—became irresistible when *Division Street* found a mate: Peter Guralnick's *Lost Highway*. It was Guralnick's second compendium of dispatches from the world of roots music, and its mingling on my nightstand, in my hands, on my desk, with *Division Street* that incited me. I picked it up for a couple bucks in a small bookstore next to the Uptown Theater on Connecticut Avenue in Washington D.C., and I devoured it like a novice reading the Gospels. Guralnick's stories, poignant and atmospheric, spotlighted Bobby "Blue" Bland, Otis Spann, Charlie Feathers, Sleepy LaBeef, and others living in the shadow of Elvis Presley.

The impulse to hear these artists' stories for myself and then connect them to their music drove me to scan concert listings for artists whom I might interview, and book and record stores for background on them. By the summer of 1985, closing in on nineteen, I was sitting on a motel room bed in Bethesda, Maryland, listening to the blind harpist Sam Myers as he reached back for stories about trade schools for the blind, switch-blade fights, and Elmore James. And tape was rolling.

Then there was blues queen Koko Taylor, in the night, her dark sweaty profile glistening against nearby stage lights. We chatted in her battered van that unbelievably had made it from Chicago to Fort Dupont Park in southeast Washington, D.C., while the blues of Lonnie Brooks thundered from the stage through the open window. (I would repeat a sweaty summer van interview many years later with country singer Billy Walker, only Billy—mindful of distracting noises—never rolled down the windows.) During the years that followed, when on breaks from college, I sat deep in Chicago's South Side with pianist Sunnyland Slim, in the basement of the Washington, D.C. Armory with Piedmont bluesman John Cephas, who was a carpenter there, backstage with Lowell Fulson in a New York nightclub. Through these encounters, I lived the dreams that Terkel and Guralnick had inspired.

Reflecting upon my reading of Terkel and Guralnick and my first face-to-face encounters with bluesmen and women from a distance of almost twenty years, it seems clear to me that life stories, not necessarily career stories, kept me—and Terkel and Guralnick, I gather—searching for interviews. Many of the musicians I interviewed had risen from the worst of American experiences—racism, poverty, despair, ignorance—to make an impression on American culture and articulate the plight of the poor, the oppressed, and the hopeful ones in search of escape. Their stories—shared in song and interviews—were deeply affected by the color of their skin, but they were by no means stories exclusive to blacks.

Blues performers weren't alone selling music informed by their experiences, as *Lost Highway* made clear. Like Guralnick's first book *Feel Like Going Home*, *Lost Highway* broke down music critics and scholars' barriers that divided black and white roots artists by touching on what made them cousins: their music that was their blood, their dogged pursuit of dreams, and their humble rural beginnings that informed their music and helped them maintain an artist-audience bond.

Country, I came to understand, wasn't so far from the blues. (This is a mantra that Charley Pride recites later in this book.) So when I began writing in the mid-1990s about country, the music of the white South, I found that the stories in conversations that made me forget about my questions or forget to change tapes or forget where I was were the stories about making the crop, about the candy pullings where fiddles and dancers converged, about the white-knuckled negotiation with the Depression. Of course my interviews covered much more than life and grind around the ol' homeplace, but that core subject and its place in my subjects' music fascinated me.

Country music, like blues, is often judged by the performer's origins. That's a standard we hold for few other musical genres. Do people care if a classical pianist comes from Hazard or Hamberg? No way. But many look askance at country artists who haven't grown up in rural American settings or who do not at least acknowledge country roots in some way. This umbilical connection between rural America and its country music is sacred and often defended with righteous indignation when cut into by radio consultants and recording executives or anybody else. The indignation heightens precipitously when men and women who broke through as country artists attempt to forsake country music's roots. Just ask Eddy Arnold, Ray Price, or Faith Hill, artists who were raised up in the rural South but who weathered critical storms when they began edging toward a purely pop sound. An artist's bond with the country or with country music roots remains central to his or her music's veracity. Country music scholar Bill C. Malone echoes this opinion: "If I'm unable to believe that the performer has actually 'lived' the life that is sung about, I want to believe that he or she respects the culture that surrounded the music."[1] In country, it's never been about just the music. The voices of the country mean something too.

As I WRITE THIS, the soundtrack from the Coen brothers' O Brother Where Art Thou has reached five million and with every ring of the cash register, the album's effect seems to grow in kind. In a media landscape that was largely devoid of traditional music, suddenly bluegrass concerts air during public television fundraising, Ralph Stanley appears in rock arenas, and sweetly spun singing in the style of Emmylou Harris and Alison Kraus dreamily rises from Merman-like sirens such as Reba McIntyre and the Dixie Chicks. Who would have thought that the soundtrack from a film featuring a pencil-mustachioed George Clooney would carry traditional country music and bluegrass out of the American Legion halls and the obscure Saturday morning radio slots, debunking the myth that people don't care anymore? This book, even, is an outgrowth, inspired by my belief that many after all *are* interested in the lives of the people who helped bring country music to where it is today. If not for O Brother, these interviews may have lain in boxes strewn around my dark and dusty attic, trampled over by my children on imaginary adventures.

These interviewees have roots dyed in the same tradition that imbues *O Brother*. Even Eddy Arnold, who first took country uptown in the late 1940s, grew up steeped in the culture that hewed country music. He soaked up Jimmie Rodgers' records on a wind-up player and the local fiddle wizards who cavorted in his midst, and—as his early Tennessee Plowboy billing suggests—he knew well the back end of a mule. Experiences such as these, which Loretta Lynn, Charley Pride, Chet Atkins, and the rest share, infuse their music with meaning true to country music's origins. It is only relatively recently, within the past twenty years, as these historical artists have receded from the day-to-day musical mix, that country music has strayed from its rural moorings.

Arnold, Lynn, Pride, and Atkins, of course, were admitted to the Country Music Hall of Fame in return for their contributions to country music, and others spotlighted here, Hank Locklin, Sheb Wooley, and Billy Walker, for example, who may never make the Hall of Fame, still receive honor for their lifting on behalf of country music. Locklin and Walker are regularly invited back to country music's mother ship, the *Grand Ole Opry*, and they are remembered for their many hits: Locklin for "Please Help Me I'm Falling" and "Send Me the Pillow that You Dream On," and Walker for "Charlie's Shoes" and "Cross the Brazos at Waco."

But there is yet another tier of artists considered in this book. They bubble and flare like magma in the subterranean, below the Hall of Famers, below the journeymen. Their names—Red Kirk and Ginny Wright—are virtually unknown to those who discuss, listen to, and write about country music; they are barely footnotes in country music history, but that doesn't mean their stories deserve to be muted. In fact, their insights tell us a lot about toil outside fame's glare, outside Nashville, where Ginny Wright seems never to have worked and where Red Kirk trod only occasionally. Furthermore, their relative obscurity means their answers to questions crackle with newness, unlike those who've unceasingly repeated recollections for historians and reporters. Perhaps their responses are tainted by the bitterness of fame denied, but they are nonetheless fresh and informative. Their stories also remind us that for every Marty Robbins or Tammy Wynette who emerged from rural obscurity to find lasting appeal in the spotlight, there are hundreds who got close and failed. There are hundreds who try today, and there will be hundreds who try tomorrow. Most will find work in fields other than music, perhaps in agriculture, computers, or retail. But many will surrender their dreams at some point. Red and Ginny didn't. Even after seeing that they would never be *Billboard* monarchs, they continued returning to the studio, picking up a weekend gig, or pitching a song to someone who could do something with it. (Kirk died shortly before a planned song-pitching trip to Nashville.) Nor did they forget that except for a few mis-calculations, the plotlines of their lives might have developed differently. Their stories, as presented in this collection, are among the best.

All of the artists herein show us a variety of stages and faces in country music. Red Kirk hung around Knoxville, an often overlooked farm team city to the major league town of Nashville, where he slouched in sedan back-seats with giants-in-waiting such as Don Gibson and Chet Atkins on mid-night rides home from school house shows. Ginny Wright witnessed intimately—too intimately, she might say—the dealings of Fabor Robison, who figured prominently in the careers of Jim Reeves, Johnny Horton, the Browns, and others, yet left a world in which nary a person spoke well of him. Billy Walker toured with Hank Williams in the singer's final days upon this earth and witnessed Elvis Presley's first big Memphis show; Hank Lock-lin muddled along in the mire of song publisher and Four Star Records owner Bill McCall, who a few years later would stymie Patsy Cline with unreasonable contracts. Artist and repertoire (A&R) representatives Chet Atkins and Anita Kerr reveal glimpses of the Nashville studios and the per-sonalities who haunted them. And, in turn, artists in this book peer back at Atkins and Kerr and at country music's other great producers: Owen Bradley, Don Law, Steve Sholes, and Jack Clement.

To be sure, oral history is not the perfect telling of history. It often suffers from warped memories and perspectives. In editing this collection, therefore, I discarded what seemed too warped, and where statements seemed obscure on first glance, I added notes for clarification. I also attempted to place the interviews in context with introductions to each of them, and by adding fur-ther elucidating information such as *Billboard* chart data, dates, places, and so forth.

Readers should know that in addition to throwing out responses with dubious probity and adding clarifying notes, I took other measures, such as rearranging the order of questions to improve readability and deleting ques-tions and responses that seemed irrelevant to the discussion of country music and the artists' lives and careers.

In the final analysis, the artists featured in this book deserve to be heard from directly, and judged accordingly. They are voices of country, fiber of the music.

Note

1. Bill C. Malone, *Don't Get above Your Raisin': Country Music and the Southern Working Class*. Urbana: University of Illinois Press, 2002.

Eddy Arnold
Seems Like a Dream

EDDY ARNOLD HAS ALL THE MARKINGS of a man's man. His tall, rugged appearance and deep, homespun voice suggest the mingling of John Wayne and Andy Griffith: solid guy, charming, practical. He's loyal to his friends and business associates—as I learned when my biography of Arnold angered his manager back in the 1990s. And he gets along as easily with the governor of Tennessee as he does with Bobby the glass cutter who rents a building from him.

But Eddy wasn't always so together. Such was apparent early in his career when shady wheelers and dealers fleeced him of newly earned money, and when RCA executives, hovering about recording sessions in the 1940s, made him quiver. In my interviews with him, he remembered clinging to one engineer at those sessions, friendly Jeff Miller: "He was a familiar face. I hope you understand where I'm coming from. I'm a boy from down South. I know I'm fooling with Yankees, and I don't know 'em and they don't know me. I don't know whether they liked what I'm doing or not. I knew what I was doing was doing pretty good. That's the reason I wanted the same engineer. He understood me, and I could talk to him."

Such comments and others in the following interview reveal a country boy—later a man's man—negotiating the bends in a road to fame. And even though that road often veered away from country tastes and sounds, it never really left the country. Arnold was inescapably country, fashioned by its music, insularity, and day-to-day challenges, and that's hard to keep in mind when listening to his fabulously lush hits of the 1960s, such as "Turn the World Around" and "Then You Can Tell Me Goodbye."

Chester County, Tennessee, in the 1920s and 1930s was flat-land farm country east of Memphis and south of Jackson, the kind of place—like the hills of southwestern Virginia or the plains of Texas—that birthed and nourished country music. When Eddy was growing up there, he heard traditional fiddles and ballads on surrounding farms, and encountered real rural hardship: back-breaking work, fickle markets for farm products, and splintered living conditions. There was tragedy, too, the kind that showed up so often in Carter Family songs and Vernon Dalhart ballads: on his eleventh birthday his father died, leaving widow and children to face accumulated debts and the auctioneer's gavel. Their land was sold on the bank steps in nearby Henderson on a mid-December day in 1930, and the Arnolds, once fairly prosperous landowners, faced Christmas as lowly tenant farmers. So, Eddy knew about life's bite. When he sang on his first Victor record about a woman who abandoned her child to "go out on a party," he related to a child's loss of a parent, and sympathetically recited the chorus: "Mommy, please stay home with me."

ONCE KNOWN AS THE TENNESSEE PLOWBOY because of his farming origins, Arnold is the sole surviving member of an exclusive fraternity that accelerated country music's hard-charging commercial momentum. Working from a foundation that Jimmie Rodgers and the Carter Family laid in the 1920s, Arnold, along with other titans such as Ernest Tubb, Red Foley, and Hank Williams, carried rural sounds to the ever-growing record markets and filled the expanding mass media space that by the mid- to late 1940s saw a proliferation of disc jockey shows and programming featuring live country music (much of it modeled after Nashville's *Grand Ole Opry* and Chicago's *National Barn Dance*).

Ultimately, Hank Williams rang loudest through country music history, thanks to his lurid flare out early in life, personal charm, and sexy rhythms and lyrics. But back in the 1940s nobody equaled Eddy Arnold's record sales. And nobody appealed more to listeners beyond the South and the farm. With performances spun with soft fiber, such as "Molly Darling," "Anytime," and "Bouquet of Roses," Arnold foraged into the mass, urban-based markets, clearing a path to country music's future viability.

In the 1950s and into the 1960s, Arnold strove to complete the transformation, to be known as something other than a hillbilly singer who occasionally crosses into the mainstream. "Eddy Arnold was going to have a new image—not a phony one, but a true image, as true as anything I could ever hope to be," he wrote in his autobiography. "People would know it and they would accept it."[1] With the assistance of his A&R man Steve Sholes at Victor Records and New York–based management (obtained after dumping huckster-ish manager Col. Tom

Parker in 1953) the transformation began. He left the Nashville studios for New York, dropped the fiddles and steel guitar from his band, recorded with jazzy groups and large orchestral ensembles, and strove for television stardom.

Initially, the experiment failed, doused in the storm of rock and roll and stymied by Arnold's unease in a purely pop-oriented musical environment. He was more at home in Nashville, which was plain to hear on his sluggish renderings of "September Song" and other pop standards. "I think he was still basically a real true country singer," observed his 1950s arranger and comanager Charles Grean. "I don't think he could, even today, sing songs that are pop."[2]

Arnold found the anecdote to his 1950s doldrums when he steered his career back to Nashville. There, in the 1960s, RCA producer-guitarist Chet Atkins and arranger-conductor Bill Walker constructed a pop-oriented sound in the studio that melded beautifully with Arnold's country-hewn vocal style. A new career exploded like flood water over a levee, thanks also to his new manager: aggressive Jerry Purcell, whose loud barking could intimidate the most unflappable of RCA officials. After years away from the top tiers of the country and pop charts, Arnold returned and, with Purcell's television and concert contacts, the singer became an international figure and a regular presence on network television.

The one time plowboy was forever established as a country-pop star, close to the goal he had set for himself in the 1950s. In conversation, he revels in his status, dwelling little on his setback in the 1950s. One might expect him, then, to deny his rural past. But this balladeer, who performed in a tuxedo for many years, speaks of his rural roots in great detail, although not with great passion. As a practical man's man might say, his rural roots are just part of who he became.

Dick Wright. That was my mother's father, and he came to live with us when I was a little boy. I became his pet. I'm serious about that, really his pet, because he was blind and I was his eyes. I led him everywhere he went. We had outside plumbing in the rural area. I led him to the toilet. I led him wherever he went. He was the jolliest old man. He had cataracts. If he was alive today, they would remove them and he could see.

He used to tell me stories. I just hope to live as long as he lived and be as good natured as he was. I used to play tricks on him. He'd sit on the front porch. People in the country sat on the front porch in a swing.

Particularly in the spring and the summertime, he'd sit there because the poor old fellow was blind. He couldn't do anything else. I'd get out of the back part of the house and go down the little road that went up to the main road and then I'd walk into our house. He'd be sitting on the front porch and I'd change my voice. Of course, he was looking for somebody to come in and sit down and talk to him. I'd change my voice and say, "Hello Mr. Wright." He'd say, "Hello there. Come on in and sit down. Talk to me." Then I'd go in and he'd realize that it was me. Then he'd grab me, put me across his lap, and play spank. I'm sure I entertained him a lot by doing that. I played tricks on him, but he thought the world of me. Wherever he went, I went with him.

They told me when I was a boy that my Grandfather Wright fought for the South and my Grandfather Arnold fought for the South, but he had a brother who fought on the other side. But you know families were split over that war. It was the most useless war, probably, that's ever been fought. Anyway, they fought it. I made up my mind since I got older and did a lot of reading. I say, "Why did they fight and kill one another over this?"

You mentioned that you had outdoor plumbing. Did you have electricity?

No. Oh gosh, no. We had lamps that you'd put kerosene in. We called it coal oil. Our heat in our house was a wood heater. Not like the wood heaters that you can buy today that really put out a lot of heat. We didn't have a fireplace. We had this heater and stove pipes. They came down the chimney and then out of the wall. The stove pipes came down to the heater. We went to bed pretty early, bank the fire so you'd still have coals the next morning to start another fire, bank the coals with ashes. It was tough, but at that time I didn't realize how tough it was. When you're a little boy, you don't know much about that. You grow up in it and it was part of life as far as I knew.

You had a windup Victrola.

Yes. Later on. That's where I heard a lot of music. I used to hear records by different people: Jimmie Rodgers, the Carter Family, Gene Austin, Kate Smith. Golly, I can't think of all of them, 78 records. I have now a windup record player like the one we had on the farm. It was a cabinet. My sister was older than me, and she went away to St. Louis and got her a job. She worked in a store in St. Louis called Famous Barr; it was a big department store in St. Louis. One Christmas she sent us that record player. We didn't have money to buy a record player. She sent us that record player: a Victrola.

Up until that, I had heard other people's [record players]. At a farmer's house, some of them might have a Victrola. Not all of them. I finally knew one man that got a radio. It had a battery in it, a great big battery. I'd go over there sometimes at night and listen to that radio. It was a real novelty.

I've read that you listened to Atlanta radio station WSB and heard Pete Cassell.

Yeah. And I listened to the Nashville station [WSM], and I listened to the Chicago station, WLS.

A woman who knew you in childhood told me, "He never would date nobody. He just dated that guitar."

That's right. I didn't have any money. I was embarrassed to date a girl. Until I got a little older, I didn't have any money to buy an ice cream cone. That's what you did then, go to Henderson to the drug store and get an ice cream cone. I wasn't a boozer. You didn't do those things then.

The same woman remembered you talking by the woodpile at school saying you were going to make some money with your voice and not farm anymore.

That's what I wanted to do because I couldn't see any future in being [a farmer]. I couldn't buy a farm. I had no money to buy a farm. All I knew to do was work. There was one family that lived on one side of us, the Stovall family. There were three daughters, and I used to help their father work on the farm, Mr. Joe Stovall. He was a good man. From time to time, he needed another man, another helper.

After my father died, they had an auction sale and auctioned off much of our implements. They auctioned off our cultivator. They auctioned off some of our mules, some of our cows, and we didn't have a cultivator then. Mr. Stovall had an extra two-horse cultivator. I bought it from him and paid him in labor for it, so we could cultivate a crop. In those days a two-horse cultivator was worth something to a farmer. I used to go help him work when I wasn't working at home, whatever he had to do, if he was hauling hay or if he was cutting firewood or fixing a fence or anything.

I was very good friends with Mr. Obe Latham and his sons. I used to go over and play with the Latham boys. That's where I was when my father died. I knew what was wrong. It was in the afternoon. The bell always rang for what we call lunch, but in the country it was dinner. My mother rang that bell. It was a big bell. You always knew when dinner was ready. You'd work in the fields until that bell rang. When it rang in the afternoon, I knew it was my father because he was in bad health. He had high blood pressure. Of course, in those days they couldn't control it. They didn't have the medicines to control it. And I'm sure he worried a lot about his debts. That may have hastened [his demise].

Did the fact that the land wasn't in your family anymore sharpen your resolve to leave?

Didn't own it, and as I kept growing, I wanted to do something to earn a livelihood.

Somebody remembers you cutting hair and another remembers you selling Cloverine salve.

Yeah. I don't apologize for it. You'd sell anything to earn a dime. That all seems like a dream to me. I did. I'd do that. I'd work. When I got just a little older, I'd work in the summertime. I'd get a job cutting timber. I remember very well, I worked for a fellow that was cutting piling which was cypress timber and they made telephone poles out of it. It was cut off the place we lived on. It was in the swamps and they would dry up in the summer. Otherwise, you'd be in mud and water up to here. In the summer, you'd cut it, throw it, skin it to take the bark off, snake it out, that means drag it out. I did a lot of things like that. Anything to make a dime. It was just hard to get something to do.

It would take two men, another person and me. We were not the only ones down there cutting. There were other people cutting. When you're cutting a tree, and it's a high tree or any kind of tree, you got to know how to chip it down here to make it fall this way or that way. I learned how to do that. I was strong as an ox for a guy my size because I worked all the time.

A lot of people said that they were skeptical about you leaving and saying you were going to earn a living with your music. Were you aware of that?

I suppose they did. So many rural people have problems seeing past their nose. They don't know what's out there. I thought I knew what was out there. I went and seldom ever went back. I just went. I tried to send my mama money when I'd get a little money. My mother . . . I don't think she ever realized really what happened to me. I tried to tell her a couple of times. She lived with me. She died in 1950, and I was already earning a lot of money at that time on records, earning *a lot* of money in anybody's book.

At what age did you leave the farm and go to Jackson?

I think about 18.

You sang on WTJS radio in Jackson.

There was an act down there. A fella by the name of Bill Wesbrooks had a little act that was on the radio everyday. This was after I'd been there one time. I went down there one time when I was going to school and our school went down and did a program on a Saturday. And then after that.... In the rural area, you always sit on the front porch and I did. And there was a man that came by selling subscriptions to the newspaper, the *Jackson Sun*, which owned the radio station. The fella came by there selling, and I strummed him a little song. He invited me to come down and take an audition and I did and I went down there. Later on, I got a call from this fella Wesbrooks that was on that station because he had a little group. He wanted me to come down and join him, and I went down on that station. I got a little job and didn't make hardly any money. We'd do some little appearances and make a little money. But I got a job on the side there working in a funeral home which gave me a place to sleep. They had an ambulance service at that time. I did a lot of work on that extra. I got paid by the job.... I did more work on the ambulance than I did on the funeral side. In those days, the funeral homes owned the ambulances.

This was an ambulance that would pick up . . .

. . . people who'd been injured, a woman going to the hospital to have a baby, a woman going home from the hospital after having a baby.

There's a story about someone dying . . .

. . . in my arms. Oh gosh, yeah. A young fella that had shot himself. We got there before he died and we put him in the ambulance to take him to the hospital. I never forgot that. A young man like that. I'm serious. That shook me.

[The man who owned the funeral home] and I one day buried a man, just the two of us. A bum had died. We didn't know who he was. We had no name. There was no funeral, just Mr. Smith, George Smith [and I]. We buried that man, if you don't think that'll shake you up. Oh man . . . I'll tell you, it will make you think.

You must have gotten used to people being bloodied. At some point you get used to that.

I guess you would. That helped me along the way, I'll tell you. I helped haul more mothers-to-be to the hospital and mothers that had just had babies that came home. I did more of that and learned how to pick them up with another person. They taught me how to place your hands under their body, one man here, another man here to pick them up without hurting them.

You played in the morning on WTJS?
Usually around noon.

Would you get paid by the radio station?
Seems like very little. I might get a dollar or something, very little.

But you were able to get some money from gigs, people would write in for you.
We'd go out and do performances at schools and that kind of thing. We didn't play clubs; we didn't have that kind of group. It was more show, song, funny stuff, that kind of thing.

Can you recall the songs you would have done?
I used to sing a song that Gene Autry had. I know you never heard of it. Of course, I used to sing one he made popular called "Silver Haired Daddy of Mine." But he also had another one that I really liked, "If You'll Let Me Be Your Little Sweetheart."

How did you first meet your fiddler Speedy McNatt?
Oh! He lived out in Luray. His father had a little store out there. He came down and we both worked on [WTJS], and then we all went over to a station in Memphis [WMPS] and we were there a couple of weeks and then they fired us. Speedy and I caught the train and went to St. Louis. . . . I went up there and my sister and this older half brother, they were living together, my sister and my half brother, so we stayed with them for just a few days. We got out and got us some little bookings in a little club and went up and auditioned on the radio station and got on the radio station and got us a place to live on the corner of Euclid and Laclede. Some things you don't forget.

You all lived very frugally.
Ate a lot of hamburgers. I think it was a White Castle. A hamburger for breakfast. A hamburger for lunch. A hamburger for dinner.

Were you and Speedy known as the Golden Lager Boys?
Yeah. Delighted to get [the sponsor] . . . never dreamed. . . . Times were so hard, and I wasn't well known. I hadn't made a record. I just played in clubs.

I wasn't a name so I couldn't do concerts because I didn't have the drawing power. I had not *arrived*.

I read that a fellow named Emil Houseman helped get you on KWK in St. Louis, and he did a program sponsored by Griezedick Beer. Did that gentleman help you get on the air?

Yeah. But Griezedick Beer wasn't our sponsor. That's a well known beer in St. Louis. Let me tell you something about Griezedick Beer: On that station KWK, which was physically in the Chase Hotel, one of the funniest things I can ever remember happening [happened]. Griezedick Beer is a prominent family in St. Louis. (You wouldn't think so with a name like that. Griezedick Beer! Good God!). They owned this beer company in St. Louis. I guess it would be 1938. We were on this station, and they elevated a new pope. There was two announcers on that station at that time. Allan C. Anthony was the chief announcer there and a good one, who later was the announcer on one of the network programs for Milky Way candy. He had a very good speaking voice. Then there was another announcer by the name of Bill Edwards on that station. He was in one studio and Allan Anthony was in the other, and Bill wasn't listening to what Allan Anthony was saying. He had a button and when he punched that button, his microphone would be live and he'd start talking. He was about to do a commercial, read a commercial. They were getting ready to take the network feed, and the pope was going to speak from Rome. Allan Anthony, in one studio, said, "And now friends I hope you'll stay with us because the next voice you will hear will be the voice of Pope [Pius XII]." And with that Bill Edwards pushed the button and said, "I'll take Griezedick Brothers Beer." The station manager, the program manager, secretaries and everything fell out of their offices because they were getting ready to hear the pope. I think Speedy and I were up there just fooling around. It was in the afternoon. That was one of the funniest things that ever happened. [Guffaws].

Did I tell you why I called him Speedy? He was slow. He had a hard time waking up. He was prone to being late, a little bit. So I just called him Speedy. He and I we were broke, but we had laughs. We really did. Single . . . didn't mind nothing.

What were the songs you were singing in St. Louis?

To tell you a particular song would be hard. I'd do some of the Jimmie Rodgers because I saw some of his folios in that time and some of the Gene Autry folios. I can't remember a song at this point.

Did you do popular songs?

Sometimes, but mostly the country type.

You left St. Louis to join Pee Wee King.

I was working in St. Louis and I had an old car that had a little radio on it. I drove down to west Tennessee to visit my mother, and I'm listening to the radio station that Pee Wee was on. He was on in the morning, around eight or nine o'clock. I just happened to catch him accidentally when I turned on that station. I flipped over there and there he was on the radio. Of course, I was familiar with him. I noticed that his male singer wasn't on with him that day, and I thought, "Well I wonder if he needs a male singer?" So when I went back to St. Louis, I wrote him a letter and told him that I sang and I played the guitar and so forth. If he was interested in what I could do, I'd send him a transcription. We didn't have tape then. So, I was working on a little station there in St. Louis called KXOK, and I went down and there

Eddy Arnold with the Pee Wee King outfit. Left to right: Arnold, Joe Zinkan, Pee Wee King, unidentified, unidentified, Texas Daisy, Speedy McNatt, Redd Stewart. Courtesy of Library of American Broadcasting.

was a program director by the name of Blaine Cornwall, mighty nice man, and I told him I wanted to do a few little songs on a transcription. He said, "I'll do it. I'll help you." So I went in the studio with my two or three musicians and did two or three things and mailed it down to Pee Wee. Obviously, I didn't know what his management situation was. It turned out his father-in-law was his manager, a man by the name of J. L. Frank, and I heard back from Mr. Frank.

They sent me a little note that said, "Come on down here."

Did Pee Wee dub you Smilin' Eddy Arnold?

Yeah. He and his father-in-law. I don't know what that meant. I don't know how that helped, but we did that. I worked for Pee Wee for about three and a half years. Didn't make any money because times were tough. Of course, I wasn't known. Nobody knew me. I wasn't a name is what I'm saying. I really became his master of ceremonies. I was capable of doing that and played the rhythm guitar. Sometimes sing solos and sometimes I'd sing in his trio, he had a vocal trio. I got a lot of experience with Pee Wee.

You did the Camel Caravan with him.

I did. We went to seems like every military camp that existed. Had a truck fixed up where the side planks would unhinge, you could let 'em down, and make a stage. It wasn't a bad stage at all. We had lighting. We had a sound system that we carried with us. That's how we performed for the military, you know. Took along pretty little girls in little shorts, and they had trays of cigarettes and they would just wander through the audience, the soldiers, and give away cigarettes.

Do you remember the reaction of the soldiers?

They loved it. They saw pretty girls in tights. The soldiers were hungry for entertainment, hungry for it.

We went to Panama, the Panama Canal Zone. We began to wonder if we were ever going to get home from Panama. Finally they had a plane. One of the generals down there arranged to fly us to Guatemala. We stayed there, I think, two or three weeks waiting for another plane to get out of Guatemala to Brownsville, Texas. When we got to Brownsville we were in the United States then, and something tells me . . . I'm trying to remember if our equipment met us in Brownsville or was it Houston to get back to Nashville. I remember riding on the back of that truck all the way from . . . it may have been Houston . . . there to Nashville. Rode on the back of that truck and was glad to get back.

That two or three weeks in Guatemala, you were just waiting around?

It was the dullest thing I ever did in my life. Guatemala. There wasn't anything for us to do. We'd stay in the hotel, get up in the morning, and get breakfast and get out on the street and stand around. There wasn't anything to do. We were just killing time, trying to get out. 'Cause the war was heating up. I'll never forget one day I was standing out in front of the little ol' hotel and I look down and I saw a man coming up the street carrying a living room suite, a couch and two chairs, on his head. He had that couch up on his head and had a chair sitting on top of that on one end and another chair on top on the other side. Trudging up the street. I've never seen that before in my life. I'm sure the guy had no truck. He just had to carry that living room set home. That really hit me.

Did you get a deferment because you were with the Caravan?

No. I had a little problem. They examined me and sent me home.

Were there problems traveling with Pee Wee, gas rationing, synthetic rubber? Did you have many accidents?

I had one accident. I was traveling with Pee Wee's father-in-law and a truck hit us, a truck with a trailer. We were going from Knoxville to Asheville and met a truck on a curb. It was raining. It was slick, and the trailer just slid clear around and hit us in the side. It didn't hurt us. It didn't hurt me. But it did quite a bit of damage to the car. I was working with Pee Wee, but I was traveling with his father-in-law. The two of us were in the car, just us.

We had one other little accident when we went to Louisville and spent the winter up there. I remember a place in Indiana when one night we were driving back into Louisville. We were doing early programs and then working out at night, which meant we didn't get enough sleep, never. Wherever we stopped you had to rest or I did. Pee Wee would kiddingly call me "the singer." We were going down the highway and everybody got tired. I heard somebody say "Let's make the singer drive." Well, the singer started driving and I went to sleep and went off the road. Didn't damage the car luckily and didn't hurt any of us. But I went off the road. When we got straightened up again I said to Pee Wee, "I guess that'll teach you to make me drive at night when I'm worn out."

Later you saw the opportunity to perform as a solo.

One day I went to the manager of the radio station [WSM] who really helped put that Camel Caravan together, but he was general manager of the radio station. A man by the name of Harry Stone. I was a young fellow. At this point, I had my mother and I had my wife and I wanted to do a little better financially. I knew Harry Stone really liked what I was doing. He told me two or three times when I was out with the Caravan. He'd hear me sing and hear me talk. He liked what I was doing, and I knew that. So one day I walked around to his office and I said, "I want to go to work for you. I can't really get ahead with Pee Wee. Pee Wee's a wonderful person, but I'm not progressing and I'm a young man. I'd like to go to work for you." He said, "I don't see any reason why I can't use you." He made it possible for me to get little spots on the radio station where I'd earn money. Things began to click on radio for me.

He helped me get a record contract. He went to Chicago to a [National Association of Broadcasters] meeting, and he had lunch with an old gentleman in the music publishing business there that he'd known for a long time. A very successful old fellow, Mr. Fred Forester, and he had lunch with Mr. Forester. Mr. Forester was very close to the executives at Victor Records and at Decca Records, all of them. I had auditioned for all of them except Victor and none of them needed me. Harry went to lunch with Mr. Forester and told Mr. Forester, "There's a young boy down there on my station doing pretty good. He's young; he sings good." Mr. Forester said, "When you think he's ready I'll make a pitch for him at Victor." A man ran Victor at the time by the name of Frank Walker. I didn't know him. Harry said, "Well he's ready now." When Forester picked up the phone long distance to Frank Walker in New York and told him about me, I got a wire from Frank Walker asking me if I'd be interested in making records for the Victor company.

They first recorded you in Nashville at WSM?

They had no studios here then. I went up in the radio studio and did a couple of sessions. I just got my guys and got around the microphone. The engineer and I kind of worked it out. I was singing the songs; I'd done all of them dozens of times. That's what I did. They released 'em. There wasn't a hit in the bunch, but they made money. The Victor company realized there was something here. I got a letter from Mr. Walker telling me he was going to leave the company and he was going over and form a record company called MGM and there would be a young man taking over his duties in the Victor company by the name of Steven H. Sholes. That scared me to death. I didn't know Mr. Walker much less know Steven H. Sholes and being young and green the first thing I said to myself was "What in the heck will happen to me? I don't know Mr. Walker much less Mr. Sholes."

I didn't meet Steve, but he listened to the records they had released and I got a long distance call from him. Of course, I was very apprehensive when I got his call. I thought, "What's he going to do, cancel my contract?" On the contrary, he liked what he heard. He wanted to bring me into Chicago to their studio and record me. So I did. I went up to Chicago and took my musicians. I got, I believe, two hits out of that session. I got "I'll Hold You in My Heart," and I got "That's How Much I Love You."[3] "That's How Much I Love You" was released and just in a few weeks it was a hit. Jukeboxes meant a lot then. It was on every jukebox everywhere.

He was the greatest thing that happened to me, Steve was. Because he liked me. It wasn't very long after he got there that I became a good seller. He found good songs for me. After I went into Chicago a couple of times and recorded, he started bringing me into New York. I'd go to New York and record because there were no studios here. I'd go on the train, take my guys, my musicians. I wouldn't take a bass player because Charlie Grean would play bass for me because he was good.

Did Grean also help with arrangements?

In a sense. There wasn't much arranging for what I was doing. I usually had learned the song before I went there. It was me singing a chorus, the steel guitar would play a chorus and me sing another chorus. It was about over then. But they were selling.

One time I went up [to New York]. It was just when I had several hits, and I didn't realize really how much I was selling. I was selling tremendously well. And I thought all those pop artists were selling a lot more records than I was. It turned out, I learned in later years, I was outselling all of them. It didn't cost anything to make my records. They'd have a pop date with Como or Mindy Carson or Vaughn Monroe or somebody and have twenty-five, thirty musicians. Well, somebody's got to pay for that. I'd go into the studio with five musicians. Voom! The man running the record division by the name of Jim Murray, he was Steve's boss. I'm up there and going to record. Steve's got me on the phone and says, "Mr. Murray wants to meet you." I said, "Okay. What does he want to meet me for?" He said, "He just wants to meet you." I'm very naive at this stage. I thought, "What's he going to do to me. He's a big shot, he'll cancel my contract." I didn't know. He said, "Come a little early." I was going to meet him on 24th Street. They had a studio on 24th Street. That's where their offices were. It wasn't RCA back then, it was just Victor. Well I went early and he took me around to Mr. Murray's office. Mr. Murray stood up and shook hands with me and said, "Be seated young man. I've been wanting to meet you. I see the sales figures come across my desk every Monday morning and I want to know what you look like." I said, "Well fine, sir." I realized then I was selling a lot of records. Their profit margin was very good. I was selling *a lot* of records. I'll never forget that day.

On your first session [in 1944] you recorded "The Cattle Call." Was that the first yodeling you had done?

No. I'd been yodeling a long time, but the yodeling thing sort of went out with Jimmie Rodgers. People would yodel but it wouldn't sell records for some reason. There was a guy on radio in between there that could really yodel up in St. Louis, on a station there. I'm going back to the days when you'd use live talent on radio stations. He was popular. He could really yodel. Whoo! He could break that wall right there. Skeets Yaney. And he made some records, but nothing happened. That's the reason I never did a lot of yodeling. The only time I would yodel was when I had a reason to yodel. "Cattle Call" was a reason. That's authentic.

You knew how to do it.

Oh yes, I know how to do it. I learned it from listening to Jimmie Rodgers, Gene Autry. When I heard those guys yodel, I could do it. I don't know why I could do it and somebody else couldn't do it, I could just do it. My voice couldn't go as high as some guys, like Skeets, Elton Britt. But it didn't mean nothing on records. It just didn't mean anything. So I said, "The best thing for me to do was find me a good love song and sing the song." I did "Cattle Call," and I did one other song, "Cowpoke" [in 1962].

When you went to New York to record was that the first time you'd ever been to New York City?

Yeah.

What were your impressions?

Big city. Oh, God.

On one of my trips going up there to record, was when I met Gene Autry for the first time. This is 1946, and he was just out of the service. He was on his way to New York to appear at Madison Square Garden at a rodeo and I was on the train, left here about four o'clock in the afternoon. I'd take a Pullman, the little train would go to Cincinnati. Gene, unbeknownst to me, got on in Cincinnati. Don't know what he was doing there, but he got on the train in Cincinnati going to New York. So I had already been in the dining car, eating my food, and I went back to my little compartment and sat and read a little bit. Then I thought, "I'll walk up in the club car." Walked up in there and there sat Gene talking to one of the executives of Columbia Records. I didn't interrupt. They were talking and I waited until they were finished their conversation. At this point, I had a hit on the jukeboxes. "That's How Much I Love You" was a hit already. Now, I'll give Gene credit. He already knew about it. When the Columbia man left, Gene was still sitting there and I walked over and introduced myself to him. He was very, very nice to me, very nice to me. He knew about the record, and we became friends and have remained friends all these years.

He was somebody you had heard as a youngster?

I admired him greatly because of the way he conducted his business. I already knew about that. I had a lot of his records. I bought his records when I was a boy on the farm out of the Sears Roebuck catalog. This was before he made movies. He was singing on WLS in Chicago. The station was owned by Sears Roebuck, World's Largest Store.

I've never forgot Gene for that. I was young, a new artist. He was already a big, big name at this point. Gene was very big and he could have fluffed me off, but he treated me very nice. I always remembered it. We just chatted. He told me he had heard my record. Wished me well, so forth and so on. I told him I had been an admirer of his all the years. I had his records of "Silver Haired Daddy of Mine," "I'm Thinking of You Little Girl," and several things. I know this sounds insignificant, but it was something to me to meet somebody that I really admired and knew something about.

On the personal appearance side, you went out with the Jamup and Honey tent show in the mid-1940s. Is that the only touring you did early on?

No. I had done a little road work out with a quartet. I didn't sing with the quartet. There was a quartet called the John Daniels Quartet, not Jack Daniels, but John Daniels. They did gospel kinds of things. I did a little work with him. I was also on the radio alone. We were all doing those early morning radio broadcasts. I think they paid me $10 a day. I wasn't known, hadn't made any records. I was glad to get it.

Wally Fowler was in that quartet.

He wrote a lot of your early songs?

Yes. He and Grayden Hall. As quickly as I started making records, a lot of people would have songs for me. Nobody had ever bothered me about songs before that. Before that I was really hunting around for songs that I could sing.

Your name was on a lot of the ones Wally Fowler wrote. Was that done out of gratitude to you?

Mostly.

After the first couple of years you were charting, Wally Fowler didn't write for you.

That's right, 'cause he wasn't writing good songs. I went for the good songs. It didn't make any difference whether my name was on it or not. I wanted good songs.

Mr. Forester, who helped me get my record contract, gave me a bit of advice early on. He said, "Young man, I want to give you some advice. When somebody brings you a song that's a good song and it's good for Eddy Arnold, you record it even though it might be written by your enemy." He was right because you're only as strong as your songs. So your enemy might write a good song.

Do you remember the first time you met Tom Parker?

I was just starting and I was on radio station [WSM] then. There had been an article on me in a magazine called *Radio Mirror* and he saw it. And he was up here and he came and introduced himself to me because he had seen that article. He was obviously interested in finding a new, young artist and I was that young artist, turned out to be. He had been working with Gene Austin, an old pop singer. He had worked with Gene for several years, and Gene, his popularity had gone down and he wasn't doing too well. That's how I met him.

Parker did a lot of wacky things to promote you.

He did. He did. He was something else. You know, I'm kind of conservative. I'm not flamboyant. That's why it worked so well with him and Presley. Presley was flamboyant, and Parker, the sky was the limit for him.

So you'd be embarrassed.

Yeah. A lot of things he'd do would kind of embarrass me. I'd say, "Gee Tom . . . "

Tom and I dissolved our working relationship in 1953, and then he got with Presley [in 1955].

He continued, though, to handle some of your live performances.
He did. He kept booking some of my things which kind of surprised me. I didn't know that he would want to do it, but he did.

Your popularity was growing in the 1940s, but because you were on the Opry *wouldn't you have to be back at the Ryman on Saturday nights?*
One thing nobody remembers or is conscious of: Beginning in '47 I was on the Mutual network five days a week for the Ralston Purina people. People always want to give the *Opry* credit and the *Opry* was important. But I was on the network five days a week which nobody remembers. And I did that for eight years. I introduced lots of records on there.

That was more national exposure than the Opry.
Yeah because the *Opry* was one radio station. I left the *Opry* in September 1948 but I still did the daily radio show.

Did you do the Mutual show out of WSM?
No. I used to feed the network from another station here that was affiliated with Mutual, a station called WMAK. The studio was in the old Maxwell House Hotel. This radio station occupied studios in the lower floor there. It greatly helped me so far as being known, even though it was on at noon. I'm always running into people now and they have a little age on them now, like I do: "Man, I was in college when you had that noon program. I used to go to my dorm room to hear it." No telling how many times people say that to me.

Tom Parker arranged for the show?
Yeah. The advertising agency that handled the Purina account wanted me. They wanted me. Of course, I was very popular on records and I got them an audience. I sold a lot of the merchandise. I used to do their commercials. When I started that program they had an announcer who would billboard the show, put it on the air: "Here's Eddy Arnold" and then do the commercials. One day I went to rehearsal and one fellow from the agency said, "I want to hear you read a commercial." I read him a commercial. He says, "You do them from now on." So from there on, all the announcer did was billboard the show. I did three songs. I had a group with me and they did one song. Four songs in the show.

Would you do that show from wherever you happened to be, if you were traveling?

I've got to answer that two ways. Sometimes I would do a pickup. But most of the time, in the beginning, I would be here. They finally got to where they let me transcribe two shows or three shows if I was going to be gone. We're talking about wax.

Did you do more traveling after you left the Opry? *Did it liberate you to do more shows?*

Tom was managing me at the time. Before I left the *Opry*, I had already stopped using the billing of the *Opry*. They wanted us to pay 15 percent off of our gross to use the name of the *Opry*. I didn't need to use the name of the *Opry*. People knew me who didn't know anything about the *Opry*. We stopped using the *Opry* in our billing altogether. Tom did all the booking anyway. We made out fine. I kept doing the daily program. That's what I did for several years. I also did a Saturday night CBS show. I think we did that for a year or eight months or something, but I don't remember how long. We did a half hour.

And then you did some television. You had your own show.

That was later on, that was '54. I got a fellow to produce it in Chicago, a man by the name of Ben Park. He was with NBC in Chicago. I got to know him because in the summer of '53 I did a summer replacement show on NBC for Dinah Shore; she did a quarter-hour show on NBC for Chevrolet, three days a week. When she went on hiatus in the summer then I'd do the summer replacement on NBC out of Chicago. All the time I was still doing the daily show on the Mutual network. I was busy.

Then after it was over I did the syndicated show, and I did it out of Chicago. I did it at a studio called Cling, Cling Studios.

In 1949, you debuted in Las Vegas at the El Rancho Hotel. Did you have to give that a lot of thought before you played there?

I'll tell you what I had to give some thought to. I kept hearing stories about artists appearing out there and gambling away all their money before they left, the money they were paid to perform. I'm not really a gambler. I might play $2 at a slot machine, but gambling don't mean anything to me. I'm not addicted to it. I got to thinking. I heard about the Rich Brothers playing at the El Rancho, gambling all their money away. You'd go in there and stay two weeks, sometimes three weeks. I thought maybe the hotel management might expect me to gamble. So I got a hold of Tom Parker and I asked him: "Tom, they may be expecting me to gamble out there in Vegas." He said, "I'll check it out." He got a hold of the William Morris Agency who booked me in there. In a few days the word came back and Tom said, "Don't worry they're not expecting you to gamble." But I thought maybe they would. When I got there I learned about a fellow by the name of Hayes, who conducted the orchestra at that hotel. He was addicted to gambling. He had gambled and was in hock so much that they said he would work there for many years to pay off his gambling debt. That's what they told me.

Were you worried about what your fans might think about your playing Sin City?

I thought about that, but it didn't seem to make any difference. You can usually tell by the mail that you get. As I remember it, that was '49, I went back out there in '53, not to that hotel. I went to the Sahara. That hotel burned, the El Rancho Vegas did. I got a couple of letters then. I answered them. I answered to the fact that I had nothing to do with the gambling side of the hotel. I sang in the entertainment room, but that's all I ever got on that subject. I always remember when I went back out there in '53, I followed Nelson Eddy in the Sahara there. He was an awfully nice man, a real nice man.

I had no act at that time. I didn't have it worked out: the timing of the stories, the timing of getting into a song. All of those things, I hadn't put [it] together at that point. I was a lot different then in later years when I finally got the act together. I try to do a performance now. You have to learn. There's a lot you have to learn as a performer, I mean performer. I'm not just talking about a guy who sings and makes records. You have to learn how to perform. There's so many things you need to do and you do not need to do, to get the attention of an audience and hold them. It's not easy to learn and nobody can teach that to you. You got to learn it. You got to look at them. I've gone to see acts perform, both lady singers and male singers, and I watch them and they come out there and they can sing like a million dollars, but they can never look at the audience. You got to learn to look at the audience whether you can see them or not. Many times you can't see them, but you got to learn to look at them. In this stage of my life, I'm an older man, and I have people who come back all the time and say to me, "You looked like you were just singing that song to me." I say, "I was." That's what I want them to think. You have to learn how to do that. I've thought a lot on that subject. I used to come off the stage in my early days and I'd say to myself, "What can I do to get to those people?" After a while it came to me and I don't know how to explain it, only you got to look at them and you got to have your timing down, your rhythm of going from one song to another or one subject to another, just like a man making a speech. I know you have gone and heard people speak and they lose you in two minutes and you could have a guy that delivered in a great manner and say the same words and you'd be with him. The same thing, a preacher, a speaker, you have to learn how to make a speech.

In the 1950s, you began to experiment a little bit with your music.
Yeah I did, a little bit. In '55 I experimented and it worked pretty good. I re-recorded "Cattle Call" with Hugo Winterhalter and his orchestra. He was a very fine arranger and conductor. He arranged all the hits Eddie Fisher had. He was it. He made a trip down here with Steve Sholes. He came out to my house and we got to talking. We decided we'd do a couple of things with Hugo. He had these French horns and everything. We did "Cattle Call" and of course it came off great. It came off, let me tell you. We did a little over a half million single records in 1955. I did, I think about four tunes with Hugo.

Was that an easy transition for you, recording with a larger ensemble?
I wasn't accustomed to hearing that many instruments at one time. It was all right but I had to get accustomed to hearing that many instruments. Now it wouldn't bother me at all, I've done so much. And I enjoyed old Hugo. Dad gummed he was a nice guy. He was a Pennsylvania man. Boy, his arrangements were fantastic.

When you went with Joe Csida as a manager in the 1950s, after Parker, did you sit down with him and say, "This is what I want to do. I want to do more in New York. I want to do more songs with a pop appeal?"
I don't know if I had that kind of conversation with him or not, but it just kind of fell in that way. I did several things. They were not sensations, though.

Was there a reason why you went with Csida?
Charlie [Grean]'s really the cause of me to start thinking about Joe. One time I saw Charlie and he knew Parker and I weren't together anymore and he said, "Why don't you think about Joe Csida. We've started this company, and I think Joe Csida would be good for you." That's how the Joe Csida thing happened.

In the late 1950s, a time when you were struggling and trying different things, you recorded some things with Latin band leader Juan Esquival that were never released.

It didn't come off. I was trying to find my way. I didn't know quite what to do. I was beginning to think, "It's about all over for me." Very frankly, as I go back and listen to things I recorded during that time, I was singing better then than I had *ever* been able to sing. I did an album in 1961 called *Our Man Down South.* Do you have that?

Yes.

You listen to those vocals. Boy, I wish I could sing like that now.

Bill Porter was the engineer on those sessions.

He had a touch. He was partly responsible for that good sound. It's so pure. He had a touch. I can't explain it. He just had a touch. It was fantastic.

Did you ever think during that period that RCA might drop you?

Well, at the end of the '50s, early '60s they might have. They could have, but even though I wasn't having hits, I was still selling records. I guess that's why they didn't want to get rid of me. One time my contract came up and there was one guy [Bob Yorke] there who wanted to get rid of me. He wanted to get rid of me. (Steve had moved to the West Coast.) But the guy running the record company [George Marek] said, "You go down there and sign him again." So he came down here and I played golf with him, but I never would talk to him about a record contract. I was P.O.ed at him. The thought that I had sold so many records and I had been good for the label. . . . I wouldn't sign with him at all, so Ben Rosner fixed up a contract and I signed with him.[4]

The artist who was doing the most at RCA was Elvis.

Beginning in '56. Oh yeah, he was hotter than a firecracker. Whoo!

Did you feel RCA made him a priority rather than you?

Well they might have, but he was doing slightly different songs than me. He did a lot of rhythm things, "One for the money, two for the show ..." He did a lot of things like that, that I couldn't do very well. I'm a ballad man.

Was there ever any effort on the part of RCA to have you do that kind of music?

No. But Presley, of course, got red hot. Then he went into the service.

Do you remember meeting him for the first time?

I met him before he ever happened. I met him in Memphis about 1951. I went into Memphis and I played a theater in Memphis and he came backstage. I had a group appearing with me called the Jordanaires, and he liked the Jordanaires. And he came back stage. He wasn't known at all. But it was my first meeting. He was always very nice. ...

Did you meet with him after he became popular?

Oh yeah. Several times. Being friends with Tom, if I was in California, Tom would send a car to get me at the hotel. He always tried to have a luncheon. If Presley was doing something at Paramount, Tom had offices there. Sometimes he would do something at MGM, he had offices there while Presley was working. I'll never forget one time Tom invited me while I was out there and Mr. Abe Lastfogel who ran William Morris. You know by the name the man's Jewish, a very fine man. Tom had a luncheon in his suite of offices out there and invited Mr. Lastfogel and several people. I was one of them. He had sliced country ham. I know he did purposely. Mr. Lastfogel ate it. "Great Colonel, great Colonel." He sliced and ate that country ham. Tom would do that. He'd do that. When they were gone, I said: "You son of a gun. You'd do that to that man." He said, "He enjoyed it, didn't he." Tom wouldn't have passed that up for anything. He did it purposely.

Jerry Purcell became your manager in 1964. How instrumental was he in expanding your career in the 1960s?

Very, very. Very important. I have to tell you a story. I was being managed at the time by Joe Csida and Joe all at once got an offer and took advantage of it with Capitol Records as an executive at quite a salary. Well Joe started looking around for a place to farm me out to somebody while he was working on the Capitol Records project. He had met Jerry Purcell because Jerry was very familiar over at RCA because Jerry was managing Al Hirt, the great trumpet player. Turns out I had met Jerry too. He came along with an RCA crowd one time down to Houston and I was appearing in Houston. He wasn't trying to manage me. He just came along with Steve Sholes, Ben Rosner, some of the RCA people.

He farmed me out with Jerry and I stayed with Jerry about a year or maybe a little more. I liked what he was doing because he knew all the TV production people, talent managers, the people who book people on television shows. He knew them all on the Sullivan show, the Steve Allen show, the Godfrey show. He knew all the people, which is pretty good. I wanted somebody like that. But as we went along Jerry put me on several of those shows. We went along, and I liked what he was doing for me. All at once, Joe, who I liked very much, he was out at Capitol Records.

Joe wanted me to come back then with him and I was in a tizzy. I liked Joe very much. I liked Jerry very much, and I liked what Jerry was doing for me. As a country boy would say, "I didn't know whether to go blind or wind my watch." I had to make a decision. So I had a meeting with the two of them together. I didn't know how to resolve it other than that. I wasn't going to tell one, "You go work it out with the other guy." I asked for the meeting with the two of them together. I said, "Gentlemen, this is one of the hardest decisions of my lifetime. I like both of you people very, very much and respect both of you. But I have to make a decision for my longtime life. Joe, something tells me in the back of my mind that another record deal will come to you, another company will want to hire you because you have record company experience. And I would take it that you'd probably want to take it again and if I went back with you, you'd have to farm me out again. I like what Jerry's been doing for me. It hurts for me to have to make a decision, but I wanted to do it this way. I'm going to stay with Jerry. Now if you gentlemen want to get together and make some kind of settlement that's up to you, but I wanted both of you to hear it coming from me at the same time." That's the way I resolved it. And I haven't been sorry. I think a lot of Jerry.

Was that partly Jerry Purcell's idea to go try the pop sound again in the 1960s?

Yeah. Kind of. We were in agreement on it. We had talked quite a bit. We thought that I could make a little move, not deserting the country, but just dressing it up a little bit and it worked. I was going on and on not having any hits and all at once I was having hits. I never really wanted to desert the country side. I just wanted to broaden my thing. I thought there was an audience there that I could get if I just reached for them a little bit. And it turned out that I could.

I was riding along in the car one day, wondering what I could do. The way I was making records earlier was just singing and having a guitar and a steel guitar. There's no freshness about it. Every record sounds the same. I got to thinking, "Now wait, why don't I take some violins and put 'em on my records, see if it don't work." And it did. I made a record called "What's He Doing in My World" there in about '65. I had the Anita Kerr Singers working with me, and I got Anita to quickly write some violin parts. I believe we used four violins or something like that. I made a record called "What's He Doing in My World" and boom!

The first top-ten record for you in ten years.

Yep. I said, "Ohh. I thought this might work." Steve, Chet, they thought maybe we better do an LP along those lines. I said, "All right. I got an idea for a title. We'll call it *My World*. Which would be Eddy Arnold's world and not necessary all world songs, but it was Eddy Arnold's world. Of course, we were going to put "What's He Doing in My World" in that album. And I remembered hearing a girl singing "Make the World Go Away." I had already heard Jim Reeves and Ray Price and somebody else sing it. They didn't register on me very much. But I heard a girl [Timi Yuro] sing almost a rock version of it. So I said to Chet, I'm talking about Chet Atkins who was producing my records at the time, "That might fit this album." So I found the song and I checked to see how many records the girl had sold. Say she had sold a half million records or a million records, I wouldn't attempt it, but she had sold, about two years before, 50,000 records. That's all she had sold. I said, "That don't bother me if that's what she sold." I did "Make the World Go Away" and we were in the studio and I was just doing it for the album and we started listening to the playbacks and we all looked at one another and we all said, "That sounds like a single record." Sure enough it was a worldwide hit. So that's how I got started using strings.

Purcell was concerned about the kind of songs you were getting up to that point. Was that a concern of yours?

A little bit. But I will say that after we had "What's He Doing in My World," we started getting the good songs. The publishers started bringing me the good songs. It's funny how that works.

I never wanted to be about political songs. I didn't want a writer to think he had to give me half of his copyright to get me to record it. I never wanted that. I did it because first I didn't think it was right, but second, I wanted the writer to bring me his good songs and for the most part they would because they knew they didn't have to share the copyright with me. If I liked the song, I'd record it.

You did a lot of television in the 1960s, a lot of television.

Yes I did. It made a national personality out of me. I was on television enough that I became known nationally. I wasn't just a little boy down South. I did Skelton's show, a special with Danny Kaye, a special with Danny Thomas. I did the *Ed Sullivan Show*. I did the *Kraft* [*Music Hall*] for several years where I was the host. After I did the *Kraft* show, I did a lot of guest appearances. You know who I really liked that I did guest

Eddy Arnold with talk show host Mike Douglas when Eddy was guest cohosting the show in 1967. Author's collection.

appearances with? Red Skelton. He was a wonderful man to me. I really liked him. I liked the others. I got along fine. Danny Kaye, golly, was nice to me. Danny Thomas was nice to me. Ol' Red was really a warm human being. I never forget the last appearance I did with Red. He lived in Palm Springs, and we were about ready to start taping. We'd been rehearsing two days or three days. Red came to my dressing room and said, "I want to tell you goodbye and thank you before the show starts because when the curtain goes down, I'm out the back door and in my car. I'm going to Palm Springs." He said, "I wish you'd visit me up there sometime 'cause you and I can talk." I found out that we were politically aligned. I didn't know it before, but he wanted to talk.

I've seen a picture of you and the Rolling Stones.

I met them in London in 1966. I went over there, Jerry and I did, and I broke a record over there with "Make the World Go Away." Of course, if you break it in England, you got the Scandinavian countries and everything.

An interesting thing happened with that. I'm talking about politics. Went over there and RCA had recorded "Make the World Go Away" with a girl over there in London and it didn't happen. I went there to get them to release "Make the World Go Away" by me. They didn't want to. They had a guy who did promotion for RCA in London that had a political deal with the music publisher. They were trying to get me to release another song published by them. I said no. If you're not going to release "Make the World Go Away," I'll just go home. I said right now "Make the World Go Away" is in the top five of the pop charts in the United States. Why would you think it wouldn't become a hit here?" I said, "Either release it or I'm going home." I said, "Screw releasing another song." I went on the BBC on a Friday night. They had one of these programs where you lip synch your records, *Top of the Pops* or something like that. I went on and did a lip synch job of "Make the World Go Away" on Friday night. Monday morning it was a hit.

And you did a few dates in England and Ireland.

Yes. I went to Northern Ireland. But it was at the BBC where I made a picture with the Rolling Stones. They were so tired and bugged out when we made that picture, they had just as soon I would have dropped dead. They maybe have grown up a little bit by now.

Eddy Arnold with TV host Ralph Emery, 1990s. Author's collection.

Was your Carnegie Hall debut in '66 as dramatic as it's been made out to be?

Yeah. It was very successful, very successful. I tore up the place. That audience was on fire. It sure was, and I was too. That was really a time in my life that I never dreamed would come about. A country boy from Tennessee in Carnegie Hall? Never in my life, never. As a boy growing up I didn't even know what Carnegie Hall was. Never forget that.... I did a full-length performance with ovations, standing ovations and all those things.

After the symphonic pop you recorded in the 1960s, you began letting more country sounds back in your music.

I was just looking for something that would sell. I was reaching.

Bill Walker wasn't doing your arrangements any more by the 1960s. He built a real symphonic sound.

Yes, he did and it fit me.

Jerry Purcell told me he wasn't so happy with your production and the kinds of songs you were getting at the end of the '60s.

I was more dissatisfied with how they were promoting them. You've got to, of course, realize that sometimes you make a record and it's a good song and it just takes off. Boom! Go! I had a lot of records like that, but some records need work, promotion, marketing.

Jerry wasn't happy with Chet's production?

Jerry was less happy with him than I was. I wanted the company to help me a little bit. Chet can't get out on the street and merchandise the record. He can just make the record and make it available.

I understand that Jerry said, "I want Eddy and I to pick the songs." But Chet said, "They're RCA artists; I have to have a hand in it." Then Bill Walker left.

I wasn't involved in that. I know Jerry made those remarks to me a good many times, but as I look back on it, I think it was just sort of a time that I had to be reborn again. Chet ... he produced good records with me. I wasn't as unhappy with Chet as Jerry was. Chet started farming me out to other producers. Now, that I didn't like. The poor guy, I guess, got so dad-gummed busy that he wanted to farm me out to other producers.

I had been lucky with him. I didn't care about going with other producers. When Chet started farming me out, I kind of lost interest and I told him.

You left RCA in the early '70s to go to MGM. Were you satisfied with your work at MGM?

Yeah. But while I was there Mike Curb sold the company, and he was out. It wasn't the same without him there. After he wasn't there, I asked out of my contract and I told Purcell, "Get me out. Mike's gone. It's not the same. I'd rather not be under contract to anybody. Get me out." So he got me out and RCA called and said, "We'd like to have you. Come back." So I went back.

Why did you leave RCA?

Well, we thought we could do better. We got a little higher royalty going over there at MGM. I'm not sure now that it was a wise move. As I look back on it, it might have been an unwise move. I was still young enough and my career was still going along pretty good. I guess you have some valleys and some hills in your career.

When I came back to RCA after having been on MGM, we did a song [in 1976] called "Cowboy." We almost had a biggie. It got going.

In the early '70s, your son was in a car accident.

It almost destroyed the two of us. He was unconscious nine and a half weeks, got a head injury, went through the windshield of a little MG, been out of college just three weeks, four weeks or something. I have to give my wife more credit, but we nursed him back, worked with him.

That was 1971. He was driving a buddy back to school at the University of Alabama to pick up his clothes. His buddy had graduated too and they had them a little room down there and my son had already brought his clothes back because he graduated. His buddy wanted to go back and get his clothes, so my son [said], "I'll take you down there." They had the wreck right outside of Bessemer. They took great care of him. The ambulance picked him up and took him to the Lloyd Nolan Hospital, that's outside Birmingham. They were wonderful people. They were marvelous to us. I'll never forget them as long as I live. Mrs. Arnold was given a room across the hall from the intensive care unit. She was in the intensive care unit many times a day for the simple reason that they were trying to bring him to. The head doctor, he was of the opinion that a familiar voice, a voice that he was accustomed to hearing might bring him to.

He stayed there seven and a half weeks and then we brought him back to Tennessee and stayed in the hospital. It was two weeks, then, before he came to. Then we brought him home. Then is when our work really began. When you come out of an injury like that, a young man, they begin to notice what's happened to them. They can't control their temper. You have to handle them. You gotta handle them with kid gloves, but we did. When we brought him home, I took me a horse trough, well I went down and bought one of them. We had him in a room on the lower floor where you could just step right out on the ground. It was flat back there. Every morning [through the sliding glass door] I dragged that thing in there right by his bed and I got me a water hose. I had it rigged up where I could put it on the faucet and I filled it with hot water and I put pillows in the bottom of it and then I'd pick him up and I'd put him in it. And I'd keep running the hot water. We were told, and it sounded logical to us, that maybe the heat and the water would bring the feeling back in his arm. I did that everyday and then I'd give him a good rub down with cream. We became pretty good nurses. They wanted us to send him away and we said, "Nope we'll take care of it." It was a long thing, but now he walks and drives his car and he has a job.

Eventually I started to work again. Mrs. Arnold really took over. She had trouble tying his tie for him. He couldn't tie that windsor knot. He'd get mad. She'd say, "Come over here and tie his tie." She just wasn't accustomed to tying a man's tie. He'd look at it in the mirror and he'd be mad. I'd tie his tie. Got him a dog. The doctor told us to get him a dog. I got him a bull mastiff puppy and he loved that dog. He'd take that dog outside with a leash. He wasn't walking good, but he was walking. He'd take that dog out there and that dog was a puppy and he started growing. The dog was strong because it was a bull mastiff. He named the dog Hoss for Hoss Cartwright. The dog would start running around him and playing. The leash would get wrapped around my son's legs and make him fall. As soon as he'd fall the dog would start chewing on his shoes. He called Hoss a few names.

We got him home from the hospital and he said a couple of words at the hospital. I had a booking. I went to Lake Tahoe. I was booked in a hotel out there and I got a call from home, from my wife and him. He had just said a word. She woke me up. I was already sleeping out there, and she put him on the phone with me. He was able to say "Daddy" and that was the most beautiful sound, the prettiest sound I had heard in a long time. It really was.

Interviews with Eddy Arnold were conducted on August 24, 1995, April 26, 1996, June 10, 1996, and June 11, 1996.

Notes

1. Eddy Arnold, *It's A Long Way from Chester County* (Old Tappan, N.J.: Hewitt House, 1969).
2. Interview with Charles Grean. February 8, 1996.
3. The two hits were recorded at separate Chicago sessions. "That's How Much I Love You": March 20, 1946, and "I'll Hold You in My Heart": May 18, 1947.
4. Rosner, a former assistant to Steve Sholes, was at this time RCA's manager of pop A&R.

Chet Atkins
The Best I Could Do

Weary of interviewers who popped up like broken strings, Chet Atkins frequently served up for publication the same old quotes time and time again. Before his death in 2001, the retiring gent would yawn and tell his guests about the day he realized that running RCA-Nashville had just about overwhelmed him. At the studio one morning, he would say, he looked down and saw two different shoes on his feet, a symptom, he reckoned, along with his colon cancer, of the enervating, never-ending push to produce the next hit record, while keeping up his own guitar-playing career. He soon after resigned the top post at RCA-Nashville.

Such well-worn stories always drew a chuckle, spicing his otherwise matter-of-fact telling of a spectacular career. Interviews naturally dwelled upon his guitar virtuosity—he ranks in guitar lore with Les Paul, Charlie Christian, Tal Farlow, and Django Reinhardt—and his role in constructing the countrypolitan Nashville Sound, the subgenre of country music that neutered the steel guitar and fiddles for the sake of reaching a larger audience. Beginning in the late 1950s, he and fellow A&R man Owen Bradley of Decca Records polished the rough edges of performers such as Jim Reeves and Patsy Cline, delivering country music to the era of the Nashville Sound. In forty years of press interviews, often at the expense of any conversation about his guitar playing, he would have to account for taking wax and buffer to country music.

This interview with Chet Atkins follows Eddy Arnold's because I conducted it in the midst of researching my Eddy Arnold biography. The one-on-one by no means spans Atkins' entire life and career, focusing instead on his work with Eddy Arnold. However, in focusing on the Arnold-Atkins relationship, a rarely seen dimension of Atkins' career unfolds. Instead of general remarks about his childhood, guitar-playing, and formulation of the Nashville Sound, a view of the producer's day-to-day burden emerges. Through the discussion about Arnold, we see not the guitar-producer superstar, but a tired executive, scratching his head while trying to keep an artist's heart pulsing.

Producing Eddy Arnold in the 1960s was no easy ditty for Chet Atkins. The producer usually worked with young talent who had no choice but to listen to him. However, in Arnold's presence, at least early in their partnership, Chet shrank back, becoming the star-struck fan waiting outside the the Ryman Auditorium for an autograph. Arnold, a twenty-year veteran of the music business, politely offered his own ideas about recording. Exacerbating his unease with Arnold was short-tempered Jerry Purcell, Arnold's manager. An ex-con who also controlled the careers of trumpeter Al Hirt, singer Gale Garnett, and others, dealing with Purcell could be like trying to muzzle an angry Rottweiler. Purcell and Atkins clashed incessantly over Arnold's recording, from song selection to the location of sessions. "He caused me a lot of trouble," Atkins told me.

Ultimately, Purcell's ranting injured Arnold's career, driving away Atkins and arranger Bill Walker, who together created a delicious sound around Arnold that fueled his amazing popularity in the 1960s. In their absence, Arnold's record sales sputtered.

Atkins' recollection of his work with Arnold—the good and the bad—demonstrates that for all the romance lapping up around his work in the RCA studios, there was also a lot of toil and stress.

Born June 20, 1924, in Luttrell, Tennessee, young Chet Atkins never guessed he'd be an A&R man, or even knew what one was, but he sensed a kinship with the guitar. "My mother and I went to Knoxville and saw a blind man play guitar on the street for handouts," he told the *New York Times* in 1974. "He was happy, all alone and just 'digging' time and I loved him. It made me cry—not out of pity but out of envy. The most important thing in the world it seemed to me then, was to be able to play guitar for a living, even if it meant being blind."[1] Inspired further by his older brother Jimmy, who played guitar with Les Paul and Fred Waring, and the sizzling picking of Merle Travis to whom he listened on WLW out of Cincinnati, Chet was blind only in his passion to play. By the age of 16, he was hired to play on WNOX in Knoxville, a station whose talent fed the *Grand Ole Opry* some 180 miles to the west. On WNOX, the youngster joined a cast of performers including Homer and Jethro, Archie Campbell, Bill Carlisle, and Red Kirk (who is featured later in this book).

Billed as the Guitar Wizard, he rode the Tennessee-Virginia-North Carolina circuit with his fellow WNOX stars until 1945 when he enlisted with WLW, the former home of his hero Merle Travis. The station, a 50,000-watt giant whose signal tore into the eastern United States, offered a stage as wide as the Ohio River. But Chet sank. Whether due to budget cuts or because his playing was too urbane (the story varies), the Guitar Wizard tumbled from station to station in search of solid ground. "Each time when I got fired, I'd say, 'Well maybe I'll get the respect I want somewhere else.'"[2]

"Somewhere else" in 1946 was KWTO in Springfield, Missouri. He had answered a call from Si Siman, a producer at the station. Siman brought him to the attention of Steve Sholes, supervisor of race and hillbilly recordings for RCA-Victor, who promptly offered the bashful guitarist a recording contract. Atkins was on the road to respect.

Chet with boss Steve Sholes at RCA's country roster, early 1950s. Sitting, left to right: Henry "Homer" Haynes (of the duo Homer and Jethro), Pee Wee King, unidentified, Eddy Arnold, Curtis Gordon, Ken Maynard. Standing, left to right: Bob McCluskey (RCA promotion), Steve Sholes, Chet, Betty Jack Davis (of the Davis Sisters), Skeeter Davis (of the Davis Sisters), Minnie Pearl, Charline Arthur, Louis "Grandpa" Jones, Hank Snow, unidentified, Porter Wagoner, Ken "Jethro" Burns (of the duo Homer and Jethro). Author's collection.

SI SIMAN IN SPRINGFIELD, MISSOURI, he had a show called *Corn's A 'Crackin'*, and he would transcribe the show and sell it to stations. He told the guy in Chicago who did the pressing, "Listen to this guitar player." Well, he got Mr. Sholes to listen. This was in early 1947. Steve liked what he heard and wanted to sign me, but he called around trying to find me and I had been fired from Springfield. I was out in Denver with a cowboy band and he didn't find me for quite a while. He finally did call me and wanted to know if I wanted to record for RCA and I told him yes. I was working with Shorty Thompson's band ... and he said, "Who's going to sing on your records?" I said, "I am," and he said, "Hell, you can't sing." I said, "Well, I'm going to sing." So he came back in an hour and fired me. That was another time. I was fired about eight times. That was the reason that particular time. It's funny now. But it was sad then. I didn't have any money and I had a wife and a baby.

When did you first become aware of Eddy Arnold?

It was right before I went to Cincinnati, so it would have been 1944 or '45. I remember his very first record was "Mommy Please Stay Home with Me." I used to perform that song. It was about a woman who went out on a party and left at home her baby son and, of course, some bad things happen and she should have stayed home with him. So it was a tear jerker. And then I heard him emcee on some shows and I thought he was a terrific emcee I loved the way he talked. Then I finally met him in '46 backstage at the *Grand Ole Opry*, backstage where we rehearsed in the dressing rooms. The first thing that struck me about him was the volume he had. I never heard a singer sing with so much volume. He was rehearsing and, boy, he was knocking out the walls in that little dressing room with his volume. I never heard anything like that before. He was, of course, nice to me. I was there for about six months in '46, and he autographed a picture for me when I left, I remember, which I still have somewhere.

He would have been out by himself at that point.

Yes he was, and I remember hearing him singing with an orchestra at WSM along about that time. They had a staff orchestra then and I guess he did a guest appearance with him or something. I don't remember what it was, but I remember hearing him rehearse. That's where the music business was in those days. We'd hang out in the halls of WSM radio which was on the corner of 7th and Union. A lot of the business was conducted down in the coffee shop of the Clarkston Hotel. It was kind of next door, and then we hung out, too, some at another restaurant called Jimmy Kelly's.

Then when I came back in 1950, he started using me as guest on his transcribed radio shows for Checkerboard. Also around '50 or '51, when Steve Sholes would come down here to record, he would use me as a sideman on his records. Boy, [Eddy] was nice to me when I needed it. Shortly thereafter, he tried to hire me and I thought about taking it, and I talked to my next door neighbor, Don Punch was his name, and I told him [about the offer]. He was in the insurance business. He said, "You shouldn't do this. You're earning power is going to be from now until you're about forty or so and you shouldn't tie yourself down to one salary." So I didn't. I didn't take the job. So he hired Hank Garland, but he never held it against me or anything.

About 1954, somebody hired me and Eddy to entertain at the Belle Meade country club, and I played a few tunes and he sang. We probably did some things together, I don't know. There was a guy there from ABC television who put us on as a summer replacement from Springfield, Missouri. We would fly up [on a chartered plane] every week for about four months. . . . I used to get irritated at Eddy because I thought we'd be safer if we flew when it's daylight. But he'd be late getting out to the airport and we'd fly into the sunset. And you know we never had any bad weather. We didn't have one damn weekend of bad weather. It was amazing. We flew in a twin engine plane of some kind.

But we did that show up there and had on a lot of famous guests like Brenda Lee, Helen O'Connell. A lot of pop acts would come on the show, and I was featured for two or three numbers, but it mostly featured Eddy, and we would do tunes together.

Steve Sholes signed up Elvis and became a big man in the company. So I inherited his job of producing all the Nashville acts and some of the pop acts that would come in from California and New York. But Eddy continued to record in New York for a little while with Steve Sholes. But, by and by, he started recording with me. We had kind of a renaissance there of hit records. We got lucky. We had "Make the World Go Away," a whole bunch of world songs. And he had a good resurgence there in popularity which I was proud of.

Did you think "Make the World Go Away" would be the one for Eddy?

No. We were just trying to make records on that one. That happened to be a real good song. I remember one thing that happened during that time, a little later. Burt Bacharach and Hal David sent a song down here, "Raindrops Keep Falling on My Head," and I turned it down for Eddy. I didn't think he could sing it because it gots a lot of octave jumps in it. Everybody in town really turned it down. Ray Stevens turned it down.

But I don't think [Eddy] liked that much. When he thinks of me, he thinks, "He turned down 'Raindrops Keep Falling on My Head.'" But those things happen when you're running a record label. You can't get every hit. Maybe I'm rationalizing. But we always got along well, and he was always well prepared. He reads music, you know, and I always felt that was a little to his detriment. I'd always tell him: "Put a little more Eddy Arnold in it. Forget those damn notes. Put Eddy Arnold in there." Because he has a heck of a style. We never had any differences.

Was there any resistance as you moved more to the pop sound?

I never had any resistance. I tried to make crossover records all the time. I didn't try to make pop records, but for a long time I didn't use country fiddle or steel because that would keep a record from crossing over. I had a lot of success with Jim Reeves doing that before I had a hit with Eddy. It worked.

Steel was not accepted until Bob Dylan came down here and did *Blonde on Blonde* and used steel guitar and then it was all right with the pop folks after he did it. I love steel guitar; it was just at that time it would keep a record from crossing over in the pop field.

That's interesting that you saw Eddy with an orchestra as far back as '46.

Yeah. I remember him rehearsing with an orchestra and maybe a vocal group. I don't know if it was a Christmas song or what it was. He would probably remember that. But Eddy is the type guy who is slow to come to a decision, but he takes things very serious and he'll look you right between the eyes and tell you what he thinks. I admire him a lot for that.

I remember one time I had an appointment with him and we were going over songs and Jerry Reed bounced in. Jerry Reed is that type of guy. He'd just open the door and come in: "Hey Chief. You should do this and do that." Eddy, a day or so later, talked to me, and he said, "Now when I make an appointment with *you*, I want it to be with you. I don't want it to be with Jerry Reed." I said, "You know, you are right. But Jerry Reed is a genius and I get a lot of good albums out of him. I get hit songs from him. All kinds of guitar licks from him." Or words to that effect. I'm paraphrasing. I don't know what I said. But he was right.

Bill Walker said that Eddy didn't like songwriters being in the studio because they'd try to tell him how to sing the song.

We would have pretty much closed sessions. I don't remember that particularly. But I do remember that he would sing much better if I got some pretty girls in the control room. I'd invite some of the office girls in, pretty girls, and he'd perform a lot better. He would sing and dance around, kind of do a little show and get a little life into the song. I never told him that of course. It's all right to tell it now.

He was the most popular artist I've ever known. Back in the late '40s, he'd have two or three hits in the top ten or the top twenty. He was just all over the damn charts. And I remember hearing when I was in Knoxville in '45 that he was making $1,500 a day. Damn, I couldn't believe that. I was making $3 or $4 a night when I went to work.

A lot of his success should go to Steve Sholes because Steve worked so hard at finding good songs for him. Of course, Eddy worked at that too. I'm sure it was a mutual thing. Steve was a workaholic. He died [in 1968] when he was fifty-seven or something. He was overweight. He thought about every artist's career and what he should do, what type tunes he should do.

Is this the '60s when you were working with so many people?

Yes. I probably started working with Eddy about 1959 or '60. I don't remember ever recording him over at McGavock Street where our first studio was. My first memories are of Studio B, and that was 1959 or '60. At 1525 McGavock Street, he built two studios in a building, Cliffie Thomas did. The Methodists were in [one], and we were in the other. There was a place down on 12th and Broadway, where RCA would bring portable equipment to record. We made several hit records down there. They'd just bring a recording machine and a spring unit out of a Hammond organ for echo. And a little console and we'd set up in there. Because they were union [National Association of Broadcast Employees and Technicians] and the RCA engineers couldn't come down here and use other equipment. They had to bring their own equipment. RCA couldn't record anywhere else except with NABET engineers. It was a photography lab really and some guys were trying to produce 3-D pictures and they spent a lot of money, and they worked it out, but it was too expensive.

When Eddy started to record more often with a large number of instruments and more complicated arrangements, did he adapt pretty well?

He was always prepared. I don't remember ever disagreeing on material. Back in those days, I had, and I still have, pretty low self-esteem, and Eddy was a big star and I was kind of a nobody. It was harder for me to work with him or Perry Como than it would be some unknown that I pick up and make a star myself. Anita Kerr would make the arrangements, maybe Bill Walker would sometimes. Anita was a fine arranger. She had perfect pitch. She didn't need a keyboard to sit down and write you an

ASCAP awards ceremony in Nashville in the 1960s. Left to right: songwriter Cy Coben, Chet. Author's collection.

arrangement. And sometimes we'd record and have her vocal group in, The Anita Kerr Singers. We'd decide that we wanted to add strings and I'd hire some fiddlers and she'd grab a pencil and write out lines for them to play.

It was simpler then. We got a lot of our songs, in those days, out of New York and California. Not near as many writers then in Nashville. Now we get all the songs out of Nashville, 99 percent. But in those days it was different.

Eddy has said that the song selection was much better after he hit with "Make the World Go Away."

Oh yeah. That always happens. When you get a hit going then everybody starts pitching you a song.

What was the process that a song came to Eddy, through you?

That one probably came to me through Hank Cochran because he wrote that. He was always hanging around my office trying to get me to record his songs. . . . It may have been recorded in the pop field before Eddy did it. They would bring me a demo of it, and I had a drawer full of songs. I had a file for each artist and when I'd get a song that fit Eddy or somebody else, I'd stick in the file and play it for him when he came in. That's the way I usually did it.

But sometimes they got the songs, too. Jim Reeves was always finding songs. Eddy may have found some too; I don't remember.

Why did you move away from producing?

I had cancer in '73 or somewhere along there, and I figured stress had a lot to do with it, so I started backing out and turning the artists over to other people. . . . When Steve died, I started backing out. I worked for Steve, I didn't work for RCA. I remember one day when I was working really hard I went in and looked down at my shoes at about 11:00 and they didn't match. And I thought, I've been on the job too damn long. So I just started gradually turning the artists over to other people. I gradually got out of it and hired other people to run the place. I left in 1980. But for years I didn't do much at all.

When you were producing so many artists, obviously it wasn't healthy for you. But what about the artists?

Well, they all had hits if they stuck around long enough. It was amazing how many hits we had. But sure, I spread myself too thin. But that's the way all the labels did it in those days. You'd make a bunch of records and just throw them out and see what stuck to the wall. If you got one started at just one little place, you could spread it all over the country usually. That was the M.O. in those days.

I remember one song we did [with Eddy in 1961]—I just loved it and it didn't do anything—called "Jim I Wore a Tie Today." It was written by Cindy Walker who had written a lot of hits. . . . But the country wasn't ready for it.

That song was recorded in the early 1960s, a lean time for Eddy and a time in which he says he thought about retiring. Did you get the sense that was going on?

No. Back in those days people bought sounds; they didn't buy looks. Today they buy looks. And Eddy was like Hank Snow. You know Hank Snow, until videos came along, hell, you could make hits with him 'cause

Chet with Eddy Arnold in the 1970s. Author's collection.

he had a hell of a voice and he could sing. The same thing with Eddy. I think I felt all along that we'd have hits if we found the right song because he had such an appealing sound to his voice. There were some artists I had doubts about, people who Steve wanted me to record. But not Eddy. I just stood in awe of him. I thought he was one of the great country singers of all time, and I don't think I was surprised when he started making hits again.

Jerry Purcell, his manager, had a role in bringing on that resurgence.

He was a thorn in my side. . . . One day we were going to record and we'd moved offices and I couldn't find the key to my desk. And he got upset because I couldn't find the material and called up New York and tried to get them to fire me.

Eddy knows he's not one of my favorite people, because he caused Mr.

Sholes a lot of heartache and Mr. Sholes was a great man. . . . But I could always get along with Eddy just fine.

[Purcell] made the charge that you owned a piece of every song that Eddy recorded.

That's the biggest fuckin' joke I've every heard. I never owned a piece of any song anybody did. I had a little publishing company before I went on the payroll. I think Jim Reeves wanted me to publish one of his songs. That's completely false. That job was just a sideline for me. I just did it for Mr. Sholes. I was making $50,000 or $100,000 a year in royalties off my guitar playing. So I didn't need that. Mr. Jim Denny of Cedarwood Publishing would send people over and say, "If you record this, you get 10 percent." And I said, "You know, I don't do that." He made that charge? I can't believe it.

There was a point at which he wanted to choose the songs for Eddy Arnold.

I never heard that. He probably put that on Mr. Sholes. He certainly didn't ask me. But he may have asked Mr. Sholes. But we get along fine now. I see him once every five or ten years. And it's all right now. They tried to get me to record Al Hirt again, and I said, "No. I'm through with him." Because Al didn't come to my defense. And I love Al. He sends word up when people see him in New Orleans. "Tell Chet hello." I love him and all that.

Jerry had Al independently produced and then wanted to bring him back to you?

Yeah. And they didn't make any hits, I guess. I don't know what the reason was. I remember Steve came and asked me to do it again. I had the idea that Purcell instigated the call, but I'm not sure of that. I was asked to do it again, but I said no. The same way with [RCA-Nashville artist] Dave Gardner. I had a run in with his wife, and he didn't make anymore hits. I'm not patting myself on the back. But I just refused [to record him]. I didn't have time for all that stress and people fussing at me and trying to get me fired when I was trying to do the best I could do. I was just amazed people would do stuff like that.

But Purcell actually handled some of your bookings for a while.

He tried to, yeah. He wanted me to sign up with him once and I didn't realize what it was. I said, okay. Because I'm a forgiving soul. And then Steve saw it and called me, 'cause he ran a picture or something. I don't know how it evolved; he probably could get me some TV shows. And

Steve was kind of disappointed in me, so I called him and called it off. He never booked me on one thing.

Certainly things changed for Eddy at the end of the '60s. He started dropping off ...

Well, careers go that way. You have a few hits and then they start playing somebody else. It will happen to Reba. It will happen to Garth. It will happen to everybody ... eventually. Eddy had a great career. He was hot from '46 and then we got him hot again in the 1960s, which was amazing. But he was just one of the greatest damn singers that's ever been. He was the hottest that I've even known. Hell, he would have three or four hits in the top ten. It was just amazing how hot he was. He had an awful lot of appeal and I think that's why we were able to bring him back in the '60s.

Any recollections of Bob Yorke wanting to let Eddy go?

No. But Bob may have. He was kind of a wild guy. . . . But Steve Sholes shielded me from an awful lot of that stuff. Because I was making hits and he didn't want to bother me with financial things, financial planning or anything like that.

I had to do it finally when he got so busy, and, of course, after he died. I started quitting after he died; I started quitting when he died. I worked for him, I didn't work for RCA. They paid me, but I really worked for Steve and tried to please him.

Did Eddy fill a void that Jim Reeves left after his death?

I wouldn't speculate on that. It could be, but I don't think anybody could fill Jim Reeves' void. Eddy was too different from Jim. Now, Jim [Ed] Brown tried to fill the void and so did Stuart Phillips, he tried to sing like Jim Reeves. They had minor success, nothing like Eddy Arnold.

Toward the end of the '60s, the pendulum for Eddy was swinging so far to pop, almost totally symphonic, but then he reached a point where he swung back. He started incorporating more traditional instruments. Do you have recollections of that?

Was I recording him then?

Yes sir. There was an album called Love and Guitars *released in 1970 that you did with him.*

I don't remember that. That's what the record business is about. You try

Early 1990s promotional photo. Author's collection.

different instrumentation and if it sells, then you go that direction, and if it doesn't, you try something else. That's just the way it works. If I'm credited with the Nashville Sound, that's just how it happened. I was just trying to keep my damn job and sell records. That's all it was about. It was a business. That's what Owen Bradley and I were trying to do, keep from getting fired. I had been fired from every job I'd ever had. We were just trying to survive. To survive you've got to have hit records.

Interviews with Chet Atkins were conducted on August 28, 1995, and May 16, 1996.

Notes

1. John S. Wilson, "You Can't Take the Country Out of Chet," *New York Times*, April 7, 1974.
2. Nicholas Dawidoff, *In the Country of Country: A Journey to the Roots of American Music* (New York: Vintage, 1998).

Anita Kerr
Arranger

C het Atkins hired Anita Kerr in 1961 to help him with a roster that read like a *Billboard* popularity chart. It included Hank Snow, Porter Wagoner, Hank Locklin, Jim Reeves, the Browns, Skeeter Davis, Eddy Arnold, Johnnie and Jack, Don Gibson, and others. And Kerr, officially the assistant A&R director, would support them by producing sessions and writing arrangements.

Kerr signed on during the rise of Chet's Nashville Sound, when the recordings rolling out of RCA were glossier than ever before. To replace the fiddlers and steel guitarists whom Chet was banishing, there were string ensembles. And that's where Kerr was especially critical; she hired the violinists and cellists and wrote arrangements for them and the other musicians. Arrangements told the musicians—classical and otherwise—what to play and how to play it, which hastened the session toward a desired sound. Arrangements also cut down on expensive musician overtime, which the RCA brass loved; musicians could just play the arrangement without having to learn the songs on the fly (standard practice in Nashville), while the wary musician's union clock ticked away.

Ironically, rhythm musicians—guitarists, bass players, drummers, and the like—who dreaded arrangements and who by and large couldn't read music, seemed not to mind the regimen that Kerr brought to the scene. Nashville guitarist Wayne Moss loved to see her coming: "I felt more at ease in the studio with her than any other arranger I've every worked for. There was no pressure. It was fun. She had such a kind spirit about her. You could just see love emanating from her. She had such a pleasant aura about her. She just had a way of making everything work without anybody getting upset, nervous, or getting uptight in the least bit. That's a real gift."[1]

The Anita Kerr Singers at work with an unknown guitarist in the mid-1950s.
Left to right: unidentified, Gil Wright, Anita Kerr, Dottie Dillard, Louis
Nunley. Author's collection.

Alongside arrangements in their march into Nashville were background vocals, another embellishment that chased away the fiddles and
steel. In that department, Kerr also proved invaluable. Her Anita Kerr
Singers were mainstays on the Nashville session circuit and had been
since the very late 1940s when Paul Cohen of Decca Records began
hiring them for occasional sessions. By the late 1950s, however, every
Nashville producer demanded background vocalists, and they wanted
the Anita Kerr Singers and Elvis's quartet of choice, the Jordanaires. As
Kerr points out in the following interview, the Kerrs were particularly
sought after because she could write arrangements and her singers could
learn them as quickly as it took Chet Atkins to tune his guitar.
Comprised of Gil Wright, Louis Nunley, Dottie Dillard, and Kerr
herself, the quartet, with its two women, often added another dimension
to recordings by playing foil to male singers or virtually becoming a duet

partner: Listen to Jim Reeves' "I Love You More" (1958), Hank Locklin's "That Inner Glow" (1958), or Eddy Arnold's "Mary Claire Malvina Rebecca Jane" (1964).

Kerr remained on staff at RCA for only two years, exiting when she realized that freelancing around town would be more lucrative. Throughout the late 1950s and into the 1960s, Anita Kerr and the Anita Kerr Singers never wanted for work, as Kerr vocalist Louis Nunley observed: "Back in those days we were working three and four sessions a day, seven days a week. There weren't very many studios, so they had to use them all the time. So you'd go from one session to the next to the next to the next. Grab a sandwich and eat it while you were learning the song."[2]

In the mid-1960s, Kerr departed the frenetic Nashville for Los Angeles, where she made her own records for Warner Brothers and worked closely with labelmate Rod McKuen, scoring music that accompanied his poetry. For this and other performances out west she received awards and fortune, but her deepest imprint lies in Nashville where she helped create a new sound in country music.

THE WOMAN WHO RAISED the sophistication quotient in Nashville called Memphis home. Born Anita Grilli on Halloween of 1927, she was only a teenager when she took the organist's bench in her church and began directing the choir. In the mid-1940s, she also appeared on radio station WHBQ. This was the same WHBQ that a few years later would gain cachet in blues and rock lore by hiring Dewey Phillips, the eccentric, rocket-fueled disc jockey who dished out rhythm and blues on his *Red Hot and Blue* show.

Pre-Dewey, Anita broadcasted in a more staid era, appearing with her family on an all-Italian program. The language, the music, everything was Italian, and the star was Sophia Grilli, Anita's mother, who performed operatic standards and played the piano. To her side, little Anita played an accordion so unwieldy that someone had to perch it on a stool to keep it from dropping to the floor. Anita's brother played saxophone, and her father read commercials in Italian.

Anita also sang with her sisters on their own program, and she rose to become WHBQ's staff musician. As staff musician, she organized choruses and other on-air talent, honing her arranging skills and learning to corral sound. There was nowhere to go but up, observed program director Gene Allan Carr, who worked closely with the wunderkind: "I can't exaggerate Anita's talent. She was eighteen by then, and showed huge promise."[3]

As if taking Carr's cue, Anita married a young announcer on WHBQ, Al Kerr, and the two moved to Nashville in search of her promise. In Music City, she easily found work on the radio and soon was rounding up background choruses for Red Foley and other country artists. A 1950 session log places her behind the organ on an Eddy Arnold session, her first with Arnold. (It was also the first Arnold session for a lanky guitarist named Chet Atkins.) As her session work accelerated throughout the 1950s, Kerr found herself planted on the factory floor as the Nashville recording business transformed from a jerry-rigged endeavor to a humming assembly line.

Because she was a trained musician with perfect pitch, could quickly write arrangements, and carried with her a crack group of singers, she was an obvious choice for producers looking to varnish the hillbilly grain in country music. Her role in giving form to the vision that Owen Bradley, Chet Atkins, and others producers saw for country music cannot be underestimated. Yet it is. Even histories dealing specifically with women in country music virtually ignore her. A gracious woman who today lives in Switzerland, she would never complain about the oversight.

I MOVED TO NASHVILLE IN 1948, and knew no one there and needed work. So, I started out just playing dance jobs and clubs just to make money as a pianist and singing. A lot of times, when you did those things, they wanted you to sing—if you could. Then I was hired at one of the smaller radio stations in Nashville [WMAK] as the staff pianist, and Jack Stapp at WSM heard about me, and I had already gotten together a vocal group. I had found a girl at Peabody College and three other guys, and we used to get together and sing. I wrote arrangements and we sang just for the fun of it. I went to another station [WLAC], we used to go and do a program there a couple times a week, just for the fun of it, no money. Then Jack Stapp at WSM heard about me and the vocal group; so then he called me and asked me to talk with him. So I went to WSM and he hired me to direct this eight-voice choir which was on a regional network there. It was called *Sunday Down South* with Snooky Lanson. So, I started writing and conducting and singing with this eight-voice choir and then the A&R man from Decca Records, Paul Cohen, was in and out of WSM all the time because that was really the beginning of all the recording in Nashville. So, [at WSM] there was always an A&R man from somewhere. So, Paul would come and he heard the group and he wanted a choir on a religious song that Red Foley was doing. He asked me if I would write the arrangement and the choir sing with Red on it. That was the beginning. He was really the one who gave us the name the Anita Kerr Singers. We had no name. We were just the choir on that show. He asked me, after we recorded, "What do you want me to call you?" I said, "I don't know. I haven't even thought about it." He said, "You're name's Anita Kerr. How about the Anita Kerr Singers?" [Cohen] hired us quite a bit for the first year because we did things with Burl Ives and all of his other artists, even Ernest Tubb. Then we began to be hired by other artists and other A&R men with other recording companies. It was sort of like a snowball. I was very lucky because I never had to go and say, "Will you hire me?" because the phone was ringing quite a bit by then, wanting the group. Not all the time, but I would say 50 percent of the time, wanting me to write the arrangements.

During this period, Chet was A&R man with RCA. He is the one really that hired me for the first session with Jim Reeves. They would just call me and say, "How about you working with Jim? Will you write the arrangements and bring your singers?"

Are you saying that the first time you recall working for RCA was with Jim?

I don't know really if that was the first time. I remember it as the first time, but it was so long ago, I just can't say definitely. It was one of the first times. Let's put it that way, but I really can't think of anybody else we sang with. I don't know if Eddy Arnold was first. Even back then I did some things with Willie Nelson. This was at the beginning of Chet's career as an A&R man with RCA.

Across the board in Nashville there was certainly an increased use of background vocalists on country records.

At that time, in the last half the '50s, there were two vocal groups in Nashville, the Jordanaires and The Anita Kerr Singers. . . . We worked with the same musicians all the time. In fact, we knew them better probably than we knew our own families because we were in the studio with them all the time.

Did the two groups have different roles, different strengths that a producer would want?

Naturally, the Jordanaires were four men. We were two girls and two men. That's a different sound right there. The Jordanaires couldn't read music at all. And we could. So, I'm sure, if I was hired to write the arrangement and they say, "Bring your singers," they know if I wrote it, the singers could read it. I think the things we did were closer to pop because we could read [music] whereas the Jordanaires—most of their sessions were faked. But then it just depends. We did an awful lot of sessions for Owen Bradley when he was an A&R man for Decca. He hired us for almost everything, except for Patsy Cline he always hired the Jordanaires. He just felt that their sound—four men—would fit better with her. He didn't want any females voices to clash with what she was doing.

I think there for a while we were about the only vocal group that Chet was hiring, except Steve Sholes produced Elvis and, of course, Elvis always used the Jordanaires.

Since you mentioned Steve Sholes, can you compare his producing style with Chet's?

Chet being a musician, his approach was entirely different. He could walk into the studio and he might have an idea, say if we were faking the session, he would have an idea for an intro or something and he knew how to tell the people what he wanted. Or he would pick up the guitar and play it for the guitar player. Steve's approach was different. He would naturally leave all the musical decisions to the leader of the musicians in the studio. He would just say whether he liked it or didn't like it which was very good, too, because he always had very good taste or, as we used to say, "a very good nose for what the public would like." But so did Chet, but he just went about it in a different way.

During the 1950s, do you recall people like Chet specifically saying that he had to drop the fiddles and steel to compete with rock?

Country just became more and more pop. It grew out of the Roy Acuff, Ernest Tubb, and Bill Monroe sound into more sophisticated sounds, and eventually it seemed like we were going to meet head on with pop music. That was, of course, before hard, hard rock hit. A lot of times, they would use strings and particularly us because they wanted to try to break into the pop market because at that time, if you got into the pop charts, you would sell much more than just being in the country charts.

You sang on Jim Reeves'"He'll Have to Go" [in 1959], a huge pop hit. What are your recollections of that?

I was amazed at how well he sang it. It really showed off his voice because when he sang low it was absolutely beautiful. It was a very easy-going session. Chet would walk in and make suggestions [about piano, vocal groups]. I can't think of anything different to say about that.

The Kerrs keep it country. Left to right: Gil Wright, Louis Nunley, Anita Kerr, and Dottie Dillard. Courtesy of R. A. Andreas.

Tell me about Jim Reeves.

He was always very nice to work with, extremely quiet. He was a quiet man. He sang very softly and he did demand quietness in the studio. He didn't like it if people were noisy. Maybe it messed up his concentration. He was always nice about it. I can't think of one time that I've ever heard him raise his voice or look like he was going to.

We did a tour to Europe together.

That was just before his death.

I think that it was just a few weeks after returning to Nashville that he died. I couldn't believe it. It was hard to imagine because we had just spent four weeks traveling around Europe. But that was a lovely trip too because everything was just smooth as silk. Not one problem with him or anyone else. I can't think of anything bad to tell you.

I'm interested in your group's role in his recording sessions.

We sang on all of his sessions, and I arranged them for the vocal group and for the orchestra. I would get together with him and set the keys, and go home and write the arrangement. Some artists when you walk in, they just tear the arrangements apart. "Why did you [do] the introduction this way? Change it." But he never did. He just walked in and did it.

In those days we did everything at one time. Today you go in and do a vocal alone. The vocalist just hears his accompaniment through earphones. But then the band was in the room with you; the vocal group was in the room with you. So you had a lot of those sounds leaking into your microphone. We were forever behind big baffles, wooden boards they would put up all around us. Then everybody was complaining about the boards because you would hear the rhythm section later than you should. But still for me it was more fun that way than the way they started doing it later. When you worked with the band and the soloist the feeling was there. If everybody did a good performance, it was really moving. It was a different type of way of selling a song in those days.

You would meet with him before the session?

It was necessary because I first of all had to set the right key for him and after that, just find out what he had in mind. Chet was always there, too. So it was the three of us talking about what we thought should be where and how the song should be treated. Once I went home and wrote it and got back the next day (Chet didn't ever give me too much notice), he would just breeze right through them. He always knew his songs very well, and had wonderful vocal control. He sang really good, I thought.

You mentioned that Jim was a very quiet individual. Many people have said that he was very difficult to get to know, but once you got past that, he could be a good friend. Do you feel like you got past that with him?

I worked with so many different people that I never became really close friends with any of the artists that I worked with because the group that I hung around with were entirely different from the people who I worked with. I hung around musicians and other singers that sang my kind of music.

He was a very introverted person, Jim was. He wasn't really outgoing. He wasn't the kind who would come up and hit you on the shoulder and say, "Hey. That was really great." He would come up and say in a very quiet way, "That was good." That's about what he would say. But he was a quiet person and introverted.

As opposed to Eddy Arnold ...

Oh ... he would come up and laugh and slap you on the back and say, "Hey that was something." And Jim was just the opposite.

Jim and Eddy were very similar in that they sang country music "nice."

They were very close to pop. That's what I meant about moving toward more of a popular sound.

When I compare the two, Eddy seemed to have more of an ability to interpret a song, to put feeling into it. Although Jim's voice was better, Eddy seemed to have more feeling.

I would say that Jim when it came to singing a song, it was very simple the way he sang it. Very smooth. I don't want to say no emotion, but he never changed. It was just the same all the way through the song, whereas Eddy would go up and down. He would have a little more emotion in his singing. But then, on the other hand, I always felt that Eddy sounded still somewhat country, whereas I thought Jim had gone further away from country in his sound. But Jim when he really killed me was when he would narrate something. That, I really loved the way he did it.

I loved the one about the voice in the choir.[4] That was my favorite of all that he ever did. He could narrate something, I thought, with lots of feeling.

Do you recall working with Jim on his ABC network show?

I remember doing it, but I can't remember anything exactly that happened, except we had to be there almost everyday and then run after that and do a couple of sessions. Again, it was very smooth. Jim knew every song. I even have some airchecks of it here. I was filing away a lot of my airchecks and cassettes and things about six months ago and I put a couple of them on and actually, when he talked on this show, a script was written, he did it so well. You never would have known that this man was reading. Whereas when some of the other people on the show said something, you could tell that it wasn't natural, that they were reading. But with him, it just fell out of his mouth.

Did you write arrangements on those shows?

Yes I did, particularly on the things that Jim sang.

As far as your European tour with Reeves, Henry Strzlecki, the bass player on that tour, says he was struck by the reception the troupe received.

It was amazing. They loved the country music. We were well received everywhere. I thought it was a very successful tour, and I'm convinced that that helped country music get started in Europe. I think it's why it's as big in Europe now as it is. That was the beginning, the first tour.

Many have said that Jim was frustrated with the night-after-night schedule of that tour.

Most of the details were very well taken care of on that tour. They had everything very organized. But he did like to be waited on. He was a little bit of a star that way, of course, but who isn't? But at least he was a very nice star, let's put it that way.

There's a point at which he's presented with a silver record on a Norwegian television show. He said something like, "I'll melt it down when I get home to see if it's really silver." Which seemed a bit ungracious.

I vaguely remember that. I remember us thinking that wasn't too nice of a thing either. He like everybody else could have his bad moments or his good moments.

For the most part he kept his displeasure under his cap, as far as you know.

At least when I was working with him he did. Now how he was with his band that he traveled with all the time, I don't know because I saw him mainly on sessions and the tour was the first time I really was with him for that length of time, nonstop. Of course I wasn't with Jim really because I was with my singers and we kind of hung around together. Jim hung around his guys in the band. In other words, we didn't mix that much.

You were hired on as staff for RCA?

I became on the A&R staff. But I got off the staff. I asked Chet to let me out of it because I was missing a lot of sessions with my singers. And to be truthful about it, I was losing money. The salary that they were paying me didn't make up for the sessions that I had missed. I really enjoyed the singing and the arranging more than I did the A&R. I stopped being on the A&R, but Chet kept me exclusively as an RCA arranger. That's how I ended up being on the staff.

Tell me about making records with Eddy Arnold. Did he require any special attention?

I would set the keys for the arrangements with Eddy before hand. Of course, he was a very sweet man to work with, always extremely nice.

When he came in he knew his stuff. . . . There really were no problems and he always seemed to be happy with the arrangements. Some artists want to change every note that you've written for some reason or other. But it was never that way with Eddy. He was always very complimentary and very nice.

Would you sit down in his office to go through the arrangements?

And sometimes in Chet's office. We would talk it through. I wouldn't tell him what I'm going to write because I wouldn't know until I got in front of the score paper. We would set the right key and we would say, "Eddy will sing it through once then The Anita Kerr Singers will sing a few lines or the piano will play a few lines and then Eddy will come in at this point and sing it on out." We always tried to keep them under three minutes at that time because the radio stations, getting play on the stations. The whole routine would be completely figured out. He just wouldn't know exactly what I had written for the intro or for the ending or for any of the instruments playing underneath him. It was always the same routine. He always seemed to like it because he never changed them.

Musicians who played with Eddy who played your arrangements and then later played with Bill Walker's arrangements say that you allowed a lot more room for improvisation.

Definitely. Of course, I started working sessions around '49 way before Walker got there. One of the sounds of Nashville was the fact that every note for the guitar players, and the bass players and the pianists—all in the rhythm section—they weren't written out. All they had were chord sheets and they made up their own little fills. The pianists did: Floyd Cramer, he made up his own fills. The bass player did. Everybody, because I thought that was the sound of Nashville. Whereas you could go to New York and write every note for them all to play and get it played, so the arrangements sound only like me, like things I would put down. Then I could go to California and do the same thing, but it would still sound like my arrangements. Whereas in Nashville it was my arrangements, but I gave them chord sheets, and between Chet and I, if we didn't like what they were playing, if he didn't like it, he would tell them or if I didn't like it, I would just walk over and say, "You know that fill that you're playing just doesn't seem to fit what I've written, the feeling of it." That's exactly why I wouldn't do it. To me that was the Nashville Sound. And most of them couldn't read [music] anyhow. It's changed in Nashville and it did when Walker was there. Many of the musicians could read then. But the ones I was working with were all self-taught. They couldn't read music, but they could read chord changes. It was almost beside thinking that was the sound, I was kind of forced to do it that way, too. Because if I had written every note for them, they wouldn't have been able to read it.

Violinist Brenton Banks says that you brought him to the sessions.[5]

Definitely. I was the one who got him started working on things.

Were you working with strings before that? Or was that the first time strings were used on sessions at RCA?

We had tried strings from the symphony orchestra and they just didn't play right on the beat. They either were ahead of the beat. I knew that Brenton besides being a violinist was a good pianist. I knew he really played the piano with a beat. I said, "What they really need is someone in charge to tell them to play with them that they can follow and to tell them when they are ahead of the beat or behind the beat." In those days, those violinists weren't raised on hearing rhythm as much as the younger violinists are now. All they played really was symphony music. They just weren't raised with a lot of other kinds of music. They needed that help. He added an awful lot to that. They got to the point where they really did great.

When they did play the arrangement, they weren't right on the beat. Brenton, as leader of the strings, the concertmaster, they had to do what he said. He played beautifully, but even though he played beautifully, the second reason we really wanted him to be the leader was because they needed help in the rhythm department.

So when you hear that so much of the studio work was done with head arrangements, that really wouldn't be accurate in terms of sessions you worked on?

If I remember correctly we did a lot of head arrangements too, in fact the whole band and the singers. We did some with Eddy too when we just walked into the studio and didn't know what the song was going to be, didn't know what it went like. We would just stand there and work out our part of the arrangement along with the musicians. So we did do some, I'm sure ... probably, maybe, at the beginning. Because when arrangements started being furnished on sessions it got to the point where a lot of the country artists wanted arrangements written. I think it was mainly the very country ones that there was nothing written. Like Porter

Wagoner, I worked a lot of sessions with him, but I never wrote anything because he was a lot more country than Eddy, who was almost pop, I thought.

The sessions seemed to have been routine, despite the fact there was often great music coming out of them.

As I said, we would have the routine worked out. But Chet never changed notes on any of my arrangements. He never changed anything, even the little fills that the band was playing, where I really didn't write out the notes, just the chords. He never changed what they were playing, unless he thought it was not in keeping with the song or the arrangement.

In your position on the A&R staff did you have any role in choosing songs for Eddy Arnold?

Not for Eddy, because Chet was the A&R man for Eddy. I recorded other artists. I produced Skeeter Davis, "End of the World." But most of the time, Chet picked out the songs because he had an excellent nose for songs, that's the way I put it. He could just smell a hit. So that was really his domain.

Did you have Dottie Dillard and Louis Nunley and Gil Wright from the start, was that the makeup of the Anita Kerr Singers?

When I had the eight-voice group at WSM, it wasn't them. It changed gradually through the years. Then we did the Arthur Godfrey show in 1957, and Godfrey just wanted four, he didn't want all eight. I just used Dottie and then Gil and Louis and we went to New York and did that talent show and we won. After that, we were going back and forth from Nashville for five or six years. There would be two weeks in New York and then four in Nashville. That's another thing that made our work pick up considerably. It got to the point that when we were home, we were offered more sessions than we could do. I had to refuse some of them because we were always booked.

So the appearances on the Godfrey show increased your profile?

Oh definitely, I think. I don't know if anybody would admit it.... It started rolling and just kept picking up speed.

Interviews with Anita Kerr were conducted on May 25, 1996, and June 4, 1997.

Notes

1. Interview with Wayne Moss, Nov. 17, 1995.
2. Interview with Louis Nunley, Nov. 16, 1995.
3. Interview with Gene Allan Carr via electronic mail, Feb. 11, 2003.
4. Kerr is referring to the song "Trouble in the Amen Corner," which Reeves recorded in 1961. The Anita Kerr Singers appeared on the recording, and it was written by Archie Campbell, who figured in the career of Red Kirk, whom we'll meet later.
5. Probably the first African American session player in Nashville, Brenton Banks began working sessions with Kerr in the early 1960s.

Ginny Wright
Little Country Girl

A few readers may be inclined to skip this interview with Ginny Wright. After all, who's Ginny Wright? Her music has seeped from the consciousness of anybody acquainted with country music; she performs nowhere, save perhaps in church or in her shower; and a quick check of reference material shows that she recorded a mere two country hits in the 1950s.

But those two hits reached the top five: "I Love You" in '54 and "Are You Mine?" in 1955. There should have been more for Ginny, her piercing voice and chart performance suggest as much. But she married not long after "Are You Mine?" and embarked on family life in her home state of Georgia. Like her singing voice, her departure from music was boldly assertive: she shrugged off an oppressive manager-producer and chose love over the mirage that fame can be.

But the mirage turned out to be marriage. Two of them dissolved, leaving her wishing that she hadn't fled so quickly from music. When she sought a way back, there were no doors open to her, and the disappointment drained her: it was difficult to realize that she had missed something big. But when she recounted for me her fame and fall from it in hours-long interviews, I was amazed that she never cried. She calmly told the story of a woman's life and career.

BORN IN TWIN CITY, GEORGIA, Ginny Wright was one of eight children. By the 1950s, she was living with a sister in Cleveland, Ohio, where she took voice and guitar lessons. Soon, her clear-as-a-bell voice and comin'-at-ya delivery found a home in a country band that performed in clubs and on television. She recorded for a tiny Cleveland record label, and in 1954 took a ticket to national prominence from Fabor Robison, the co-owner—with drug store owner Sid Abbott—of Los Angeles–based Abbott Records.

A Fabor Records' publicity photograph of Ginny Wright. Courtesy of R. A. Andreas.

Through Ginny Wright, we glimpse intimately Robison, a man with a Cheshire-cat grin who helped build the careers of major artists such as Jim Reeves, the Browns, and Johnny Horton. Reviled by most anybody with whom he worked for his alleged withholding of royalties and dictatorial style, Robison is one of the most enigmatic figures in country music. He revealed little about himself to those around him and remained elusive throughout his life, dashing from town to town—from country to country, even—searching for the next big thing.

Other figures in music history fleetingly tremble to life in Wright's recollections. She paints humanizing portraits of Jim Reeves, one of country music's most influential stars, and Elvis Presley, who was on the cusp of fame when he and Ginny crossed paths in Shreveport, Louisiana. Ginny was their mate, traveling the same roads, treading the same stages.

Reeves and Presley kept to those roads and stages. But what of those who didn't? Ginny knows. She relinquished her limelight before it dimmed.

I WAS IN CLEVELAND, OHIO, and I was working for General Electric and helping my sister in a restaurant at night time. I was putting all my tips away so I could buy me a guitar, which I bought me a D-28 Martin with my tips. I loved country music. I was taking opera lessons, and my teacher didn't want me to sing country music, but I slipped around with this country band and sang. We sang for businessmen's clubs, and we started doing TV shows. And we had this great big barn dance every Friday and Saturday night I sang at. I started singing with a girl and we went by the name of the Blue Star Girls, but she got to where she was boy crazy. The owner of the band let her go and he kept me. I was scared to death of having to sing by myself. I got out there one night and it's a big barn dance and they served cold drinks and coffee and hot dogs and stuff. I got up and the first song I ever sang by myself was "Precious Lord, Take My Hand" and of course nobody danced by it. Everybody just stood up and listened. Everybody come out from behind the concession stand—I was real young, about 18—and listened to me. I was scared. I was about ready to say, "Lord do take my hand. Take me off of this stage."

I was doing everything I could to find somebody that would record me. I didn't know anybody, but I struck up with people up there in Cleveland, Ohio. I was going around just singing with this little local band, and they told me about Jack Gale. He was more or less recording pop music. He had recorded Johnny Ray with "Cry." It was a real big hit record for him. But I think he sold it to a major label because he wasn't in a position to push it like he really wanted to.

I went down there to his office. He had a partner with him and I walked in and I was talking to his partner; I forgot his name now. I said, "I sing country music." I couldn't play the guitar [well], so I took one of the guys in the band down with me to play the guitar for me while I sang. I knew every one of Hank Williams's songs at that time. I reared back and did "Kaw-Liga" and "Your Cheatin' Heart." And he listened to me, and he said, "It sounds pretty good. I got a guy down the hall here that's my partner. He's got a little country music show and he does different voices." Anyway, I went down the hall and Jack put his feet up on the desk, and he reared back and said, "Okay, let me see what you can do." I sang "Kaw-Liga" and two or three other songs for him. He said, "I'll let you know something." He told me to call him at 12:00. Man, I couldn't wait for 12:00 to come and I called him. He signed me up on this little Triple A label, which he owned. He cut "Goin' Steady," which Faron Young had out, and "You're Under Arrest," which Ray Price had out at that time.

He put it out locally. The thing just started taking off on his show, and right around Cleveland and places. It just so happened that Fabor Robison was going to Detroit, Michigan, to pick up Jim Reeves who was playing in a big nightclub there in Detroit. He was coming through and he knew Jack and he was punching around on the radio and he heard this record Jack was playing. He called him up and he said, "That's the girl I want to put on my new label." He owned Abbott Records at that time. He said, "I'm going to start Fabor Records, and I'd like to sign her up."

Jack didn't want to let me go. They talked about it and everything. It must have been two or three weeks later, I went up to the radio station. I used to go up there and aggravate Jack, cut up with him. He'd call a taxi and send me home; I wanted to get on the air and be a disc jockey, too. He always laughed at me because he took me around to get my picture made one time and the photographer was pushing my head this way and that way. And I said, "You quit, you hateful thing." So that's Jack's saying. Every time he calls me, he says, "Hey you hateful little thing." But anyway, he told me, "This guy came through who's got Jim Reeves." And at that time that label was hot because he had Johnny Horton. Of course [he also had] Mitchell Torok; he recorded him with a song he wrote called "Caribbean." It was a pretty hot label. He said, "He'd like to sign you up, but I ain't going to let you go." Man, I pitched a fit. I said, "Jack you can't do nothing with me. You don't have the money to push me and promote me. I don't have it. You give me that man's number and let me call him." So, I called him out in California. And he said, "Yeah, Ginny, I like your voice. Put me about ten songs on a tape and send them to me." I still couldn't play guitar very good. So, I went and got one of the guys out of the band and went up to the radio station where Jack was at and Jack made ten songs for me. He didn't want to, but he did. He said, "Boy, you got the nerve." And I said, "Well, I got to get somebody to put me on tape." So I did ten different country songs, a lot of them Hank Williams, a lot of them Webb Pierce, different ones, and sent them. I quit my job at General Electric and I was just working nights with my sister at the restaurant. Everybody said, "You crazy for quitting your job." I said, "Shoot! I'm going in show business." All the waitresses said, "You ain't never going to hear nothin' from that." About two months went by and sure enough I didn't hear anything. I thought, "Well my God, ain't nothin' gonna happen, I guess."

I was out there one night and I was working and I had to make a whole lot of milk shakes for these jockeys that ride horses. I was mad as heck and I looked up and I saw this Cadillac pull up in front of the restaurant. It was Manner's restaurant, kind of like a Shoney's restaurant. I saw this guy pull up and it had a California license plate on it and he had on dark glasses. Well I reached back and pulled off my apron and laid it up on the counter. My sister said, "Where do you think you're going." I said, "*I'm* going to record." She said, "You're crazy." I said, "I bet you that's Fabor Robison." I met him at the door and said, "You're Fabor." And he said, "You're Ginny. I've come by to get you." I said, "I'm ready to go." He said, "We'll leave out in the morning." I was living with my sister at that time and I went home and packed me a suitcase. And he said he'd pick me up the next morning. He was on his way to Detroit, Michigan, to pick up Jim [Reeves]. And Jim had the big hit record "Mexican Joe" at that time. He came by and got me and I was scared to death. I got me a pillow and I put it in between me and him. He said, "What you got that for?" I said, "I've heard about you men. You better not dare even come across this pillow." He had a black Cadillac at that time, so we went on up there to Detroit, and I was young, didn't know what to do, and I said, "Lord have mercy. I'm going to get to meet Jim Reeves." He was a big artist then.

So we went on to the nightclub that night and Jim got up and sang, but then he came down and said, "Ginny, do you know 'Dear John [Letter]'?" I said, "Yeah. I know 'Dear John.' I know just about every country song." He said, "What about getting up and singing it with me?" So I got up and sang it with him. The people in there were applauding and everything. So he said, "Why don't you do one by yourself?" So I got up and I did [Goldie Hill's] "I Let the Stars Get in My Eyes." Another artist had out "Don't Let the Stars Get in Your Eyes."[1] She had out the answer to it. Anyway, I sang that thing and you go around on one verse and if you don't sing the other one, you get tangled up and you just keep going around and around and you can't end the blamed thing. So I sat up there and I sang the same verse over and over about five or six times, and I just backed up, just quit. Jim come up there and said, "Ginny don't let that get you down. Do another one." I was scared to death, but I went ahead and did another song. That's where Fabor got the idea of doing me and Jim on "I Love You."

At intermission, [Jim] came by and sat down and this woman walked up to me, kind of a young woman. She had short, bobbed off hair and she had on pants like a man. She was patting me on the shoulder and just putting her face up in mine. "You don't need a microphone. You got the strongest voice. Your voice is really strong." Back then it really was. I could yodel and that kind of stuff. She was patting me, and Jim looked up at her and he said, "You get the hell away from her!" I kind of looked funny. I kind of opened my mouth. I didn't know that artists did fans like that. I said, "Jim she's a fan. What are you doing that for?" He looked at me and laughed. He said, "Ginny, you don't know what she is?" I said, "She's a woman. She's a fan. She came up here telling me that she liked my voice and everything and I'd be a great singer." He pulled up his chair by me, "Honey, I know you're a little country girl but I'm going to tell you about the birds and the bees. You stay away from women like that." Of course, he explained to me all about it. I didn't know nothing about it. I just couldn't believe that a woman went with a woman or a man went with a man. I was just green.

After the show that night, we drove straight through from Detroit all the way to Shreveport. Fabor would drive a while and Jim would sleep in the back seat. I'd sit up there in the front seat and then when Jim would drive he would sing songs to me that he wrote. He wrote this song "Please Leave My Darling Alone," which I recorded, which was not put out until after I got mad and left Fabor and came home and got married. He sang me another one that he wrote called "I've Forgotten You," which Fabor wouldn't let me record because we were only going to do four songs on the session. Anyway, later on Hank Snow recorded it.

After we got down to Shreveport, the radio station [KWKH] stayed on 'til one o'clock. So we recorded from one to daylight. And that's when we cut "I Love You." And Jim cut "Bimbo" that very same night. I cut two of Mitchell Torok's songs, "I Want You to Want Me," which was on the back side of "I Love You." And then I cut another song that Mitch wrote—it's called "Where Were You?"—which was later put out, too. We did those songs, and we all had to sit around one microphone. It was quite different back then, recording, than what it is now. Like it is now when your record and make a mistake, you can go back and take that mistake out. Back then, you couldn't do it. So they like to sing me to death. I remember the guy that was doing the recording, the engineer, he said, "My God, Ginny hasn't made a mistake and you all making all kinds of mistakes." But Jimmy Day was on steel guitar. Jim played rhythm and Floyd Cramer played piano and Jerry Rowley was on fiddle.

You also appeared on the Louisiana Hayride *in Shreveport?*

They would take the first half hour from the *Louisiana Hayride* and record it and send it to the soldier boys overseas. One of the soldier boys wrote a letter to Horace Logan: he was the head of the *Hayride* at that time. And he asked me would I go read it. I said, "Oh my God." I thought I was gonna die. I had never been in front of that many people, but I went out and read the letter and that was my first appearance on the *Hayride*. When I come back off the stage, Mr. Logan said, "Well, Ginny I heard your song 'I Love You' and you got a hit. When you go out to California and get out there and write the disc jockeys"—because Fabor wanted me to go out there and start writing disc jockeys and everything—"come back and I'd like to put you on the *Hayride* as a regular." It seemed like "My God. Am I Cinderella or what? What's happening?" Everything was so great.

When I started to leave, Jim come bent over the car and said, "Well, Ginny, don't stay out there too long. We got a hit on our hands." He didn't know at the time that "Bimbo" was going to hit, too. "Bimbo" hit and so did "I Love You." I went on out to California and stayed out there and wrote disc jockeys, and then I left and come back to the *Louisiana Hayride* and joined up as a regular. Of course, Jim and I would do "I Love You" every Saturday night and he'd do "Bimbo," and we'd book around in Texas and Louisiana and New Mexico. We went out to New Mexico quite a bit.

What kind of places would you play?

Big auditoriums and we played a few nightclubs, but not very many. I just didn't like nightclubs. We played fairs and different things like that. One night we played a big auditorium in Hobbs, New Mexico, and we got out there and we did "I Love You." Well they just encored us one time after the other. So we got tired of going out and singing "I Love You." Jim says, "Let's fool them. Let's do something else. Do you do 'Dear John' in the same key?" I said, "Yep. Key of D." So we went out there and the band took off and I sang, "Dear John . . . ," and I mean the audience just went crazy. They thought that was something. We'd pull tricks like that. Jim was real easy to work with.

Mary would go with us a lot, his wife. She would stay at the motel. She very seldom would ever go out to the show. "We'd be riding along and singing songs and the guys would be talking, but one thing about it. Jim was such a gentleman until those guys—some of them might take a little drink—but if any of them got to telling nasty jokes or cursing or something like that, he would immediately stop them. He said, "There are ladies in the car. You don't do this." It was just a wonderful world for me. I loved it. I loved every minute of it.

I know that night we played the big auditorium there in Hobbs, New Mexico, this guy came up and he ran a nightclub and he invited everybody after the show to come to the nightclub and sing and he would furnish free drinks. Well I went and got my guitar, got my little old cosmetic case, and I started heading out to the car and Jim says, "Ginny where do you thing you're going?" I said, "I'm going with you all. I'm invited. I'm on the show." I know Johnny Horton was on the show that night. There was quite a few big artists that was on it. He said, "You just go get in my car. I'm taking you back to the motel. You're staying with Mary. You all start packing up because we're leaving and going back to the *Hayride* right afterwards." I said, "Lookee here! Who do you think you are? I got invited too." He said, "You ain't going to that place." He just looked after me. I guess he knew that I come from pretty good stock. I don't know what I was going to do going to a nightclub like that because I didn't drink. It was so funny, I got mad at him and I come back to the hotel and I'm crying. And Mary said, "What's the matter with you?" I said, "Jim won't let me go. They invited me." She said, "He knows what he's doing. You ain't got no business going to that place."

How well did you know Mary?

When we was in Shreveport, when Jim would be booking out by himself and I'd have some days to myself, Mary would come and pick me up and we'd go out to a movie and go out to eat. We went out to rodeos together, and went on picnics together. A lot of times Jim would be with us. We went to the fair. We just more or less stuck around like artists do. I didn't know anybody else. The Rowley Trio would go with us and Carolyn Bradshaw. We would go to different places like that.

When Mary wasn't traveling with Jim did she feel left out?

I don't think so. A lot of times she would go with us, but she would never go to the show. She would go and stay in the motel. I asked her one time because I was kind of curious. We had a big barn dance in Hobbs, New Mexico, and Tibby Edwards was on there and Johnny Horton and me and Jim and several other people was on there. I said, "Mary why don't you get ready and go with us?" She said, "No. I don't want to go. I don't like to see the women messing over Jim. If I don't go, I don't see it, and I don't know anything about it. I'd just rather not." She'd stay at the motel, and we'd do the show and then we'd come back. Most of the time, we packed up and leave right then, and go back to the *Hayride.*

She must have been a strong person, given that they were married and Jim was a well-known star, he was out on the road, he was popular with women, certainly had opportunities with other women. What about her allowed her to handle that?

Just like you say, she was a strong person. I don't think I could have handled it if it would have been me. She handled it really well. If she ever was jealous, she never did let on like she was. She answered his mail. She was more or less like a secretary for him. I guess when he was on the road, she spent most of her time just helping him. I played a lot [of] shows with him, and Mary went with us a lot, and sometimes she wouldn't. I've seen things happen like girls coming on to him. Jim was a man and there would be some nice looking girls and sometimes he would sit and talk with them.

When [Fabor] came to Cleveland, Ohio, to pick me up. I was helping my sister do waitress work and he came to pick me up. I was scared to death of him. I went with him, and I made sure that he got me a room by myself. He came back to the car and said, "They ain't got but one room." I said, "That's all right. I'll sleep in the car." He laughed at me and said, "Get on out chicken. I got you a room." I remember definitely this girl. I couldn't understand it because I had been raised so close by my mother and my daddy. At that time, I wasn't married, I was single, I was a virgin. I couldn't understand how people could live like that. But that's the way the world is. There she was with a husband, and she slept with Fabor and she slept with Jim. I couldn't understand it. I guess that's just the way life is. I remember Jim telling me, "Jenny don't slip up and say anything about that woman." That was in Detroit.

Getting back to your work in Shreveport, did KWKH book your shows?

Pappy Covington I think his name was. He was kind of a heavyset guy. A lot of times he'd book me out alone. And I would get my guitar and I flew. I caught a plane. I used to book a lot in Carlsbad, New Mexico. That's where one of Jim Reeves' fan club presidents was at. Her name was Lucky Brazeal. I used to go and stay at their house. She had a daughter and a boy and we used to go out horseback riding in the mountains and camp out and shoot skunks and everything else. I just had a ball. She was a wonderful person and she made a lot of my costumes for me, too, a very good seamstress.

Jim would stay out there, too, when he would go. "Bimbo" got real big so he started booking out a lot by himself, too. They would allow us to maybe book out two times a month, but the rest of the time we had to stay on the *Hayride* because we had a contract with them.

Jim and I were supposed to cut another song called "I'm in Heaven" and I know it would have been a nationwide hit, but something happened between him and Fabor. I don't know what it was. They had a misunderstanding. So instead Fabor cut me with that song with Tom Beardon. And Tom was on the *Louisiana Hayride*. Well, Tom's voice was kind of deep. It wasn't like Jim's. Later on the Browns, on RCA-Victor, cut this record, the same one that I cut, but Jim and I were supposed to record that and in fact we rehearsed it and it was great. It hurt me very much that Fabor wouldn't let Jim record it with me, but he had Tom Beardon record it with me. It did good.

[Tom] was a real tall guy and I'd go out on stage at the *Louisiana Hayride* and we had one microphone and I had to take a Coca-Cola crate and stand on it to reach the mike. Or make Tom Beardon have to bend over. And the audience would holler about that.

Of course, I was on the *Louisiana Hayride* the first night Elvis Presley came on there [October 16, 1954]. They had Jim and Slim Whitman and Mitchell Torok and myself were considered the main stars on the *Louisiana Hayride*. But Elvis came just as a guest with the two members of his band and he was scared to death. I went on right ahead of him and he come up to me biting his fingernails and walking the floor. We used to have one waiting in the wings and one waiting on the stage. It was all unrehearsed. We just put down the songs we were going to sing on Saturday to the next Saturday. And the band was so great. They could just pick up anything, the *Louisiana Hayride* band. I was out waiting in the wings and Johnny Horton was on right ahead of me and Elvis was coming on after me. And he liked to walk himself to death. He was just a walking and a walking. And he come up to me and said, "How can you be so calm?" I said, "I'm not calm. I'm scared. Just take a breath and go on out there and sing." We kind of laughed about it, and he went out there and sang. The first song he did was "That's All Right Mama." He had that out on Sun Records. He was such a nice guy. He had a picture. It wasn't even a glossy picture because he couldn't afford them. Elvis didn't have any money back then. And he signed, "To Ginny. Elvis Presley." I still got the picture here with me right now and I wouldn't take nothing for it. But I threw it over in my guitar case. After he got off the stage, he didn't get all that big of applause. He was kind of nervous about it. You see, those people like country music and "That's All Right Mama" kind of threw them off. They didn't know what to think about it. So I told him, "That's all right. They'll catch on to it. Get out there and sing you a good country song." And they had a little coffee place right out from the *Hayride* and in between our songs—we'd sing them one at a time, you know—we would go down and have coffee. Elvis and I went down there and had a cup of coffee together and we talked. He talked to me about his mother and all them things. He got back out there and he did—I believe it was— "Old Shep," about the dog, you know. Of course, the audience responded a lot better.

And then Fabor called me and wanted me to come out to California and cut "Are You Mine?" which Myrna Lorrie and Buddy DuVal wrote. So I caught a plane. I have never flown before. Scared to death. The Rowley Trio took me out to the airport. I had lost my ticket, finally found it. Fabor told me to bring a coat because it was a little cold out there. I hung it up in the airport and I got up on the plane and a man beside me went to take his coat off and I went to take mine off and I didn't have no coat. My coat was down there in the airport. I looked at the stewardess, she came by. The plane had done gone up. It was one of those four-motor planes; back then, they didn't fly jets. I looked at her and I told her, "Where's my parachute?" She looked at me and she said, "What?" I said, "I want to know where my parachute's at." I meant it. I thought you really wore a parachute. She said, "Honey. You don't wear parachutes on passenger planes." I said, "Don't you tell me that. You just turn this plane around and take me back." She said, "If it started falling, you wouldn't have time to jump out no way." It was quite comical, and I sat there and watched the motor the whole time. When I got to California, I had a crink in my neck. I was making sure that motor wouldn't stop, like I could do something about it.

But Jim was out there too, and they gave a big party for me and him, took pictures and our pictures were in the magazines and everything. Anyway, I went out there and I met Tom Tall. Tom was still in school; he was like two or three years younger than me. We rehearsed this "Are You Mine?" We recorded it where Tennessee Ernie Ford recorded all his stuff, Western Recorders. Used Speedy West and he is one of the best steel guitar players I've ever heard. That thing took off like a bullet after Christmas. "I Love You" stayed on the charts for twenty-two weeks. Well, "Are You Mine?" stayed on there something like twenty-six weeks. Back then songs did that, but now they don't. They hit number one and stay on there one or two weeks and drop back down.

Fabor called Mr. Logan and asked him could I be dismissed off the *Hayride* for a while. He said he wanted to book me out there. He started doing that and I was going to have to go back to the *Hayride* later. We booked all up and down the coast, all over California, Oregon, Washington, and everywhere with that song.

In the meantime, Fabor started this thing with me and Jim and the Browns and Tom Tall—this was before we cut "Are You Mine?"—called the String Music Show. We just went everywhere. I believe it was about six weeks we were on the road. We traveled in Cadillacs. I was the featured girl singer; Jim was the featured boy singer. They sent out these advertisements ahead about the String Music Show ahead. We played one-night stands. We went everywhere. We started off in California. Of course, Jim and I sang "I Love You" a lot. Tom Beardon was not on there with us, so Jim Ed Brown sang "I'm in Heaven" with me. We finished up on the *Louisiana Hayride*.

Reeves' guitarist Leo Jackson told me that on the String Music Show Fabor wouldn't let the men and women mingle.

There was a lot of problems going on, but Fabor was mingling himself. He didn't mingle with me, but he was messing around. I went into a room and was going to talk to him because I was getting aggravated at everything. He had pressured us so much, and he was making life miserable. We couldn't go nowhere. We couldn't even go to the swimming pool. He went back [to Hollywood] to record and he caught a plane. It wasn't too long after we left on the tour. He told us all not to go swimming. So, me and Shirley Bates and his secretary, we all wanted to go swimming and we all went downtown and bought bathing suits. This little Alvadean Coker, she was a little tattle-tale. Well, she told that we went swimming and man he just raged and went on and carried on until Shirley Bates called her boyfriend. He come up and got her, and the police had to come out to the motel to keep Fabor from jumping on her boyfriend. I was going to leave, too. I wasn't putting up with that. I was going back to the *Hayride*. I'm not used to taking stuff like this: somebody telling me what to do and clamping down on me like that. Jim came and talked to me and said, "Ginny you're the featured girl and I'm the featured guy. Without me and you there's no show. Shirley we can do without because she's just a fill-in. We can't do without each other. You've got to stay." I said, "If I stay, he better keep his mouth off of me from now on and I mean it." So, I went into the room to talk to him and him and Alvadean . . . he had his hand up her dress tail and all that kind of stuff. He was just that way, and he used to try things with me, and I told him, "My daddy'll kill you if you don't keep your hands off me." He said, "Well, I got other women." I said, "You take those other women. You do what you please. If you don't want to make an artist out of me, I'll go someplace else and make an artist out of myself. I don't need you."

So he didn't want any of the women swimming.

I think he just didn't want us to get in contact with any men or anything. He was always jealous. I dated an Air Force guy in Shreveport while I was on the *Hayride*, and he was a good-looking guy, and I just dated him a few times. He also drove a race car, and I went out and rode in the lead car with him one Sunday. My God, Fabor found out I was dating him and that's when he really started making plans to pull me out to California. He took me off the *Hayride* for a while and pulled me out there.

Then there was this young boy that I had met on the *Louisiana Hayride*. He had come [from California] to be a guest star on there one night. He wrote a lot of songs. He was a young good looking guy and I was young, too. There wasn't anything wrong with me. I wanted to date and see people. He told me, "If you come to California, call me and let me know." So when I got out there I called him. I was playing with the Squeakin' Deacon, one of those Riverside Ranch Shows.[2] Fabor had to go someplace—Chicago—to record somebody or on business. He made Mary [Robison, Fabor's wife] drive me, and he told Mary not to let me out of her sight. That boy wanted to take me out to eat after the show. I told Mary and she said, "You know what Fabor said. You better not go out with nobody." I said, "Well look Mary, I'm not going home with you. I am not. You can follow behind us if you want to. I want to see the ocean. I haven't seen the ocean since I've been here. We are riding down by the ocean and get us something to drink and then I'm going home." She followed us all the way. Everywhere we would go, she would go. So, that's the kind of atmosphere I had to live in.

So Fabor was booking you also.

He was my manager and I didn't much go for that. I don't think Jim went for it, too. I think that's one reason that he left and went with RCA. He'd come out there when I was in California, right after I cut "Are You Mine?" and me and him had a long talk. And me and him and Fabor went down to a restaurant to eat and I thought him and Fabor were going to have a fight because he told Fabor he wanted to be released. "Bimbo" was hitting big then. He just told Fabor he was getting out of the business, he was quitting. All the time, he was fixing to go with Steve Sholes of RCA-Victor. Fabor got mad and got up and left. And Jim told me, "Ginny. You got a contract if you want it waiting right there with RCA-Victor." And, see, that's where I made my big mistake. I should have left, too. Fabor finally released Jim, but Jim had to turn over all his royalties to Fabor. I had to do the same thing, eight years later when I was married, before he ever would release me.

Tom [Tall] and I booked a lot of shows and "Are You Mine?" was really hitting big. We were on the *Hometown Jamboree* out there. We were on several different jamborees in California. We were on TV with the Collins Kids, Lefty Frizzell, and a lot of big artists. Him and I, we had a show and had to go to Phoenix, Arizona, and I had just bought me a brand new car, couldn't even drive the blamed thing. I didn't have any license. So I left it out there. Tom drove his car and we went to Arizona and we played this big show, a great big town hall dance. We had some television shows we played. I decided I was going home. I got mad, you know how young people are. I just threw a temper tantrum and tried to give Tom my guitar, but he wouldn't take it. He said, "Ginny, one of these days, you'll like to keep that D-28 Martin. I'm not going to do it." So I caught a plane and I went home. In the meantime, I was writing to this guy from Sandersville, Georgia. Because he was from Georgia, I wrote him. He wrote me a letter and I'd write him back. And he sent me a picture and, oh boy, he was as good looking as Elvis Presley. He had slick black hair and everything. I fell in love with a picture, I guess. I was lonesome. Fabor wouldn't let me date. He watched me like a hawk. He wouldn't let me talk to anybody. I went and called my sister on the phone one time at a pay phone. He followed me and told me I was calling some major labels. He said, "I know that's what you're doing." I said, "Would you like to talk to my sister? That's who I'm talking to." He just watched me too close. I was too young. I wanted to date and meet people and go out. I wasn't the type who was going to live a rough life or go to bed with somebody. I just wasn't that type. But anyway I got aggravated and I caught a plane and I went home. My husband-to-be—I didn't even know I was going to marry him at that time—him and his sister met me at Atlanta airport. I come home and stayed with my mother and daddy who ran a grocery store in Twin City, Georgia, not too far from where he lived. And he come down everyday and we dated and everything, that was right before Christmas. Of course, Fabor thought I was coming back. He thought maybe I'd get over my little mad spell and I'd come back. So I started singing on the *Peach State Jamboree* in Swainsboro. Man, I packed the house, I guarantee you. Every Saturday night I'd sing there with local people. When he saw I wasn't coming back, he got in that Cadillac and he drove all the way across the United States and come in there to my mother and daddy's grocery store and went back in the back to the kitchen and slammed down $200 and told me to get on a plane and be back in California. He said, "You are booked for a session and you are supposed to be going on the *Grand Ole Opry* and the *Red Foley Show*, and Paramount Pictures is interested in you." We had made a film. I had all of this in the palm of my hand and I could have went with RCA-Victor at the snap of my fingers if he would have given me my release. Jim had said, "Go with RCA because you're never going to get anywhere with Fabor." He just kept me in the red all the time. He charged me for meals that I didn't even eat. Back then it was hard for an artist. There were so many of those small labels cheating people blind. Fabor had an ear for music. There's no doubt about it. But I know he made a remark one time: "Artists are like dogs and you got to treat them like dogs." I said, "I'm not no dog and you're not going to treat me like no dog."

I left and went home [around Christmastime] and in June I got married. I took the $200 that he give me to catch a plane and went and came over to Augusta and bought me a wedding dress and got married. I thought I would go back into it. I figured I'd go ahead and sign with RCA and Steve Sholes. I got married and it wasn't but four or five months after that that I found out that I was expecting a baby. After I had my little girl, I just decided not to go back. My husband, he didn't want me to go back. Fabor came down here one time and my husband got a gun. He said if he saw him he was going to shoot him. I said, "Well, I'll just forget about it and I more or less wrapped myself up in my little girl and my family and three years later I had another little girl. And five years after that I had a boy. Three years after that I had another boy and then another boy and then another boy. I have six children. And I more or less just wrapped my life and my world up around my family.

Fabor, I think, went over in South America and started a studio and then he went to Hawaii and he called me up after eighteen years. Of course, I had found my husband with another woman and we divorced and I raised my children by myself. My oldest one was like fifteen years old. But anyway, I raised my family without the help of him and went into nursing in a hospital. Fabor found out that I was single and he called me up and asked me would I come to Hawaii, that he would like to record me again. He said he could book me seven days a week over there. Well, I thought I would go, so I made a tape for him, went over to this studio in North Augusta and I struck up with this guy who was in what you call bootleg tapes. I didn't know it was bootleg tapes. I just thought they were making soundalikes. They would come back like every month. He was an ordained Baptist preacher, one of them was. So I wound up marrying him and I went to Texas. So I got sidetracked again. I never did get in the business any more. But later on I divorced this guy because he wasn't like he should be by my children. I went and worked out at Westinghouse, the Savannah River plant. I had a real good job out there and supported my kids.

I heard about Fabor, a guy called me from Shreveport and told me that Fabor was in bad shape and was in a nursing home. So I got this friend of mine to take me down there and I went to see him in 1986. He was laying in the bed and he was smoking a cigarette and I told him, "Fabor what in the world are you doing smoking a cigarette?" He knew me and everything. His mind was still very good. I said, "You would have killed me if I had smoked." He said, "Yeah, but you was a star." He said, "One thing I want to do is get out of this bed and record you one more time. I know you can make it." That was his dream that he wanted to do this. I stayed and talked with him a long time. We took some pictures. He didn't look like himself. He was quite pitiful. After I left and come back up and two or three weeks later, I got a call from this guy that he'd been staying with and he had passed away. I didn't get to go to the funeral.

That's more or less the story of my life with Fabor.

When did you last see Jim Reeves?

The next time I saw Jim, he had the Blue Boys, he hadn't had them together long. He had his bus and he came to the Bell Auditorium in Augusta. And when Elvis came I wanted to go see him so bad and I cried and cried and cried and my husband wouldn't let me go. "You ain't going to see him. I'm not going to let you." I said, "My God, I only knew Elvis on the *Louisiana Hayride*. So when Jim come, I said, "I'm going to Jim Reeves." So we went and I knew the man who run the backstage. So we sat there and watched the show and it was just great. Jim come on last. Leo Jackson played the instrumental "Wheels" so good. He could really play that thing. Jim sang his songs. He was on RCA-Victor then. He really went over big. I told my husband, "I gotta go backstage and see him." He said, "You just got to do that." He started on me. You know, a lot of women would say go to the devil, but I was the type, I just humbled down. I said, "Please, please go backstage with me." So we went backstage and Jim was bending over his guitar case, putting his guitar up and I walked up and tapped him on the shoulder. I hadn't seen him or heard from him since I left. Jim turned around. He had on this jacket that I always loved: it had tassels on the sleeves. He had that jacket on that night and with these big old arms he reached up and just grabbed me. He hugged me. I introduced him to my husband. He said, "Leo come here and look and see who's here. You won't believe it." Leo was standing off. Leo came over and grabbed me and hugged me. All of the other guys were mostly new.

So we went out in the parking lot and we're in our car, we had a Buick. Jim was fixing to get on the bus. They were cranking the bus up and loading it up and Jim comes and pokes his head in the window and talks to us. He said, "Ginny what in the world did you get out of the business for?" I couldn't tell him why. But I did speak up. I said, "Jim there's one thing I want you to tell my husband—and I want you to tell him honest—that I did not never have any affair with you or with Fabor or with anybody else in show business." He said, "I'll vouch for that. Ginny was a lady." Of course, my husband gave me hell after that. He threw up in my face a lot of times: "People in show business are no good. They travel around with men."

There are some good people in the world and Jim always was a gentleman and he treated me like he was my big brother.

He said, "Why don't you all take this Buick and put it on the back of this bus and let's go on the road." My husband says, "I don't think so. I don't think so. We can't do it." He says, "Well Mister Joseph, if you ever get tired of her, you just send her back to us because show business loved her." That was the last time I saw Jim.

I don't talk too much and tell people that I ever sang or I ever knew Jim because it is really unreal. The people you talk with, if you tell them you sang or you knew Jim or you knew Elvis, they look at you and kind of smirk and say, "You did?"—as if to call you a liar. They just can't believe that anybody would know them. I'm a person just like everybody else. Just like Elvis was a person, I'm a person. We're just real people and lucky enough to get a break.

Interviews with Ginny Wright were conducted on October 21, 1996, August 2, 1997, and August 3, 1997.

Notes

1. In the early 1950s, four country artists enjoyed hits with "Don't Let the Stars Get in Your Eyes": Skeets McDonald (1952), Slim Willet (1952), Ray Price (1952), and Red Foley (1953).
2. During the 1950s, Carl "Squeakin' Deacon" Moore hosted programs over radio station KXLA (Los Angeles) from the Riverside Rancho, a Los Angeles nightclub.

Red Kirk
Voice of the Country

his book takes its title from Red Kirk's billing. For fifty years, whether he was visiting the *Grand Ole Opry* or serenading dancers in a cramped east Tennessee Legion Hall, he was the "Voice of the Country." The appellation might seem a bit awkward next to sexy tags, such as the Drifting Cowboy, the Cherokee Cowboy, or the Hillbilly Cat, but it's rarely set down next to such names anyway.

For a while in the late 1940s, it looked like the Voice of the Country might echo across the country and settle next to the Drifting Cowboy and the Cherokee Cowboy. He flowed in the Knoxville, Tennessee, vein that carried the likes of Chet Atkins, the comedic duo Homer and Jethro, and Bill Carlisle, and it seemed a matter of time before this boyish man with red hair and freckles rose out of the vein and struck Nashville stardom, the way Atkins, Homer and Jethro, and Carlisle had. To clear a path west to Music City, Kirk scored two big hits for the fledgling Mercury Records: "Lovesick Blues" (1949) and "Lose Your Blues" (1950). Then he made the rounds of major radio barn dances, such as the *Opry*, the *Louisiana Hayride* in Shreveport, and the *National Barn Dance* in Chicago. Kirk even took on a manager, the storied Charlie Lamb, who later published *Music Reporter* in Nashville and enjoyed as many country music connections as one man could.

A powerful brew simmered in Kirk's pot: hit records, major radio appearances, resourceful management. But the brew lost its bite. Kirk's prospects turned cold and wan. He resorted to small label deals and off-the-circuit radio jobs in towns such as Lexington, Kentucky, and Lima, Ohio. He wrote songs, but never with much commercial success, and resorted to hocking furniture to finance self-produced records. Ultimately he landed back in east Tennessee, in Kingsport, where he deejayed on a small radio station outside town.

Red Kirk at radio station WNOX, Knoxville, Tennessee, c. 1951. Left to right: songwriter Arthur Q. Smith, Red Kirk, steel guitarist Howard White. Courtesy of Howard White.

As the red hair turned to white, this old journeyman ballplayer who never climbed out of the minor league marveled that his Nashville connections, who once seemed such hot leads, had faded into distant acquaintance: "I had all kinds of friends down there," he told me. "I just didn't take advantage of it. I never was one to be pushy."

I INITIALLY THOUGHT the Voice of the Country to be a study in frustration, but he did not fit the mold I had created for him. Years after the rejections and lost shots at fame when I met him in 1998, he appeared the picture of contentment. The people of Kingston adored him, listened to his country music radio show, bought the goods he pushed on television commercials, and filled the small venues where he and his band occasionally played. At home, he and his wife lived cozily.

The frustration angle deflected, I took another tack with Kirk, scrutinizing his career to find out why a man who enjoyed every opportunity failed to capitalize and reach the big time. It was clear that Kirk's vocals were less than dynamic, but so were those of many artists who made it. I asked "D" Kilpatrick, an A&R man with Mercury who produced Kirk in the early 1950s, why the singer never made it: "At that time you had to be half or two-thirds entertainer. To be a success on radio, as little as those jobs paid, you had to be an entrepreneur. That means being a business-man, swinger, promoter, about a half thief and a half genius. Red didn't qualify for that, yet he had the demeanor of a winner. . . . And Red wasn't easy to convince. Red had a mind of his own. I'm not saying he was stub-born, and he certainly wasn't stupid, but you didn't just convince him. He was a little bit like the late Hank Williams. You could have the best idea in the world and if Hank didn't buy it, you could show it to him all day long, and he wouldn't buy it. Once you got him aboard, look out, he'd run over you. He'd improve your own idea."[1]

So was it stubbornness, naiveté, poor singing, bashfulness? Why did this man, who started at WNOX in Knoxville with a raft of future stars, lose *his* future in country music?

In '49, when Hank Williams came out with "Lovesick Blues," Homer and Jethro were on the show and Homer and Jethro came downstairs from the control room one day and said, "Red, there's a record up there that you should learn." I had been doin' these yodelin' things, you know. I learned the words off of Hank's record and started singin' it. Murray Nash was the A&R man with Mercury, and he came over one day and said, "How would you like to have a record contract?" Well, I didn't even ask how much or why or what. I said, "Where do I sign?" Back then you had to be an old pro to get a record contract. I had only been in the business a couple of years. That's the way I got my deal with Mercury, because they wanted a cover record on "Lovesick Blues."

You recorded that on the first session you did?

Yeah. We did it at WCRK in Morristown, Saturday night after the *Barn Dance.*

I had an old arch top Harmony guitar that Archie [Campbell] had already told me sounded like beatin' on a damn lard can on the air. So Homer leant me his big blond J200 Gibson to use on the session that night.

That was 1949?

Yeah. April of '49. It bein' a cover record, Mercury didn't release it 'til June. The record was done coolin' off by the time they got our cover record out on the market.

That got to number fourteen on the Billboard *chart.*

My "Lovesick Blues" did? You know I didn't even know enough to watch
Billboard. . . . I listened to Nelson King on the ol' WCKY, the *Hillbilly Hit
Parade.* I did a cover record on George Morgan's "Cry Baby Heart" and
they backed it up with a cover on Hawkshaw Hawkins's "I Wasted a Nickel
Last Night." I was either in the number one or number two spot on the *Hillbilly Hit Parade* for several weeks. One of them was number one and the
other was number two for a couple of weeks. Then they switched places.
Nelson would play my "Cry Baby Heart" one night and Hawkshaw
Hawkins's "I Wasted a Nickel Last Night." And the next night he'd play
George Morgan's "Cry Baby Heart" and my "Wasted a Nickel." I was in
there every night for several weeks. . . . We'd listen to Nelson about every
night comin' back in. We'd play one nighters, and we'd be comin' back in
off the road about the time he'd get into the top ten.

Did he play your "Lovesick Blues"?

Yes, come to think about it, he did play it occasionally. But by the time,
like I say, mine got out on the market, "Lovesick Blues" was beginnin' to
fade. But you say it went to number twenty?

It went to number fourteen on the Billboard *chart.* . . . *You recorded
subsequent sessions for Mercury in Cincinnati?*

Murray booked us into Herzog's studio in Cincinnati and that's where I
met Jerry Byrd. It took us forever to make that session because I got so
enthralled with Jerry's handling of that bar and doing the things he does with
the steel guitar with a bar, that takes most steel guitar players fifteen pedals
to do. I'd be watching him and I'd lose my place. He played on most all my
other Mercury records after that first session.

Your session sheets talk about the Stringdusters backing you.

It was Louis Innis on rhythm, Zeke Turner playing lead guitar, Tommy
Jackson on fiddle, sometimes Red Turner on bass, sometimes Jethro's
brother, Archie Burns, would play bass with us. He was an extraordinarily
good bass man. He was an especially good show man.

You did duets with Judy Perkins.

Murray had us set up to do a duet session with Patti Page. Well, just a
week or so before that session was due to take place, Patti's "Tennessee
Waltz" started goin' through the roof, and her manager says, "No more."
She had already done a session with Rex Allen, who was on Mercury at the

time, but he wouldn't even let her do another session with Rex. She was such a hot commodity then that he didn't want anybody riding on her coattails, you know. So I did the session with Judy Perkins who was on the *Midwestern Hayride* on WLW.

Were you on WLW?

No. I didn't perform there. Jerry and all the rest of the crew worked there.

Where were you based in 1949?

Forty-nine is the year I left Archie and went to Lima, Ohio. That was Jerry Byrd's hometown, by the way. I got to know his family. Jerry'd come up and we'd all go pheasant hunting together.

Murray Nash was a sales manager for a hardware company in Knoxville.

He was the sales manager for C. M. McClung Hardware. They were the Mercury distributors, so he got in as an A&R man for Mercury.

He relocated to Nashville at some stage.

He went down there to run a publishing company, Murray Nash Associates. . . .

Charlie Lamb was my manager at one time, but he didn't do much managing because I had just had my car repossessed and I didn't have any transportation to get to these places he was booking me. And all these people he was booking me with was calling him and cussing him out because I didn't show up. And he'd call me and I'd tell him, "I told you I didn't have no way of gettin' there." So he didn't hang on to me long.

You told me June Carter beat you out of a job.

This is one of those things I can't prove. The front man for Martha White Flour with Chet and Mother Maybelle and Helen and June and Anita, he got to drinking so bad that he was missing the early morning show, which is hard enough to make sober, much less when you're drinking; they had an early morning show; then they had a spot on the *Friday Night Opry* and then the *Grand Ole Opry*. Martha White finally fired him. They were auditioning people to take his place. June wanted to front it, but they didn't want a woman to do it. They wanted a man to do it. Eddie Hill who was in Memphis at the time was invited and Joe Allison and me. The three of us were invited to come down for a week each and do the morning show, do the *Friday Night Opry* and do the *Grand Ole Opry*. After everything was over, I thought Eddie Hill had it and Eddie thought I had it, but no Joe Allison had it. Well, Joe was pretty much of a known drinker . . . so I always wondered that maybe June knew the score and knew Joe wouldn't last long and Martha White would get disgusted and say, "Okay June, you can have it." And June finally got to front the show.

When something like that would happen, would it be the advertising agency that called you to come down? Or a WSM person? Or somebody who worked for Martha White?

I'm not sure, but it might have been Chet that called me. It's been so long ago. I'm not positive, but it could have been Chet. Maybe they left it up to him to make suggestions. Since Chet and I had worked together before, it's very likely. And he knew Eddie Hill, and I'm sure he knew Joe Allison. That was 1950, maybe '51.

You've talked about Hank Williams coming after you.

I'd gone to Dallas to meet with Slim Whitman's manager, Mac Makela, with the thought in mind of fronting Slim's band, doing the show opener. . . . We went to Brownwood, Texas, to do the *Louisiana Hayride*[2] that Saturday night and I did a guest shot on the show and then we went back into Brownwood after the show was over and there was forty of us and the waitresses in the restaurant threw a bunch of tables together and made one big long table. I was sitting talking to the Carlisles's guitar player who had worked with us in Knoxville. He and I were discussing old times. Down on my left, Horace Logan was at the head of the table. On his right was Hank Williams and on Hank's right was Hank's new bride. It was November of '52. I was up to her right about seven or eight people. Well, Roy and I were talking, and I heard Hank a'cussing and a'carrying on and I looked down the table at him and he was looking right smack at me. I was trying to figure out what had happened and somebody said, "Somebody's throwing packs of crackers down there and they're getting close to his bride and he's upset about it." Of course, in his condition he was awfully easily upset. Horace Logan's job was to keep him just hyped enough to keep him from getting the shakes, but not so much that he couldn't stand up at the microphone. That was Horace's job: to take good care of Hank.

So I didn't think anymore of it. They quit throwing the crackers because nothing happened after a while. And after a while, buddy, Hank started storming out down there; somebody had thrown a cracker and it almost hit her. I looked up and here come Hank. He done pushed his chair back and was coming at me with a steak knife in his hand. So, I got ready to defend myself, what good you can against a steak knife. . . . But Horace caught him and prevented my bloodshed. Anyway, that was a close call. That was the last time I saw Hank. Of course, he died about six weeks later.

Hank had never been a real Red Kirk fan. I got my record contract with Mercury on the strength of his "Lovesick Blues."

Murray Nash, the A&R man for Mercury at the time, we were in Nashville to do a session one day and Murray said, "Hank's down at Acuff-Rose. Let's go down and get him to give us one of his good songs for the session." So we went down there, and Hank was there. Murray said, "Hank, Red's in town to do a session. Why don't you give him one of your good songs." So Hank went back in there and he come out with "Honky Tonk Blues." I liked the song. But one of the things that I did wrong all the time I was at Mercury was let Murray pick the material and tell me how to do it. I'm not beyond coaching and advice but I had no say so whatsoever. And I wanted to do that song, but Murray said, "No Hank give him one of your good ones." That kind of hurt Hank's feelings so Hank went back in there and brought out a song called "Ain't Never Been So Lonesome." Murray fell in love with it. We recorded it; it didn't sell nothing. Of course, Hank recorded "Honky Tonk Blues" about two or three months later and that's history. I don't know that I'd have sold it like he did. But we would have had a better shot.

We had a song that I recorded once called "Can't Understand a Woman Who Can't Understand Her Man." It was originally written as he's an alcoholic, and she has locked up his liquor cabinet. So, Murray changed it. Nothing about alcohol in it. "No buttermilk beside my bed . . . no water in my water cup." He took the meaning completely out of the song. He didn't want me doing honky-tonk drinking songs for some reason. I didn't drink, and I reckon he thought it would offend me, but, heck, all I was interested in was trying to sell some records. Them beer drinking songs are what sold back then. That was one of the things that hindered me.

You did quite a bit of songwriting.

A song that I wrote that Cowboy Copas recorded was "There's a Wreath on the Door of My Heart." *Billboard* called it "too morbid."

The only thing that I ever did that amounted to anything was Leroy Van Dyke who recorded one of our songs called "My World's Caving In." The Mercury A&R man at the time, he went rushing down to Atlanta to a publisher down there. He said, "You're gonna thank me for getting you on the back of this one. He just happened to be the publisher of "Walk on By."

That's the biggest joke of the century, the publisher thanking him for getting him on the back of "My World's Caving In." On our side, all the musicians, all the sidemen, Leroy, all the A&R people thought that was gonna be *the* side. I've always said since then that if you can't be talented and write the hits, just be lucky and get on the back of them.

We made a pretty good piece of change off of it. All we got, of course, was record sales. We didn't get much on performances cause everybody played the other side of it. Everytime we logged BMI, I managed to play it several times, and I had all the other jocks playing it. That made us a penny or two somewhere down the line.

You also recorded with other labels such as, ABC/Paramount, Starday.

Most of those things were done on an independent session and we just sold the masters, one to ABC and a couple of them to Starday. I did one session for Republic 'cause Murray Nash Associates bought Republic from Gene Autry.

So even after leaving Mercury, you kept up your association with Murray Nash?

Oh yeah. Murray had left Mercury and the last session or two that I did with Mercury, the A&R man was "D" Kilpatrick. We'd be rehearsin' a song in the studio, and he said, "What key are you doin' it in?" I'd say, "C." "Do it E flat." He'd step it up about a step and a half; he'd want me to scream it out. That's not the way I like to do things. Of course, like I said, I'd do whatever they told me. After a couple of sessions with him, Mercury decided they didn't want anything else to do with me.

How did you get on radio in Knoxville in the 1940s?

When I was a kid growing up, my mother kept thinking that I ought to be a singer, so she'd take me in and we'd audition for Lowell Blanchard.[3] The last time before I went into the service before World War II, I remember Lowell told me that I was going to have to develop some vibrato in my voice, and I had no idea what he was talking about. A country boy from Wolf Holler didn't know what vibrato was. But I remembered the word and I finally found out what it meant. I reckon it just naturally developed and I guess I grew up too. My voice matured a little bit.

We had had a Future Farmers of America (FAA) band in Clinton High School and one of the boys that was in that band—Howard Spesser—and I, we decided [after the stint in the service], we wanted to go in and do a guest shot on the [*Tennessee*] *Barn Dance*. Lowell invited us. We went in and sung for him.

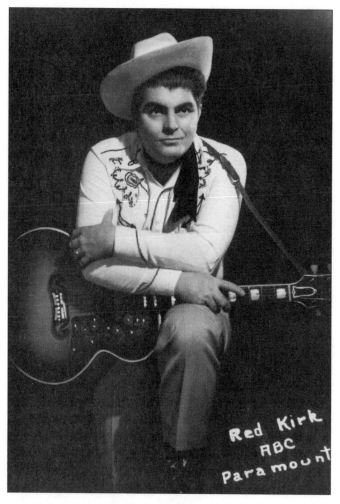

Red Kirk
ABC
Paramount

1950s promotional photo. Author's collection.

He put us on the off-the-air show while Eddy Arnold's *Purina Show* was on the network. We did the off-the-air show just for the people in the auditorium. Archie Campbell did a grandpappy character and he had closed the first on-the-air portion and went backstage to take off his grandpappy makeup. Lowell went back in the dressing room and said, "Archie, there's a fella out here that I want you to hear sing. Don't try to hire him because he's too damn smooth." This is 1947 and Eddy Arnold, him and Red Foley, were about the only two selling smooth stuff. Archie came out on stage and listened to me. When I got off, we went backstage and I went into the dressing room and talked with him, and he said, "Can you sing a part?" He said, "I need somebody to sing in my trio. How would you like to have a job?" I said, "Well, what about my buddy?" No, he couldn't use him. I said, "Well, we came in here together. I guess I'll not take it if you can't use him too." Like I was saying, that was part of that naiveté that I was so obsessed with back in my younger days. I wanted to take that job worse than a dead man wanted a casket. I was trying to be a good guy. On the way home, ol' Howard he give me up one side and down the other. "You go back in there Monday and you take that job. After you get in maybe you can help me get in. There ain't no use both of us being out."

I went back in again that Monday and I went backstage. I know I was a country bumpkin; I wasn't putting on a very good front. I said, "Mr. Campbell." He looked around with that blank look. He didn't remember me from Adam. "That job you offered me Saturday night. Is is still open?" He still had that blank look for a second. Then he said, "Oh yeah, sure is." I said, "I'll take it." I didn't say, "What does it pay?" or nothing. They was all standing around there in new $50 suits and driving them new cars. Why, Lord, I didn't know they owed their grandmas for them. I just saw myself gettin' rich right quick.

We did the *Merry-Go-Round*. Later on in the afternoon we packed up the car and headed for Rogersville. That was the first show that I worked with him. We were coming into the outskirts of Rogersville when he wheeled around. (Sunshine Slim Sweet was driving, Archie was in the passenger seat. I was in the back with Smokey White the fiddle player.) He said, "I guess we ought to talk money." I said, "I guess I figured you'd pay me whatever the going rate was." He said, "They don't pay me anything for the *Merry-Go-Round* or the *Barn Dance*." In less than a month, I found out that was a lie. They didn't pay much, but they paid him some. He said, "Lowell keeps us booked five nights a week, regular. I'll pay you $5 a night." I didn't need no darn calculator to tell that was $25 a week, the best you can make. My heart went plum in my shoes. I lost faith in God and humanity right quick.

You knew that was a pittance.

It wasn't nowhere near what I expected. I was thinking—it was 1947—$100 a week. I had put my foot in it then. I couldn't take it out. I worked for him for a long time for $5 a night. Finally he let me have a picture taken with the words to three or four songs I was singing on back of it. I sold that for a quarter and that was all mine. I was making more selling pictures than he was paying me. Then after Slim quit, Archie put me in charge of shipping out the advance tickets ... and stuff like that. And selling tickets at the show, taking charge of the money. He put me on 20 percent of the gate then. I started making a little bit of money. It still wasn't much 'cause we were only charging twenty-five or fifty cents.

I think Archie jinxed me. I think when I first got my record contract, he thought I was going to leave him. He started talking to me like, "Well ... you're good but you're just not going to make it. Red, you'll never in your life hear anybody say they don't like to hear you sing. But they'll never come flocking out to see you." It's turned out that way, but it's a jinx he put on me.

I liked Archie, but I didn't realize what he was doing. Here I had a record contract and that was something to kill for. He'd been trying forever to get a record contract and couldn't. I reckon he thought I was some kinda prize that he wanted to keep. He didn't want me going off to work for somebody else. Everytime I got a job offer he'd knock the whiz out of it. I didn't see it then. I thought Archie was looking out for my best interests. He was looking out for his best interest. I could understand it. I would have probably done the same thing. If I got a person in my band that I see potentially better star than I am, I'm gonna push him. I want the proceeds from it. I think that's probably what Archie was doin'. . . . He didn't want me to leave because he felt that I could help him make money.

You were in the war.

I was drafted in '43 . . . served in the 37th Division in the Pacific. I reenlisted. . . . They put me with the MPs in Manila and I didn't like that G.I. stuff. I wasn't used to taking no brush and lye soap and scrubbing leggings and belts until they were snow white and all that stuff. They had me feeding the Jap prisoners. To this day, I'm not a Japanese lover, but they was feeding one of the admirals. . . . And they'd have us take him food from the kitchen in one of those big gallon fruit cans we had in the service. And they'd have fruit and gravy and everything all mixed in that one can. You just fed him like a hog. I didn't believe in that, and I had to get the heck out of there. So I reenlisted under what they called the Red Apple Bill and came home for three months, and I was in the darn hospital in Oak Ridge with malaria about all the time I was home. After I got out of the hospital, I married the first girl that came down the pike, that would agree to it. The marriage lasted six years. My father said, "I'll give you six months." I was too pig-headed to go with that. I made it last six years.

Then I went up to Camp Campbell, Kentucky, and went out on a recruiting tour through the Midwest, to different fairs and so forth. I was discharged just a short time before Christmas in '46. . . . I went and signed up on my 52–20 club, go $20 a week for fifty-two weeks until we got a job. I drew that for a couple of weeks and then I went to work with Archie.

How long was your mother taking you to Lowell Blanchard?

The first time I was ever on radio I was five years old. We were still living in Knoxville at that time. We went down to WNOX. They had some kind of a talent show. They were in the old Andrew Johnson Hotel at that time. They were way up on the top floor, and I thought the elevator would never get me up there. I sang "St. James Infirmary Blues." Seems like my mother said I won the contest. I don't know whether I did or not. That was my first knowledge of WNOX. Lowell took a kind of shine to me then and I guess I was maybe fourteen when I went back again. When I was sixteen, that's when he told me I need to develop some vibrato.

She wasn't one of the pushy moms. She didn't make people plum nervous when they saw us coming.

Were you playing guitar?

Not when I was five, but when I was fourteen and sixteen.

Did you teach yourself?

More or less self-taught. I first started playing what they call a dobro now. It was a steel guitar that my cousin who boarded with us ordered and he had some books with chords and stuff. He worked from two to ten or the three to eleven shift and I'd go in and sneak out from behind his bed and play on it after he'd leave for work. Then when we moved to the country I started playing a regular, we called them, Spanish guitar back then.

I was going to South Clinton School and this lady came through giving guitar lessons. But she had to sign up so many (fifteen or so) and get paid in advance for three lessons before she could stay there long enough to give us the whole course. She gave us the first lesson and then skipped town with all the money. All she did was teach me a B7th chord, 'cause I knew E and A and I liked playin' them chords 'cause E was the best chord to sing in. That's the only teaching I had.

You were born in Knoxville and then you say you moved out to the country.

Out in Anderson County. They called it Wolf Valley. I called it Wolf Holler 'cause there's still places in there where the sun don't shine. My mother was from there. We moved out to her ol' homeplace. In fact, when we first moved out there, we moved in the house with my grandad, until they got a house built across the road. Dismal Creek ran down through Wolf Valley and emptied into Clinch River. It went through my grandad's farm.

Dad worked in the marble business at the time. The Depression didn't hit us as soon as it did a lot of people because the marble business lasted on up to about '34, when we got such hard times that we had to move out of Knoxville into the country. . . . He was a hand polisher. . . . Back then marble was treated like diamonds. You didn't polish it with a machine, you hand polished it. He was supposed to have been one of the best they had out there. He didn't make big money, but I guess for then it was. I remember him coming home on many a night and eating supper and going back and working another shift. . . . He worked many a double shift. He was always aware of what was going on in the family, but Mother was right there in the house, did the housework, and took care of the kids.

When you moved out of Knoxville, he helped your grandfather with the farming?

He was working at the textile mill then before we moved out in the country 'cause the marble business had just gone defunct. People quit buying those expensive building materials and started buying concrete blocks.

You sang smoothly. Is that connected to your childhood?

I came up listening to big band music. I listened to country, I listened to the *Grand Ole Opry*, but my favorite program was on WWL [New Orleans] on Sunday night, where they played beautiful waltz music, Wayne King and stuff like that. And I liked [Bing] Crosby and [Perry] Como.

In fact, when I was working at WROL, the program director and the music director, the program director played piano and the director was director of the Nashville Symphony, played violin. We did an afternoon program singing "Nature Boy" and pop stuff like that. We did it for quite a while.[3]

This was after WNOX . . .

Bob Mason, who billed himself as Radio's Tallest Singing Cowboy, and his band came to work on WROL in 1949; he wasn't making any money either. The station wasn't paying anything. The rights to plug our personal appearances was all we got from the radio. But he got wind of this little station up in northwestern Ohio that was pretty much virgin territory. He got to talking to them and he got with me and he said, "Let's go up there." I didn't realize I was the only one with a record deal. Why wouldn't he want me to go with him? I'm sounding like I think I'm some kind of a big shot, but I ain't. But I had what they wanted. Just because you had a record contract back then, you were pretty well highly regarded. I didn't even realize it. I just took it for granted. It came so easy that I didn't think it was any big deal. So we went to Lima, Ohio. He did pay me off in cowboy shirts and boots, like Archie said that he'd do. For weeks and weeks, that's all that I got. I'd maybe get a buck or two to go to the grocery store. We got playin' square dances and the grange halls. Started doin' pretty good.

This naiveté that you talk about, what is the source of it?

I grew up under my mother's thumb. She called all the shots, and I didn't have to do any thinking on my own. And I guess I never learned any better the whole time I was in the service. I guess I should have been cocky and I wasn't. I should have been realizing that I had something that was saleable. That's the only thing I can lay it to. I had low self-esteem. I didn't know what it was.

Interviews with Red Kirk were conducted on November 12, 1998, and December 21, 1998.

Notes

1. Interview with Walter David "D" Kilpatrick, Oct. 13, 2000.
2. The *Hayride* frequently left its Shreveport base to broadcast from other locations.
3. Lowell Blanchard was announcer on WNOX radio's *Midday Merry-Go-Round* and *Tennessee Barn Dance*. He was employed at the Knoxville station from 1936 to 1964.
4. Red left Archie Campbell's employ in 1949 after the band gave up playing dates. At that point, Campbell had moved to WROL in Knoxville; Red stayed at WROL as a solo act for a short time.

Hank Locklin
Yesterday's Gone

One night a couple of years ago I sat with my friend Mark James in Nashville's Station Inn. Mark's a Pittsburgher, and there was a time when I doubt he would have recognized "The Great Speckle Bird" had it landed on his shoulder. But he moved with his job to Atlanta ten years ago and commenced a country music education. Now, whenever he's in Nashville scaring up clients and I'm there scaring up stories, we hit the hillbilly circuit.

Mark's back and my back rested against the Station Inn's wall while we listened to a western swing band whose sideman for the night was Ranger Doug Green of the cowboy group Riders in the Sky. Green's licks and the band leader's jokes about Tennessee football flavored the sets, but I couldn't stop peeking over at the legendary bass man Bob Moore who sat at one of the banquet-style tables trading gibes with the band. Then I completely checked out. I started listing in my mind veteran country artists whom I wanted to interview. There were many, but I dwelled on two: Ferlin Husky, whose whereabouts I did not know, and Hank Locklin, who I knew still came up from his home in southern Alabama to appear on the *Opry*. (I had seen him recently on the televised portion of the show.)

Locklin recorded for RCA during the label's country music heyday in the 1950s and 1960s. There, with astonishing results, Chet Atkins polished the singer's honky-tonk edges and dipped him in the country-politan vat. Within five years of signing, Locklin tacked seven hits on the top ten country list, spending a total of 159 weeks on the charts. Among the gold-streaked records were the career-making smashes "Send Me the Pillow You Dream On" (1958) and "Please Help Me I'm Falling" (1960), both of which crossed over to the pop charts and today stand among the best-known country songs in history. So, I badly wanted to talk RCA and monster hits with Locklin.

My daydreaming about Locklin sailed on at the Station Inn. There was more to his career: a native of McClellan, Florida, he had first recorded for small Texas labels in the late 1940s (Gold Star and Royalty) before hooking up with Smilin' Bill McCall's California-based Four Star Records. McCall's reputation rivaled Fabor Robison's: many of his disgruntled artists accused him of issuing unreasonable contracts and then doling out a miserly share of royalties. Reluctant to confront McCall, the retiring Locklin suffered at Four Star for five years, squeaking out two national hits—"The Same Sweet Girl" (1949) and "Let Me Be the One" (1953)—and seeing little for it. It took an assertive Steve Sholes to rescue Locklin, extracting him from his contractual shackles in 1955. (If only Locklin could have warned Patsy Cline: the Four Star trap snarled her from 1954 to 1960.)

A refuge, RCA paid him and paid close attention to his career. He remained part of the label's family for sixteen years, but then a new

With a troupe preparing to depart for a European tour in 1957. Left to right: Locklin, Katherine Shucher, Herb Shucher, Louis Dunn, Dick O'Shaughnessy, Del Wood, Jim Reeves, Mary Reeves, Maxine Brown, Leo Jackson, Bonnie Brown, Jim Ed Brown. Author's collection.

breed of RCA-Nashville brass cut him loose in the early 1970s. His last hit came in 1971: "She's as Close as I Can Get to Loving You." He had rarely been absent from the charts between 1955 and 1971 but he failed to read the charts thereafter.

Back in the Station Inn, another UT joke and some bustling at the entrance stirred me from my list-making. To my right, I saw five people walking in, looking for a seat. The group approached our table and in single file circled it, taking seats all around. An elderly gentleman with a fisherman's beard took the chair next to me. He looked familiar to me. He smiled and turned to the band. After a few minutes, he pulled up closer to me. "I haven't heard music like this since I worked in Texas," he said. "What were you doing in Texas?" I asked. His reply was immediate: "I'm Hank Locklin."

I THINK THAT THE GOOD LORD has blessed me. I'm still singing the songs in the same key that I sang them in when I recorded them back in the '60s and even before then. It's a blessing to be able to still sing and hit those notes.

If you had to describe your singing voice to somebody who had never heard you before, how would you describe it?

I never have thought about it. If they heard it, it wouldn't bother me either way, which way they wanted to talk about it. But I'm glad that I do have the voice and as yet, I don't have any problems. I'm thankful for that.

From the beginning, did you ever consciously attempt to produce a vocal style, to sound like somebody?

When I was in Mobile, Alabama, I know I was under twenty-five, I wanted to sing like Ernest Tubb and Roy Acuff. I sang their songs and tried to sound like them. There was a sergeant in the army [Pee Wee Moultrie] and there's a place in Mobile called the Whistler Community House. On Saturday night, they had music and dancing, things like that. Pee Wee told me that "if you ever want to sound like Hank Locklin you don't need to try to sing like Ernest Tubb and Roy Acuff. Get your own style." Right after that I wrote "The Same Sweet Girl" and that was in my own style.

I quit trying to sing the songs like Tubb or Acuff or Eddy Arnold, he was a favorite of mine. I didn't try to sing like him, but I did record a song that he had a big hit on, "I'll Hold You in My Heart," but I went at it in a direction of my own thinking.

You recently recorded with Jett Williams.[1] Beyond the physical similarity with her father, do you see any of her father in her singing, in her delivery of a song?

Well, I've been knowin' her a pretty good while. I told her one time, "If you really want to branch out, I think you oughta get you some different songs, not just your dad's songs. That's good and you do a good job, but whatcha oughta have now is some material of your own." Of course, "Hey Good Lookin'" it's one that her daddy had, we sorted of upgraded it some and she done real good on that. She's doin' real good now. I think maybe she's written some songs, too, and that's good.

Do you think she'll be able to get out of her father's shadow?

Well, I don't know about that. You opened up a new keg of worms there. I think she has a lot of songs now that she's recorded. She's going to do all right. She's married to a lawyer that helped her get her money, and they've got a beautiful place. He's really a nice guy and he's got a good head about music. So they're doing real good.

I met Hank one time in Houston when I was on the radio down there. They had the Texas Corral at South Main and he was down there that night. It was the first time I ever met him. I said, "Where are you going from here?" He said, "Well, I'm going to stay here. I'll be here a couple of days." I asked him about coming up and singing on my show with me. I told him about the show at 12:45 on KLEE everyday, Monday through Friday. So, he showed up and sang a couple of songs. I had no tape recorder, didn't even know what a tape recorder was then. I can't remember what he sang, but he sang. That's the only time I ever was around Hank.

Who was your sponsor on the show?

A car dealer.

Did you have to find your own sponsor?

The guy that brought me down there wrote a song called "Poison Love," Johnnie and Jack recorded it. Elmer Laird, that was his name. He told me, "Hank, I have enough cash money to fill a two-story building." He made it during the war. He had written a couple of songs, "Rio Grande Waltz." I was on at 12:45 about five times a week on KLEE radio.

[Elmer Laird] had sold a car to a guy that was underaged and his mama had to sign for it. The morning we was going to a radio station and cut some demos, they called me and said [Laird] was dead. I said, "Come on, don't kid me like that." His mama told him to come and get the car and then he came into the little office and he was raising all kinds of sin and Elmer happened to come in about that time. So they went outside and when they went outside, I think the guy was ahead of him and he turned around and hit him in the heart with a little old knife. He fought him, running around the car for a while, but he never lived. They just threw him in the car, and on the way to the hospital he said, "Don't let me die 'til I talk to my wife."

I sure hated that. He told me, "Hank, if you'll do it my way, it'll be all right. If it don't work out, I'll do it your way."

He was acting as a manager for you?
Right.

How had he made his money?
Selling cars.

During the war?
During the war. Houston is a big place. It was big then.

As well as helping you with your career, he was sponsoring your program?
Yes. 12:45 P.M. Five days a week.

Was there a morning program?
Yes ... We had the whole band down there at that time, until he got killed. After that, his brother took over. He had a car lot, too. That's when I wrote "The Pillow." I took it down there and [the secretary] copied it off on a typewriter. I just wrote it right out. That was the easiest song I think I ever wrote. The words just fell in, everything just fell in.[2]

What got you thinking about a pillow?
Well, if you remember, there was a song out about sending different things ["Anything That's Part of You"] and it said, "Send me the pillow that you dream on. I want to dream on it too." A guy from Acuff-Rose, he called my attention to that. At that time Acuff-Rose was looking for people to write. Bill McCall had come in for a couple of weeks—that's when I was recording for Four Star—and I told him about the song. We all went out to eat, Pappy Daily, he was one of the guys who helped me up the ladder. He was sitting there eating and I told him about the song and I said, "I'm gonna let him have it to publish it." [McCall said], "Oh no, you can't let him have it to publish it. We'll publish it." I didn't talk him out of it. I just went ahead and did it.

[The Pillow] was so simple and heart warming, it's how you come across telling your spouse you love her. There are many ways that it really means something. This song really means something to every person. It's something that you touch everyday. Mine hung in there. And it's been going now for over fifty years.

You were born in McClellan, Florida. Can you tell me about your childhood?

There was a doctor who came from a little place called Munson, Florida. It was a big timber area and Baghdad Land and Lumber Company owned many hundreds of acres of timber. In Munson they had a commissary and they had a train that went from there to Milton and he came over on his horse and buggy and spent the night. I was born at 1:30 A.M., I believe, on the 15th of February. When I was nine months old, I fell off the porch and broke my arm. Nine has been an unlucky number for me. When I was nine, a school bus ran over me. Back then when I was nine years old there were single tires on the truck and they had rabbit wire on the outside of the thing and I guess they had glass in there and they had three long benches that you

Onstage in the 1950s. Author's collection.

sat on. We was trying to see which one of us was going to get that front seat. One of the guys caught ahold of me and I turned loose. But when I found myself, I was lying flat on my back and that school bus was coming around to the left. . . . It went right on across me. So I've had all kinds of luck like that. I had rheumatic fever and I overcome that. All of the kids after that got ahead of me. That was in McClellan School in Santa Rose County. I got behind. I went through the tenth grade.

What did your family do?
Farm. Two horses and two mules. We didn't have a tractor.

What did you raise?
Corn, cotton, peanuts. I remember going with my dad over in Brewton, Alabama, and there was a bank and daddy borrowed $25 to buy his fertilizer, feed to plant that year. Times wasn't all that good back in that time, but we had hogs. They killed hogs and daddy fixed it up, cut all the bones out of it and put in a barrel and put salt in it and salted it down.

In the evening when I came in, they had what you call the slops. There'd be a big ol' five-gallon bucket that momma would put [that slop in]. She'd peel potatoes and put that in there. We had one ol' sow and she was a mean gal. Looked like her head was nearly twenty inches long or it might have been two feet long. When they saw me [coming with the slop], they come to that trough and she'd come leaping down and the trough was about fifteen feet long and with that big long nose she'd go right down that trough and hogs and pigs and everything were just flying on each side of that thing. The slop would sour. It would be pretty sharp and I got the idea that I would fix that ol' gal. I went out there and I very lowly called the others and they was all in there and she comes right down that trough and when she got through there she was picking up that [sour slop]. When she left, I guess she made a round out there a good 150 feet, squealing. That sour stuff got to her. She never did do that again.

Did you slaughter the hogs?
No. I wasn't big enough to do that. They would have the pot boiling and they'd knock 'em in the head and stick 'em and they'd bleed.

That's not a pretty process.
I don't know. I didn't think about it that way. I was looking for that good hot meat. He'd salt it down. He'd take all the bones out of the hams and salt it down in the barrel for a couple of weeks and then put it in the smoke-

house and smoke him. I remember my mama going out there and the hams were hanging down there and they were about two inches thick and she'd take a knife and cut a piece and bring it in and slice it up and fry it. Man that was good eating with big ol' hot biscuits and syrup. We made syrup, too. Ate a lot of syrup and biscuits.

What did you make the syrup from?
    Cane. We'd grow cane.
    Dad bought a Model T, bought it secondhand and he might have paid $200 for it. Back in the '20s I was ten years old. Milton was about thirty-five miles and them ol' people would get together and talk, and they'd say, "Went to Milton today and come back and never had a flat."

By the 1930s, did you see the air go out of the sail a little bit with the Depression? Do you remember things getting worse in the 1930s?
    No. I wouldn't have known about it no way. Mom and Dad took care of all that. Always had clothes.
    All kids have somebody they look up to. There was a store that was about a good 1,000 feet or more away from where we lived in this big ol' house. His name was Mallory Black ... he had a store. It was during Easter and there was a little church up the road, probably a mile and a half away from the store, north. I had a pair of overalls and I was barefooted. I went by and asked him, "You reckon this looks all right." I had on a shirt and overalls to go to an Easter egg hunt. I was going up to the church. "I was wondering what you think of these overalls on Sunday." "Oh," he said, "You look fine. You look good." He took all that [self-consciousness] out of me and I went up there and had a good time.
    John Temples had a store and I remember him playing Santa Claus. He had a Santa Claus suit and he was kind of built like a Santa Claus. At the school in McClellan, maybe about a quarter mile from the store, he'd come down. They'd cut holly down and have all the Christmas things [displayed] and he'd come down there and play Santa Claus. He was the best. I liked him very much.

How many children were in your family?
    Four. They're all gone. I'm the last one. Two boys and two girls.

How did you get interested in music during your childhood?
    I'd go to church and I'd come back whistlin' the tunes [of church hymns], but I didn't know the words. Papa was a pretty good fiddle player back in

the days before he had any children, and Mama played guitar. They'd have frolics. A frolic was if you had a house and you had a big room, they'd play and they'd all dance.

Would you listen to the Opry *as a youngster?*
Yes. That's where I heard Acuff and Ernest Tubb. They were about the most popular ones that were on the *Opry*. I liked their singing.

Did you listen to any of the other big shows at the time, WLS *in Chicago* or Wheeling Jamboree *on* WWVA?
No. I knew about them. They had a battery out there in the country, didn't have no electricity. I was already gone from home when they finally got electricity.

How was it that you began to sing and play?
Just around the house. I played at school. Verdi Williams was a girl who sang with me [at school]. I didn't know many songs back at that time. That was in high school. They had an auditorium.

Did you play on radio in Florida?
The first radio station I played on was WCOA in Pensacola.

How did you get involved with that station?
Well, I had a guitar and I had a cousin down there. It was an NBC station. My cousin Radford, he was a little older than I am. He played the harmonica. Back in them days when we was just school boys, we played over that radio station then. Played a couple of songs on top of the hotel there.

My mama's sister lived down there. I don't know how we got down there, but we got down there. We went to see a cousin in New Orleans, and I played over WWL there, just the guitar and me. I was just always interested and I kept on keeping on. That's what I was doing.

I worked in the shipyards [in Mobile, Alabama]. I worked up in the mole loft, where you make the patterns . . . to make those tankers. I went down to a music store and bought me a Gibson guitar. It cost $52. A round hole. It was a good guitar. I don't know what I ever done with that one. I may have given it to somebody.

Were you doing much picking and singing before you were drafted?
No. I was working at the ribbon mill in Brewton, Alabama.

Hank Locklin and Dolly Parton recording in 2000. Courtesy of Hank Adam Locklin collection

What year were you drafted?
Forty-three. But the war [was ending] in '44. They let me come out.

You never went abroad.
No. I was at Fort Leonard Wood in Missouri, in the army.

Did you play while you were there?
No. I was glad to get out of there.

You went from Mobile to Texas?
No. I went from Mobile to Hot Springs, Arkansas. These boys had the Four Leaf Clover Boys. I played there in Hot Springs over KTHS. We went

out and played schools. Clent Holmes was a comedian [and guitarist], and we'd play and sing. One of the boys played the bass, the announcer. Clent played mandolin. Joe Avants played the bass. We'd play dances up in Plainview, Arkansas.

Then we left there and went to [KWKH] Shreveport and played with Harmie Smith [as the Rocky Mountain Boys]. [Then Elmer Laird] in Texas wanted a band. He had just built [KLEE], and he heard about us up there and he brought us down there. We was on six times a day, in the morning at 6:00 and we played fifteen minutes and we'd come back [through the day]. We done that until [Laird] got killed and that's when we broke up. Harmie Smith went back to Shreveport and went to work with Hank Williams.

You played some of the skull orchards in Texas. Were they rough?

Not for me it wasn't. For the other guys who went out and played them [it was], if you went outside Houston. I played 105½ Main [in Houston], the boy who was in charge of that was R. D. Hendan, and the Texas Corral was Jerry Irby. Floyd Tillman played there, too.

When you played places in Houston, they were peaceful.

Oh yeah. We didn't have any problem.

I went with Jimmy Swan when I came out of the service. He had a band. I played guitar for him. In Hattiesburg, Mississippi, we had quit playing and a fight broke out. It was a pretty goodsized place, 100 feet by 75 feet. This slim boy, he had just come out of the service, and the fight started, and he walked around there and Jimmy Swan run down there and I'm standing rolling up the cord on my guitar. This guy didn't have a gun but he put his hand [in his pocket] like he was going to get a gun. When he did, this guy shot him. It didn't get in the heart, but it was just to the side. They got him out and into a car, but when they put him on the operating table, the bullet had already pierced him and just the skin was holding it in on the back. He died right there on the table.

That's when Clent and them went to Arkansas [as the Four Leaf Clover Boys] and I went back with them. I left Swan then in Hattiesburg. Later on in life he run for governor in Mississippi.

Did you play Cook's Hoedown in Houston?

Yeah. A lot of times. That's where I saw Bob Wills. That's before I got to play with him before he died. The man could make the hair rise on your head when he'd open up.

2000s promotional photo. Author's collection.

How did you come in contact with Pappy Daily?

Pappy Daily helped me a lot. He's the one who got me tied up with Bill McCall. . . . He had a big record store on E. 11th Street there in Houston. I knew Jerry Jericho, and he helped Jerry. At that time, he had a lot of jukeboxes and him and Bill McCall liked to gamble and they'd go to Vegas. He bought records from Bill McCall and sold tons of them.

At that time, I had a five-piece band and they heard me on the radio. There was a lot of songs I sang other than mine, good dance songs.

You knew him from his record store. He loaned you some money to buy your house. How did you get to know each other?

I was on the radio at 12:45 everyday. Whenever I recorded for Four Star, Pappy is the one who got me in with Bill McCall. That's how that worked.

Did you learn quickly that you weren't going to get rich with Bill McCall and Four Star Records?

Yeah. I don't know how much money he got, but he [leased me] to Paul Cohen and I went to Nashville. I recorded several songs up there. "Let Me Be the One," I cut that there [in 1953] and Owen Bradley played piano. [McCall] didn't let Paul have it. It would have been on Decca if he had and I'd 'a made some money off it, but I didn't make any with him.

I was playing at the Texas Corral and they had a thirty-minute radio program before the start of the dance, and I had written a song called "To Whom It May Concern," and I sang that. And Paul and Owen Bradley were staying up at the hotel, so they come to see me. It was early in the evening and they talked to me about [signing with Decca]. I told them I was tied up with Four Star. Later on, Paul Cohen got in touch with Bill so he could lend me out to them. I came to 16th Avenue here in Tennessee to cut the records.

Had you also started doing the Big D Jamboree *on Saturday nights in Dallas at that stage?*

I don't think I started doing that 'til "Geisha Girl" [in 1957]. I went to the *Ozark Jubilee*. I went up there and sang two or three times. It might have been more than that. They wanted me to come to the *Big D*, but I kinda wanted to go up there. I thought it was a little more up. The last time I sang up there, Si Siman, I asked him, "When do you want me to come back?" He said, "Hank just don't call me, I'll call you." That was the word I needed. I never called him again, so I went to the *Big D Jamboree*.

I'd drive up there [from Houston to Dallas] and I had to go through Huntsville, Texas. I'd leave there at two o'clock. It didn't take long for me to get up there. It was a good 200 miles, I think. I had a parking place and there was a policeman who would park me, so I could get out to come back to Houston when I finished up.

Did you find you were able to branch out more with your Big D *appearances?*

Never thought about it that way. I had a lot of places I could play, but that was just me. I didn't have no band; they had the band there. They'd invite me to the *Big D*.

In Texas, you played in Texarkana. Did you ever go west into New Mexico and Arizona?

No. That was too far.

For many years you didn't keep a regular band, like Arnold who had his Plowboys, Reeves who had his Blue Boys. Why not?

I had some bread and butter songs like "Geisha Girl." . . . I had a lot of bread and butter records, and by being down in Texas, I had a big following. They had bands, and I never had no problem working with a [pick up] band. A lot of guys come back from a date and say, "I didn't like the band. They didn't know what they was doing." You heard derogatory stories like that. But I never had any problem with a band 'cause I sang the song and they had heard 'em playing on the radio all over the place. I didn't need to take a band.

That remained true in the 1960s.

Sure did.

It was easy for you to book out. Did anybody do that for you?

I'd do it. They'd call me at the radio station. Then I'd know where they were. There were two or three places that were pretty bad. Some of the boys who had a band told me, "They're some bloody buckets. You better watch yourself." When I went, I never did pay attention to the girls. I'd pick out the ugliest ol' boy out there and I'd find out his name and I'd get acquainted with him. I'd dedicate a song to him and his girlfriend. They'd like that, so there wasn't nobody going to fool with Locklin because I wasn't out there trying to take the girls. . . .

Done the same thing in Louisiana with my ol' buddy Jimmy C. Newman. I got $25 to go down there and work with him and with Happy Fats Le Blanc. He was kin to the guy who put out Hadacol [Dudley J. Le Blanc]. The girls will swing by you and want you to pay attention to them. I had black hair, and I was pretty good lookin'. I wasn't that good lookin', but I was pretty good lookin'. I never even let on like they was around. After I had been going down there I spent the night at Happy Fats Le Blanc's and the next day they had a table and the food was piled up on it. They called me Hanka Locka-lin. They said, "Hanka Locka-lin you better eat to make you fat." I'd go down there on a Saturday night from Houston. They told me, "Hanka Locka-lin, you can have any of these girls you want down here. You know that." I said, "Man, I'm just not interested." They said, "Nobody'll bother you. You can have them." If I had gone down there like some of the other guys who got in trouble. . . . When you go down there and mess with the girls, they don't like it. They treated me real good. I'd go down there, have to go through Beaumont, Texas, to go down there.

Various promotional photos. Courtesy of Hank Adam Locklin.

How did Steve Sholes come into your life? How did the RCA deal happen?

When my contract ran out, Steve got in touch with me. [Bill McCall] claimed he still had a contract with me. I had the contract and he called Steve and told him that he had a contract with me. He said, "It's going to be another year." He called me in Houston and said, "This guy says he's still got a contract with you." I said, "Don't believe that. I'll let you know.

It won't take long before I let you know." So I went directly to the head of the union in Houston and carried my contract. I said, "I want you to read this stuff and tell me if he still got me under contract." He read it and he said, "No." So he called Steve and told him, "Hank is free to go with anybody he wants to sign with. He does not have a contract with Bill McCall. It's up." That's the best move I ever made when I went with him. I didn't have nobody to talk to [for advice]. Back in them days if you wanted to get on the records, it was something to get on a phonograph record.

Pappy Daily must have been sad to see you go with RCA.

I don't think so. Pappy was a pretty good guy. He knew that I had got a bad deal. But that was yesterday and yesterday's gone.

Lefty [Frizzell] and me was going on a tour down through Beaumont and we wound up somewhere down in Louisiana. And George Jones played the guitar for us. He backed us. He could play good. At that time he was trying to write songs, and I told him, "There's one thing you can write about that ain't been written and that's about moonshine. You oughta think about it." He got together with the Big Bopper and wrote "White Lightening." It turned out real good. Jones told me, "If I could just have one hit, I'd never want another hit." I said, "You no good son of a ... you'd get one, you'd want to get another." I hadn't been long signed with RCA and I had written a song called "You're Back Again." I sang it to George, and I said, "George if you cut it,"—'cause he was fixing to record—"you can have half the song. And I'll sing it with you." That's the first time I think I ever sang tenor to anybody. And I had clear forgot it until about ten years ago. [My son] Adam said, "Dad, come in here I want to play you something. He went through two lines of the song before I could start to recognize [my voice]. I forgot about it, just completely forgot about it. It turned out real good.

Tell me about Lefty Frizzell. What were your impressions of him?

I worked all out in California with him. The gals loved him. We'd have to wait the next day, if we was going to another place, we waited until the couple of them who had gone visiting with him had gone away. That's when I met Jean Shepard on that tour.

You were talking about George Jones; both of you recorded "Why Baby Why."

He had already recorded it. Felice and Boudleaux Bryant wrote it.

When I cut it with Chet, Boudleaux was there. Chet said come on in here and sing it with him. He's singing with me on the cut. It sold pretty good, my record did.

Were you at all intimidated by the experience of coming to this large international label?

No way, Hoss. I was just glad to be there. When I had "The Pillow," it just took off like a scalded dog.

"Please Help Me I'm Falling" and "Send Me the Pillow You Dream On" are two of the most popular country music songs ever recorded and they are still being covered and sung today. How do you account for their longevity?

In every life something good comes along. By 1977, "The Pillow" had played just in the United States over a million and a half times. I was real thrilled with Dwight Yoakam when he recorded "The Pillow." Everybody who lies down on a bed, that pillow is right there with them. When I first recorded it down in Houston, Texas, that's where I got my start. . . . When I wrote the song and sang it on the radio, it was just the guitar and me. All the sudden pillows of all sizes come rolling in. It just took off like a scalded dog. I don't know what I did with the pillows. I gave them to people when I went out and played. I don't think "The Pillow" will ever die. It's something you touch everyday.

"Please Help Me I'm Falling" is a pleading song. Don Robertson and Hal Blair [wrote it]. Don played the piano [on the demo] and sent it on a lacquer to Chet Atkins and Chet played me the song. It had that slip note [piano style]. I told Chet, "If we can get Floyd [Cramer] to get that slip note like ol' Don did, I believe we might have a hit." . . . I tell you the truth, it's a first-take song. We just took it one time and that's what we got. [Floyd] really played that piano.

How was it that you parted ways with RCA?

Chet got to feeling bad, but he never let you know about things like that and he put me with another guy, Danny Davis. Danny made an album with me, but he wanted to sing. The songs he was recording was songs that had already been hits. I knew him quite well because I lived [near him]. I invited him over to the apartment and we'd cook steaks. I told him, "Why don't we make some songs together, get some songs out." But he didn't want to do it, he wanted to sing. I finally told him, I might have been ugly about it but I didn't intend to be, "What are you going to do when you run out of hits [to cover]? There's just so many hits that you can record and do with the Nashville Brass. When you run out of them how are you going to create something else?" That's one of the things [that led to the split]. That was all right. Jerry Bradley [and I] were walking up the stairs at RCA and I told him I'd like to do "Let an Angel Love the Devil Out of Me." He said, "Why don't you listen to this song . . . ?" It was something about a friend. It didn't flow. It was just a song. I told him about [my song] . . . and he said, "If you want to do it, I ain't going to fight you about it." It came out real good, "Let an Angel Love the Devil Out of Me." It was a good beat, but by that time our ol' buddy Charley Pride got "Kiss an Angel Good Morning."

I left.

Were you surprised that you never had another national hit after leaving RCA?

I signed up with [MGM], and I made a lot of records. Carol Channing and I did an album together. I was just flouncing, I guess. I didn't know what to do. . . . I've had all kinds of things like that happen to me, but I'm still going.

Interviews with Hank Locklin were conducted on August 9, 2001, and October 24, 2001.

Note

1. Locklin and Williams recorded a duet of "Hey, Good Lookin" on his 2001 album *Generations in Song*.
2. Locklin first recorded "Send Me the Pillow You Dream On" in 1949; he recorded his hit version for RCA in 1957.

Charley Pride
American

Thirty-five years ago, Charley Pride gave up a dying baseball career and a tough job slinging coal in Montana to stretch the limits of the Nashville Sound. He's best known, of course, as country music's only black superstar. But when the native of Sledge, Mississippi, embraced the sweet, easy-going Nashville Sound of the 1960s and married it to the harder, scalier styles associated with good ol' honky-tonk music, he left a mark on country music that had little to do with the color of his skin. He joined Glen Campbell, Loretta Lynn, and Johnny Cash in the cream of country music's ambassadorial corps.

Pride had long admired the lush countrypolitan recordings of Eddy Arnold and Jim Reeves, embracing their ballads and even re-creating Reeves' vocal qualities breath-for-breath in his early RCA-Victor recordings. But the singer, known early in his career as Country Charley Pride, also delighted in covering Hank Williams's songs and un-abashedly honed a subtle and natural twang that brought to mind Ernest Tubb and Lefty Frizzell. Pride evolved into the most popular singer ever to join the Arnold and Tubb styles and came to embody these two disparate aspects of country music. In the late 1960s, while fans and artists angrily debated whether modern and traditional country music could inhabit the same house (they're still arguing today), the two styles dwelled tranquilly within Charley Pride.

Pride's blend of traditional and modern seasoned with flecks of the blues and gospel he knew in his childhood stoked his dominance of the country music charts for more than a decade. From 1969 to 1983, he boasted twenty-nine number one country hits, among them "Is Anybody Goin' to San Antone" (1970) and "Kiss an Angel Good Mornin'" (1971). Furthermore from his chart debut in 1966 through 1984 only three Pride hits failed to make country music's top ten. His was a phenomenal rise, marked by Country Music Association awards, platinum records, and Grammys. This star's brilliance only dulled in the mid-1980s when a powerful youth movement led by George Strait and Ricky Skaggs galloped into Nashville.

Pride's tumble from chart preeminence came swiftly. RCA dropped him in 1986, and a three-year stint with the independent label 16th Avenue South only yielded one top ten hit, the aptly titled "Shouldn't It Be Easier Than This?" (1987). The titan of the 1970s failed to even touch the country charts in the 1990s. He remains viable only on the concert circuit, filling venues at home and abroad, where he reminds audiences of why he remained so strong for so long.

WHILE PRIDE STRETCHED THE LIMITS of the Nashville Sound in the 1960s and 1970s, he also tested country music's and Nashville's racial tolerance. Would country fans in the middle of the intolerant South accept a black man who sang the white man's lament, or would they don white hood and cloak if they thought Pride was crooning to or about white women? Such questions throbbed in the minds of record producers and managers who worked with Pride. They knew that a prominent black figure in the white man's world rarely knew an easy road. Throughout the twentieth century black musicians—band leaders such as Jimmie Lunceford and Duke Ellington, for example—toured the South under the constant threat of violence, and in Nashville's country music world specifically, treatment of black artists had been anything but progressive. In the 1920s and 1930s, the *Grand Ole Opry* treated the talented harmonica player DeFord Bailey like a mascot, little more than a cute puppy on a leash, and as late as the early 1960s, violinist Brenton Banks, who would lead string sections on many Nashville country sessions, was refused membership in the local union until Chet Atkins raised hell on his behalf. Such attitudes toward blacks prodded RCA officials to leave Pride's face off his first album. But the anger aimed at this black country singer on a major label proved to be milder than expected. In Pride's autobiography,[1] he describes a bomb threat in Augusta, Maine, and the narrow-minded promoters he encountered, but despite such obstacles he soon gained acceptance among the predominantly white audiences of country music.

One wonders, though, why more black singers haven't followed Pride into Nashville. One thinks of Stoney Edwards and Cleve Francis, men who never really stuck despite their handful of country music hits. Today a new black face in mainstream country music would seem as

Charley Pride recording in the 1960s. Author's collection.

unlikely as a Gibson Flying V Guitar on the *Grand Ole Opry* stage. In the early twenty-first century's demographic-driven country music scene, labels look for faces that look like those in the country music audience—and those faces are by and large pale. But if white audiences could accept a Charley Pride in the midst of this nation's bitterest racial conflict, as Birmingham, Memphis, and Chicago flared, why wouldn't similar audiences accept a black singer today? After all, in the past two decades, virtually the same demographic propelled Bill Cosby's sitcom to the top of television, bestowed pop status on performers such as Whitney Houston and Wyclef Jean, and elevated to royalty sports figures Michael Jordan and Tiger Woods.

In ignoring black talent, Nashville has also stiff-armed the black audience, a market that it probably never realized it had. In the absence of mass distribution of music tailored specifically for rural black America throughout much of the twentieth century, many blacks had no choice but to listen to country music, and they did so with relish. Representative of such fans are B. B. King, Bobby Bland, and Ray Charles, artists whose childhood fascination with country records and radio barn dances later inspired their recording of this music that really spoke to all colors. Almost every post–Second World War blues and rhythm and blues singer whom I've interviewed acknowledges the influence of country music, but Nashville has refused to allow that influence to come full circle by disdaining black nourishment, failing to groom black singers and audiences.

For Charley Pride's part, he is weary of such discussions and of the distinction of being the first and only black country music superstar. "You get with some reporters, and they just want to belabor the point, and elaborate on it until you've chewed your cabbage twice, you know," he complained in an interview with Alanna Nash. "We can talk until tomorrow about it, but when you get through, it comes down to this: I'm not here to be a symbol or an image, but I'm put in that position by the mere fact of being myself."[2] One sympathizes with Pride. His "first and only" designation and the chatter about race in country music that swirls around him threaten to obscure his real contributions: his huge hits that helped country music gain acceptance in markets around the world and his wonderful sound that pays tribute to the diversity that shaped country music.

YOU CAN FIND A SONG to fit any situation you're in, just about. There are three basic ingredients in American music: I think it's country, gospel, and the blues. It don't necessarily have to be in that order. I think each one has borrowed from the other over the years. It's just that way. If you listen to a lot of lines of different songs, you're really singing some of the experiences you've had. People used to say, "Country music is so sad." I say, "Well it depends on how you look at it." Sometimes it's nice to hear a sad song and then cry and then feel good afterwards. I believe music is for comfort and soothing, the right kind of music.

Was there something in you that needed to be in a profession that had a high profile?

In baseball, I wanted to be the best that ever was. When I went into baseball, my intentions was to go to the major leagues, break all the records by the time I was thirty-five, and then go into this business of singing. I was singing in the old Negro Leagues. They'd have bands at certain clubs, and we'd go in there, and I'd get up on stage and sing. People'd say, "You sound pretty good. . . . You can make a lot of money singing." I'd say, "Yeah but I want to go to the majors and break all then records." When they said, "Who hit the most home runs?" Not Babe Ruth or Hank Aaron. "Who's the last .400 hitter?" Not Ted Williams. [I wanted them to say] Charley Pride. . . . I kept doing it good. It's the way with all of us. "If you're going to do something, do it good." It starts from your raising. And when my mother would say, "Don't have no chip on your shoulder," that would give me courage to have the guts to go out there and get it done. I think all of these ingredients together collectively helped me do this. Since I didn't make it [in baseball], I'm just glad I was blessed with a voice. I'm going to tell you, all eight boys and three girls, all of us sing. I thought for a long time that everybody sang. When I lived out in the country, I didn't realize that some people can run fast and some can run slow and some can sing and some cannot. All of us sang. I thought if you could get up and eat breakfast, you could get up and sing. When I tell people I don't read a note of music, they say "What?"

What is it about baseball and country music? Jim Reeves played. Bill Anderson . . .

. . . Conway Twitty.

When we grew up, it was called the national pastime. For me, it was my way out of the cotton fields. When I saw Jackie Robinson, I said, "That's the way I'm headed. I'm going to get out of these cotton fields like that." That was one of the motivations for me. I think you can go further than that and just say it was the national pastime. That's what just what most kids loved to do.

So many people were playing the sport then.

You only had sixteen clubs in the majors, and it wasn't as wide-open as it is now. It hadn't expanded. Incidentally, I think it has been diluted. There's great players still there, don't get me wrong. . . . I think I can illustrate it better by saying this: There was a guy named Pee Wee Reese who was playing with the Dodgers that kept a guy in the minors that was in the Dodgers organization by the name of Roberto Clemente.

The other thing that gets me is when a guy gets hit, and he wants to run out there and hit the pitcher because he brushed him back. To me that was part of baseball. When I first started switch hitting, my brother and I just before we'd go to school, we'd get out by the hen house, and I'd let him throw to me early in the morning. It was cold. I'd tell him, "Don't tell me when you're going to do it, but throw it at my head so I can learn how to duck from this side."

Why should me as a pitcher, lay it in there for you to make me look bad?

I'm out there to get you out. Where is it written that I got to make sure I stay away from you and not pitch you too close or too this or too that. But you can get in there and rip the ball up through there and knock my head off if you want to. As a hitter, I could pull it, slice it, just like golf. I was a good hitter and I was a good pitcher. I'm not bragging. . . . They're giving the hitters all this room to rip it up the middle or rip it over the fence. But what about me? I want to get you out. I don't want you ripping me over the fence and ripping everything I throw up there.

There has to be a little intimidation in there.

Exactly. I'm going to loosen your tongue pallet just a little bit. Give you a little shave every now then.

It's interesting that in the 1970s you were working out with the Texas Rangers.

My first year with the Rangers, I had a AAA contract when Billy Martin was managing. The year—it was on my birthday—I got a hit off Jim Palmer down at Pompano Beach. I was a DH. I was one for two. I got a single right up the middle.

Were you just having fun?

No, I was serious that time. That was around '72, '73. I first started going to spring training in '71 with the Milwaukee Brewers. [Manager] Dave Bristol asked me to do that. There were guys like the catcher Darrell Porter and a bunch of others guy, saying "Who is this guy?" I was a young player, and I was looking good. I wasn't there trying to get a job, but I tell you this, I didn't go out there and just sit around. I worked harder than some of the guys there. Consequently, I looked good.

If I could go back to your singing career. I know I brought up baseball.

And I rattled on didn't I?

Tell me how you came to RCA?

When I was on a show [in Montana] with Red Sovine and Red Foley. They put me on the show up there, and they said, "You ought to go to Nashville." I had just gotten back from spring training with the Los Angeles Angels in '61, and then the Mets expanded in '62. Since I didn't make it with the Angels, I thought I'd give a try for the Mets. Then they ran over me in the smelter in Montana and broke my ankle. That threw me another year behind, so I didn't go in '62. I went in '63. In the year of '62, they won 40 games and lost 120. Casey [Stengel, the manager] said he wasn't going to look at me. "They'll look at anybody," that's what I thought, "when you lose 120 games." But he didn't look at me, so I came back through Nashville. Red Sovine had told me to go to Cedarwood Publishing Company. Baseball played a pretty good prominent role in how I evolved into country music.

When I stopped by at Cedarwood, that's where I met Jack Johnson. Someone had told me about him before I showed up. He had been looking for a colored guy who sang country music for a long time. When I went in there I saw [Cedarwood manager] Bill Denny standing with somebody else. Beyond them, in the back, was [singer and Cedarwood co-owner] Webb Pierce. I said, "Is that Mr. Pierce? Can I meet him?" So I met him.

1970s' promotional photo. Author's collection.

Red Foley had filled in for him on that show up in Montana that I was telling you about earlier, when I was doing those two songs and they told me to go to Nashville. I said, "You was supposed to be up in Montana last year." He said, "Oh yeah. Red Foley filled in for me on that date." I said, "I sing country music." He said, "Oh . . . get this boy a guitar." So they put me downstairs and Jack Johnson came and I did two or three songs for him, and after I did the first song, he said, "Now sing in your natural voice." I said, "Well, this is my natural voice. What do you want me to do?" He said, "Where are you from?" I said, "I'm living in Montana right now, but I'm born and raised in Mississippi." He said, "How do they take you up there?" I said, "About the way you are now, when they first see me." So I was going to let everybody in Nashville hear me, but him and [Cedarwood staff writer] Jan Crutchfield took me to the bus station and said, "You'll hear from us within two to four months."

I went back through Denver because I got two brothers and sisters who live there still, and they lived there then. I said, "Well I got time to spend. I'm on my vacation anyway. I'll just cut through Denver and see my brothers and sisters, then go on up from there to Montana." So it took me about two or three days riding the bus back. When I got back to Montana, I had a manager's contract waiting for me. I kept that thing for about a month or so, showing it to everybody 'cause I didn't like the language in it. The main thing is, I finally signed it and sent it back. Another year went by.

One guy I had met was on a small label, and he had come back through [Montana] and I was still working at the smelter. He said, "Man, you still working at that smelter?" Next time, he came back, he said, "I got my Cadillac. You ain't got your Cadillac yet? You got to live the part." I had my old Dodge. It was a Dodge that they made that had the gearshift on the dashboard. I said, "No man I ain't got no Cadillac."

Jack was trying to get me on a TV show like *Hee Haw*. Roy Clark was going to be one of the guys. It was going to be me and some other people. And it didn't materialize. He hadn't got me signed. I didn't realize he was running into all the trouble he was running into. People were saying, "Jack's going around town trying to get a you-know-what into country music. He's done gone out of his head."

I heard all these kind of things coming back at me. But to tell you the truth, my wife and I had no idea, even being raised in Mississippi and grew up in segregation, until somebody mentioned it [that there were no blacks singing country]. It just never dawned until it was pointed out. I said,

"Oh . . . that's what he's having trouble with." So he felt if we could just get on television, labels would just scramble to try to sign me.

They [sent] me seven songs to [work up, including] "Take that Night Train to Memphis," "Snakes Crawl at Night," "Just Between You and Me." They said, "Work the songs up and send them back." So I said to myself, "I ain't sending them back. I'm going to take them back." So I got in my station wagon and drove to Nashville. That's when I met Jack Clement. I had the songs all worked up, and they played the tape. So Jack took his guitar and let me sing right in front of him." He said, "I think this guy's ready now to go in and make a cut. Do you think you could cut two songs in three hours?" I said, "I can do it now." I'd never been in a recording studio in my life. We cut this dub, "Snakes Crawl at Night" and "Atlantic Coastal Line." Mel Tillis wrote both sides. August 16, 1965. I'll never forget it. Two o'clock.

Was Jack Clement still on staff at RCA or was he independent at this point?

He was an independent producer. So we cut this thing and gave it to Chet Atkins and Chet took it to [the RCA brass in] California. September 28th I got a call from Jack Johnson. He said, "You're going to be on RCA." I said, "Is that good?" They laughed about that. "The guy's going to be on the biggest label in the world and he says, 'Is that good.'" But that's the way I got on RCA.

It was Jack Clement who continued to produce you.

Yes, I give him credit for being the producer that put those together and sold those many records. In fact, he said to me, "Charley, the records we're making now, they're going to be playing them fifty years from now." We ain't got but twenty years to go, and they're still out there now.

What was unique about Jack Clement the producer?

He was tough. He was good, and he was tough.

Can you give me an example of how he was tough?

The most critical person of me is myself, and I always felt that I could do it better. He had to stop me a lot of days and say, "Go in the corner. Shut up. It's good. It's fine!" I'd say, "But I can do it . . ." "Shut up!" There were things like that.

I remember we cut one thing about thirty cuts. I still don't like the song. He was very determined that I did it the way he thought would be the best. Apparently it worked because we sold a lot of records.

One thing people say about Jack Clement is that he has a tendency to overproduce, as he did with Johnny Cash in the 1950s and the Stoneman Family in the 1960s. Did you find that working with him?

I don't know whether I should say "overproduce." But I think with him having that reputation and me being critical of myself and I wanting to do what I think is best for me . . . the stubbornness hit on both ends. But when it was all said and done, we worked it out. He started drinking a lot and doing things like that, so we just finally got so we wasn't able to work together.

By the early 1970s, Chet Atkins and others say RCA-Nashville wasn't so much fun to be around.

When I came to RCA, if you sold 50,000 albums you were a keeper. And I started right away and they never spent no money on promoting me. The next thing you know I'm selling 100,000. The next thing you know, I'm selling 200,000. By the time I won Male Vocalist of the Year and Entertainer of the Year in 1971, I was kind of a victim of my own success because 300,000 selling, one million selling albums, I helped start that. I was in the upward movement of sales. It got so that whenever they'd release an album on me, they'd press up 300,000 right off the bat. So all of a sudden after twenty-something years with them, they developed a thing, saying "Wait a minute we're losing ground on these pop stars." I remember them spending $200,000 on a guy named Nick Palmer [in 1967], a four or five city swing on him: Boston, Atlanta, San Francisco. I was playing [one club] in Atlanta, and they had him at [another], and on my break, between shows, I went over there. Of course, every night was a test for me at that time to see how they would take me, my fans and everything. We were packed, and he was packed, too. They had cut an album on him. I think they was trying [to] make another Frank Sinatra or Tony Bennett or something like that out of him. My understanding was that they were spending something like $200 grand on him. Back then, that was a lot of nugget. It's a lot of nugget now. They ain't spending nothing on me. I snuck in there and watched him, and I heard him sing. He had a pretty good voice but he never did nothing.

When I started selling all these records, all of a sudden the pop was dropping, the rock was dropping.

My stable mates were Dolly, Waylon, Eddy. I think the moguls from Capitol, Columbia, RCA [in the 1980s] said, "Why don't we slide all these off and get some youngsters here?" They put the hat on them. When I say this, I'm not talking against the singer, I'm talking about the industry that decided this. They put the hats on these guys and started throwing five of them against the wall to see if two of them would stick. That's the way it's been. I'm not complaining. I'm just giving you a collective situation of how I've watched this thing develop.

You saw this developing in the 1980s?

I saw it coming. I asked my attorney to write RCA up in New York that I would like to get a release, but I'm thinking if I get to the top it will filter down to Nashville and get them to think about what do to with a guy who's still selling two or three hundred thousand albums. But what do you know. They let me go. I had no back up. I'm devastated. It really got me because I never believed that was going to happen.

But anyway, I'm still breathing. I ain't in the soup line. [Shows] are still selling out. I still think it was a mistake for them to do that. But I think the pendulum is swinging back. I think I'm going to be able to sell some more records like I want to do. That's the thing I want to do again, sell records.

You talked about your transition from RCA in the 1980s. Then you went to 16th Avenue Records.

I didn't want to do it, but I did.

[Former RCA executive] Jerry Bradley was behind 16th Avenue.

Nothing against Jerry Bradley, I was just so put out. I wanted to wait, but my people, I did what they wanted to do rather than what I wanted to do. I'm not trying to pass the buck. Two times [I went with independent labels] and it didn't work.

Was there anything remarkable about Jerry Bradley the producer?

Not remarkable. We just worked good together. We did some good things together. We coproduced once we got together. He ended up being my second producer after Jack. Then there was Norro Wilson. I feel I can work with anyone if we can get along. I feel I can get along with anyone.

Are any of your songs autobiographical?

A bunch of them: "Wonder Could I Live There Anymore," "Mississippi Cotton Picking Town," which is about our hometown. The guy who wrote it worked for the grocery there where we grew up. "That's Why I Love You So Much." That song reminds me of when I was trying to get in baseball and my wife stuck with me. The lines of it are. "You stood by me whenever times were bad / Never once did I hear you complain / You always made the best of little bit we had / You held your head up, proud to wear my name / And that's just one of the reasons why I love you so much / You are the reason that I live / I know I got a woman no other man can touch / She gives me all the love she has to give / You sacrificed for dreams of mine that never did come true (That's when I mortgaged $400 worth of furniture and headed up to Montana.) / You've done without to satisfy my needs / And every time I tried and failed I found new strength in you (That's when I went to the Angels and then I had to come back and went down to the Mets.)

When I sing that song it reminds me of that kind of thing.

Do you ever talk to songwriters about your life and ask them to write about it?

Nope. I don't even know who wrote that. My measuring stick, is "Do I like it?" because when I cut "Snakes Crawl at Night" and "Atlantic Coastal Line" and "Just Between You and Me," I came back and told Jack Clement, "I like 'Just Between You and Me.'" He said, "No. We ain't going to release that. We're going to release 'Snakes Crawl at Night.'" They didn't want me singing love songs at that point because [racists might wonder] who was I singing those love songs to and what color were they? So all of that would dial into the equation, which I didn't kick then and I'm not kicking now because I think they had a point. We weren't even off the ground, but it ended up that all my fans want to hear me sing is love songs. When I heard "Just Between You and Me" that's the one I wanted. That song ended up being my first top ten record. I said, "So now what I'm going to try to do is if I hear a song make sure Charley, level with yourself, do you like that song?" That's what I've tried to do and still do all these years. The songs that I like the lyric content of, my fans will like it.

"Kiss an Angel Good Morning . . ."

Couldn't wait to get in the studio on that. Had no idea that it would do what it did. No idea at all. Just like I had no idea that I'd be in the Hall of Fame. I wanted to get in that studio and cut that song. I loved it. I liked it. But it did what it did.

How did that come to you, that song?

Ben Peters . . . we were working together. Jack at that time was still picking most of my material. It came from Ben Peters. Later when I started

1990s' promotional photo. Author's collection.

my own publishing company [Jack and I] would work back and forth. I'd do one from his publishing company, and I'd do one from my publishing company.

Right after that [in 1972] you followed up with "All His Children" recorded with Henry Mancini.

We did that for the movie *Sometimes a Great Notion* with Henry Fonda and Paul Newman. In fact, I think Paul Newman requested that he wanted me to do that.

Do you enjoy recording with a large ensemble?

Oh yes. I do a real good job, too. I did the National Anthem. It's still in the can at RCA. I did that with an orchestra. I did a song with an orchestra called "Dallas Cowboys" that John Schweers wrote. We did a pretty good session on that, too. I love being around eight to ten violins and a cello and the singers. With thirty people in the room, I just feel like I could sing forever.

Do you have a preference to record live with a band in the studio?
Yes. I'd rather record with a band and everybody. I don't like tracks.

When did you have to start using tracks?
I still have never done it too much. I've done it here and there, but I'm still reluctant.

In your autobiography you talk about Faron Young opening doors for you, so it's fitting that you were inducted into the Country Music Hall of Fame with him.
Couldn't think of another person that I'd rather go in with.

What is something that people don't know about Faron?
That sometimes he was one of the most obnoxious fellas you ever want to see, but he had one of the biggest hearts in the world, especially if he wasn't drinking. If he loved you, he loved you and he was your friend. That's the best I can put it, but sometimes you might not know what he might say.

In your book you said it took a little bit of time for Faron to warm up to you, were there performers who never did warm up to you?
When I first started out reporters were asking, "Now Charley, how does it feel to be the first colored country singer? How does it feel to be the first Negro country singer? How does it feel to be the first black country singer?" Now it's "How does it feel to be the first Afro-American country singer?" I say, "The same way when I was colored." They say, "What do you want me to call you?" "You can call me anything you want out of those four. Do you want to make another fifth one?" But I'm Charley Pride the American, that happened to have a permanent tan. That's just the difference in my own heart and mind. Out there in the culture, they say, "He's one of them." That's the old "them and us" factor. You have to divorce me from that when you're looking at me as an individual. If you're going to throw me in the pile, I'm going to jump out of there. And you're going to grab one and grab another one. When I come out of there, I'm still going to be Charley Pride the American.

I suppose people want you to be an R&B singer.

People say, "Well Charley, why didn't you sing like B. B. King, [you're from] a blues state?" Well, I disagree with that, too. I tell people, "Well, that depends on how you look at it, whether it's a blues state. Let me name you a few people from there: Conway Twitty, how about Tammy Wynette, how about Jimmie Rodgers, how about Leontyne Price of the Metropolitan Opera, how about Elvis." When they ask who's the King of Rock and Roll, they ain't going to say Frankie Avalon. Elvis Presley. So maybe Mississippi produces what people want to be in their own life and in their time. Somebody might say, "Why didn't you sing what I thought you should sing? Why didn't you be like you're supposed to be? That's the way you all . . ." We could talk here all day, but it comes down to the old "them and us" factor. "Why ain't there more of you all [black country singers]? I say, "Why ain't there more [black] senators and presidents?"

You talk about B. B. King and people like that. Did you listen to blues as a child?

I listened to every music you could think of. Sonny Boy Williamson, Howlin' Wolf. . . . The basis of American music is country, gospel, and blues. These guys sing that. I'm the epitome of that. If you or someone say to me, "Charley, that song you sing, that's a country song, but I hear a little bit of gospel in there, I hear a little bit of blues. A voice like yours, what's it doing singing that stuff?" Maybe this is how you sum it all up: Maybe in Charley Pride, not only singing, but hearing and being, you're hearing the epitome of American music, the American that's singing the American music.

We're all a product of our influences.

That's right.

I've interviewed blues and R&B singers like Bobby "Blue" Bland, and Bland talks about listening to the Grand Ole Opry *when he was a kid. . . .*

But the first thing they would say is, "But you didn't follow it, Bobby" or B. B. or whoever the blues guy is. "You sang the blues." It's what one wants to be and what one has the courage to go to in spite of. When I first went to Montana, the guys said, "Charley, what's going on down there." I went to Montana during the civil rights movement, just started singing in nightclubs up there. When Rosa Parks wouldn't get on the back of the bus, they said, "What's going on?" In Helena, you couldn't find one or two black families or cats and dogs out of 25,000 people. There were my wife and I and a couple others. You talk about a minority! I said, "Well, you pay your fifteen or twenty cents to get on the bus and there's a line that stops just five or ten feet from the door where you come in, in the front, and that's roped off for you all. Now sometimes there ain't but one of you all on there, and we done filled it up all the way from the back. Then we have to start standing in the aisle. There ain't but one of you all up there, and half of the aisle could sit down if the law didn't deem that we couldn't sit there. That's what happened to Miss Parks. She said, 'I ain't going to move no more.' She didn't get up, so she went against the segregation laws which are wrong, and then they put her in jail. Would you like to pay the same amount and then stand? Flip it over. You start in the back, and you leave the front seat for us and there ain't but one or two of us riding, but you still got to leave it open in case one of us wants to ride. Does that sound right?" In those kind of things, I had to take my time and explain all of that to them. "That's what's going wrong with them down there, between us and you all."

You mentioned that Jack Clement wanted you to be careful about the songs you sang early on. Does racism explain why you weren't part of a duet like Porter and Dolly, Jim Ed Brown and Helen Cornelius?

I'm sure, probably. I hadn't asked, but I would think probably so. It probably had some bearing.

In your book you say that Willie Nelson called you "Supernigger." ...

Supernigger, yes.

That surprised me, and I had to wonder if he really was being kind.

Yes, he was. It's like when friends say what they want to another friend, but then you take it outside the circle. . . . [People outside might say] "Do you hear what Willie Nelson called Charley? And he didn't do nothing. I would have probably hit him in the mouth." That's an inside thing. I'm not saying I condone it. I didn't tell him to do it. But that was his way of saying, "That [the term] nigger don't mean nothing to me." That don't meaning nothing more to me than "superbread" or "super candybar." I think it was something like when *All in the Family* came on with Archie Bunker. He loosened up a lot of things. There were a lot of things that couldn't be said on TV that were startin' to be said. It was there, but it was "*Let's just pretend it ain't there.*" But if you make friendly comical references, it takes away that sting that has been there for so many years. That's the only way I can put it. Now . . . you can talk to him. I never asked him, but that's just the way I felt that he was doing.

You played baseball in Memphis in the 1950s. Did you pay attention to Johnny Cash and others who were part of the white music scene there?

I remember Johnny Cash, Roy Orbison, Jerry Lee Lewis came to do a show at the Memphis Red Sox baseball at Wellington and Crumb, where I was playing baseball in the old Negro Leagues. I remember when Johnny came on, they didn't have many people there. They wanted to see how many colored people they could draw. (We was colored back then.) I was one of the ones in the stands, and I remember Johnny at one point stopping, "Is there anybody that wants to hear a request for anything." They wasn't reacting. Nobody said anything and then I said, "I Walk the Line." His eyes lit up just like a Christmas tree. Later [I said to him], "Do you know who that was? That was me." He said that he remembered that particular request on that particular day. He just smiled and laughed. I think you borrow a little bit from everybody that you meet that you like. If you like something about them, you might try to borrow a little something that will help you in your upward travels and onward progress.

Certainly Elvis was part of that scene.

I met him right at Lansky Brothers. He was going in to get some clothes there on Beale Street. He had on a red shirt and white pants, and I went over and said hi to him. Of course, he didn't remember that when we met back in 1971. But I told him that's where I met him. I followed him at the Hilton International in 1971 after I won Male Vocalist and Entertainer of the Year. I talked longer to his dad, though, than I did to him. He did meet me and my wife, and I went back to meet him with my daughter. I tell this onstage, he got down on his knees and played nosies with my daughter and doggone it, I didn't have a camera. I sure would have loved to have a shot of that.

The interview with Charley Pride was conducted on October 30, 2000.

Note

1. Charley Pride with Jim Henderson, *The Charley Pride Story* (New York: William Morrow, 1994).
2. Alanna Nash, *Behind Closed Doors: Talking with the Legends of Country Music* (New York: Knopf, 1988).

Loretta Lynn
Woman Enough

A friend of mine who writes about country music tells of a drive she and Loretta Lynn took through New York City. "That's where I spent the night," Lynn said to her, pointing as they passed Macy's on Broadway. My friend, who would never deny a person's imaginative streak, could only sit by bemused as her companion spun an improbable tale about a night locked in the block-sized department store. "Right, Loretta," she thought. "And nobody came searching for you? There were no security guards around to help?"

My friend knew that we all must indulge Loretta. Scrutiny will do no good: it's like stabbing at quicksilver. I learned the same a few years later.

A threat on her life when she carried the Olympic torch through Louisville in 2001? I called the Louisville police to get the details. They were befuddled. I asked her management. No, no, they couldn't recall anything like that. My reflex was to take the story back to Loretta, but I blanched. The very act of challenging this vision of grace with pene-trating blue eyes seemed too daunting and too much like an attack on Southern womanhood. Like William Faulkner's sheepish city fathers who sit in the parlor of the ancient and ambivalent Emily Grierson, afraid to just flat-out demand payment of property taxes, I could only shake my head.

As embellished as her stories may be, what needs no embellishment is her track record in country music. She has followed an amazing career path to acceptance among mass audiences and has taken country music with her.

Her story begins in Johnson County, Kentucky, in Butcher Holler, a place known to millions because Loretta Webb was born there on April 14, 1935, and later sang about it. Her father, whom she worshiped until his death in 1959, mined coal at Consolidated Number Five near Butcher Holler, but the job offered little subsistence, so her family endured life in a drafty shack, stealing bits and pieces, raising and canning vegetables, learning how to survive on next to nothing. Hardly a teenager and with little experience of the world beyond Butcher Holler, she married a World War II vet named Mooney Lynn, whom she dubbed Doolittle or just plain Doo. The marriage delivered her to fame, but its nearly fifty years of physical and mental abuse also scarred her.

Although Lynn quickly points out that she could dish out abuse measure for measure with Doo, there's no denying who endured the most. Before his death in 1996, Doo bedded their son's girlfriend, disappeared for long stretches, intermittently kicked Loretta out of their home, and often used his hands in a most unloving way. In her second autobiography *Still Woman Enough*, Lynn recounted Doo's harrowing reaction one night when she drank a beer and threw up. "He dragged me into the kitchen, run the sink full of water, grabbed me by the hair and shoved my face in the sink. He knew how scared I was of water and held my head under until I began to choke. Then he yanked me out by the hair until I caught my breath. As soon as I did, he pushed my head back under the water."[1]

Such episodes with Doo begged the thorny question—one I asked her with some hesitation—how could this woman—who suffered little obnoxious male behavior in hits like "Happy Birthday," "What Kind of a Girl (Do You Think I Am)?," and "Your Squaw Is on the Warpath"— tolerate such an abusive husband? She tackled the question in the following interview, claiming the songs were boot kicks to Doo's shins.

Somewhat ironically, it was Doo who encouraged a career that became a refuge from home life and afforded her the stage to lash out at the failings of men. He encouraged her to ply her mountain-stream clear voice on stages around the Pacific Northwest, where he had moved their family in the 1950s. A performance on a Buck Owens show in Tacoma, Washington, landed her a contract with Norm Burley, a Canadian who owned Zero Records. From there, her career shot up faster than a rock from under a rolling wagon wheel.

In 1960, she waxed "Honky Tonk Girl" in a Los Angeles studio and— after she and Doo visited countless disc jockeys to pitch the record—it rose to country music's top twenty. The record and the helping hand of almost everybody's Nashville mentor, Ernest Tubb, bought her a spot on the *Grand Ole Opry* and a deal with Decca Records. Decca's Nashville A&R man Owen Bradley would guide her in the studio for the next twenty years.

Early promotional photo. Author's collection.

In contrast to the patently assertive woman that Lynn is today, early in her career she was subdued by the new and foreign worlds opening to her. Her poor formal education and naiveté about the music business restrained her. She relied on paternal Nashville artists such as Tubb as well as Patsy Cline, kind Greyhound drivers who directed her to the next bus, and loyal fans who helped her start fan clubs. She was a waif in the wilderness, as the following scene suggests: "When I'd take my little record out and picture [to sell after a show], I couldn't give back the change. So I'd sit on the stage and sell 'em, and I was having a terrible time. The line would be way out the building, so somebody would jump up on stage and help me with the change and help me sell."

By the mid-1960s, however, Little Red Riding Hood had slain the wolf. She shook the country music world by competing head-to-head with males and aggressively confronting them in her compositions. In contrast to Kitty Wells, whose seminal "It Wasn't God Who Made Honky Tonk Angels" demurely and indirectly raised questions about men, Lynn fearlessly lashed out against cheating men and scheming women in 1960s hits such as "You Ain't Woman Enough," "Fist City," and "You've Just Stepped In (From Stepping Out on Me)." More than any other female act in country music, she challenged men in a man's world. And she was making a lot of money doing it.

Hers would become one of the monumental careers in country music. She not only blazed trails for women in her field and loudly defended women on recordings, but also helped bring country music to audiences outside country's traditional boundaries. Like Johnny Cash, Eddy Arnold, and others, she parlayed her popularity in the country base into appearances on national television and international tours. Perhaps her most significant contribution to country music's proliferation was her 1976 autobiography *Coal Miner's Daughter*. Written with George Vecsey, she unflinchingly recounted her raw childhood, stormy marriage, and the price of fame. The book hit the *New York Times* bestseller list and became a movie in 1980 starring Sissy Spacek, who won the best-actress Oscar for her portrayal of Lynn. This sort of extra-Nashville validation—*New York Times* attention combined with a blockbuster movie—was unheard of in country music circles. Only the fictionalized film *Nashville* in 1975 and the career of Johnny Cash had called so much attention to country music beyond traditional country audiences.

The momentum continues to this day, although Loretta's well out of the mainstream country spotlight these days. Still, her latest album *Still Country* hit the *Billboard* charts in 2000, and her second autobiography, *Still Woman Enough*, pierced the *New York Times* best-seller list in 2002.

And there's got to be some truth in that.

THE WOMEN ALWAYS COME UP TO ME and tell me that they appreciate what I've written 'cause they gone through the same thing I have. And the men always come up and say, "I appreciate you fightin' for your old man." [They're talking about] "You Ain't Woman Enough (To Take My Man)," "Fist City" and all that. It hit the women and the men, 'cause the woman was saying, "You ain't gonna do this" but then they'd turn right around and say, "You ain't woman enough to take my man." So I kind of hit 'em both.

Loretta Lynn with Eddy Arnold. Author's collection.

A lot of things you've sung about during your career, you never hear in country music today.

They don't have no country music now. What it is is fantasy land. If they didn't have the videos for them to show their bellies or their boobies, they wouldn't have nothin' then. If they come out on video and just sit there and sing, you couldn't sell that song 'cause the song don't say nothin'.

So you don't think country music is telling it like it is anymore.

No. Country music is not telling it. There's one girl that's out right now that says, "Pour me, pour me, pour me another glass of whiskey." I said, "Come on girl, get it." I think it's [Heidi Newfield of] Pony, Trick Pony. I kind of like her. I don't know who writes for her. She don't write. But whoever's writing for her knows she's goin' to do it. So she's not afraid to do it. So I say, "Come on." She was woman enough to get out there and sing it.

Did you take a lot of criticism for the things you were dealing with in song thirty years ago, like in "The Pill"?

I'd get down off the stage, and I'd mingle with the people who was drinking. Well, every woman told me they were on the pill. So, what's the big deal? Down South in the Bible Belt they banned the song and the preachers would preach about it. The women would go out on Monday morning to see what the heck was wrong with it. They just made the record bigger. Thank God for the preachers! Ain't that right?

They even banned "What Kind of a Girl (Do You Think I Am)?" and a preacher come backstage. He paid his way to get in, after he got through preaching. He come over to me and he said, "Loretta I have a fifteen-year-old daughter. We've been having a lot of trouble with her. We got this record for her and do you know all she does is sit and listen to it? She's not like she used to be; she don't run around. She's told her boyfriend, what kind of girl do you think I am?" The disc jockeys thought it was dirty, and they waited 'til they was told to play that record, that there was nothing dirty in it. I thought it was great when the preacher come up and told me that.

Those songs just hit you, there's no pussy footing around.

That's right. I go right through the middle on it. You don't need to go around with all this fluffy stuff.

A lot of the songs were very sexy, but not necessarily explicit.

Like "Wings Upon Your Horn." Well, you know what? I didn't know people called horns dirty. All I was doing was just taking wings and horns. Angels have wings. The devil has horns, right? Well, that was the way that I wrote. I wrote exactly what would happen if a girl went with a man. . . . It said, "Before you first made love to me, you called me your wife to be. But after that I seen the devil in your eyes." So when it got to the chorus, I said, "You're the first to ever make me fall in love and not take me." But Owen Bradley come runnin' out of the studio and said, "Loretta, honey, this song's too dirty. You'll never get by with this." And I said, "What's dirty about it?" He said, "Horns . . ." I couldn't understand that. It made me so mad that I broke that line that it gave me a little more ummph to bust that line open: "You're the first to ever make fall in love and not take me." He walked out on that song, but the song [became a hit].

Were you surprised when your first autobiography Coal Miner's Daughter *took off in 1976?*

Yeah I was. 'Cause I hadn't lived. When they wanted to write the book, I said, "I really haven't lived. I don't know what you're gonna write about because all I've done is have kids." They said, "Well, let's write one." I had three or four writers, and I picked George Vecsey. Why, I don't know. But I picked the best one.

Why do you think people are interested in your life?

I really didn't know, but when the book was written and became a best seller and then come into a movie, I thought, "What in the devil are they gonna to do a movie about?" I thought the book was a little funny, and I laughed when I read it. I'd lay awake at night and Doolittle would read it to me, a chapter or two every night. And we'd laugh about some of the things in it.

Tell me about the emotions you experienced writing your second auto-biography, Still Woman Enough.

Now and then I dream about Doo. He's never dead, and me and him are out doing something together on the farm. The other day I dreamed he said, "Loretta, take a ball of string and tie it around this stake and go to the head of this garden, so you can get these rows straight." Well, before I started getting a garden out without him, I just took my hoe down through [the dirt] and it grew just as well. Who cares if [the rows] are crooked, as long as it grows. Me and him used to fight about that. So every now and then I will dream, but he's never dead. He's telling me what I should do and what I shouldn't do. Or we're on vacation and we're in the camper and we're having a good time, I'm out diggin' up different flowers in the desert. We're doing somethin', you know. But I never dream about him bein' gone.

But I think probably the hardest thing was talking about [the death of eldest son] Jack. But I didn't tell the most hurtful things. When I was on the road, I had a seizure. I had seven seizures caused by emotions. They had taken two different [MRIs] of my head; they said there's no tumor, no nothin'. So it has to be something else. So we started going back to everyone I had, and it was when something happened. The last one I had I was in Champaign, Illinois [in 1984]. My son was drowning right at the moment I had the seizure.

Do you think you're a spokesperson for women?

I think I am, probably. Because I've gotten so much mail since I've been singin' from women asking me what they should do about this and what they should do about that. Back when I was answerin' all my mail right at the time I'd get the letter, it was so hard 'cause it started pilin' up on me and I was gettin' triple, triple, triple mail. And I was havin' to write in the car as we drove. It was real hard. Here I am answerin' questions, "My old man's gonna leave me. He's goin' with the woman next door." It was stuff like that. What are you gonna say? Sorry? I just told 'em to get a ball bat to him. He'll stay if you get a ball bat to him.

You know, I was working Vegas one night and I was singing "You Ain't Woman Enough (To Take My Man)." This is the maddest I think I've ever been onstage. This woman raised up—everyone was quiet during the show—and said, "Let me tell you something. I've been to Hurricane Mills and I *had* your old man. I had a big tail gown on, you know. I swished down and pulled up my gown and I hit the table. I was goin' right at her. They took her out before I got to her. I think I messed up a lot of people's drinks and stuff. But they took her out. Hey! She didn't have no business sayin' it. I'd 'a used that microphone over her head.

Do you feel like you have something to say on behalf of all the women back in Kentucky who are living in the Butcher Hollers there.

There's not many people living in that Holler today. My brother lives there and takes care of the old home place. But there's not as many people living there as there used to be. They got TV and they moved out to a little bit better place.

Yes ... but there's still a lot of women nursing sick husbands, raising families alone. It seems to me that during your career you've always had something to say on their behalf.

When I did "One's on the Way" [in 1971], I'm telling you I have never had so many women pregnant at my shows in my life. Half of the crowd that was pregnant looked like they was fixin' to have it that night. I thought, "Oh God let 'em get home before it happens." Some came right about the time the baby was supposed to be born. One of them did get sick at the show. That went on for about five years. I guess every song I've done, really, hit the women and the men. I didn't put the men down. I stood up to them. Men like to be fought over.

When you were first getting started what was the toughest thing about being a female in the industry?

Well, I was the only one that played guitar, and I played bar chord rhythm. I learned by myself and my little brother Jay Lee worked [with me]. The hardest thing was the way [the other women performers] looked at me when I came to Nashville playing my own guitar like that. They never expected a woman to play bar chord rhythm. I don't know why a woman had never done that.

There was just as many women in Nashville then as there is now. They just wasn't gettin' heard because they wasn't different. They wasn't first, and they wasn't great. They were just mediocre singers. The first time I knew I had any, really, competition was about a year and a half later and me and my brother was drivin' down the road and Tammy Wynette come [on the radio] with "Apartment #9." "Uh-oh, I got me some competition." It just made me work harder. Competition's great. Ain't much out there today, unless you want to show your belly button. I ain't showin' mine. I'd have to go get me a tummy tuck like so many have, have my whole body done. Somebody looks like a cartoon now, but we won't say. I'm tellin' ya! They start gettin' fat and they start takin' ribs out.

You say there were women who were trying to keep you down.

I was on the *Grand Ole Opry* twenty-two times in a row, and the girls that was on the *Grand Ole Opry* was fighting to keep me off. Patsy Cline, when she was here, she fought to keep me around. They were having a party at one of the girl's homes and she heard about it. So she called me up and said, "Loretta, you and I are going to a party tonight." I said, "What for?" She said, "I think it might be interesting. You might need to go." Later, I found out that they were meeting to have me kicked off the *Opry*. It wasn't mentioned that night because when Patsy walked through the door, she said, "If anybody in here has got anything to say, say it now." But I still didn't know what she was talking about. I just walked in smilin' and happy doin' what everybody else done. But Patsy knew. All the girls was getting together to have me took off the *Opry*. But it wouldn't hurt because the next day I just went to the *Grand Ole Opry* and told 'em what happened, and they said don't worry about it.

In your first book, you talked about Patsy visiting you from beyond. Does she visit you still?

I think she does. Somebody touched me last night. I know that it's crazy. . . . But I was laying there last night in the bed and somebody done this to me. [She taps her shoulder.] You can tell when somebody touches you. I tried to find out who it was, I named over different people, but I can't seem to.

I could see Patsy one time when I was really sick and I had a whole medley of her songs fixed up [to record], and I thought, I'll never get though "Crazy," "He's Got You," all the slow ones. And I kind of looked up, and I could just see a form of Patsy in her little red skin paints and little gold shoes. It was just like she said, "I'm ashamed of you." And I didn't even think about that medley until it was over. Never even thought about it until that was over.

What do you think Patsy wanted from life?

"Look how things have changed," she'd say. She bought this little brick home. It wasn't no mansion or anything like that. And she took me out—they didn't have the yard done even—and said, "I want you to look at my home." She was so proud of it. She said, "I won't be happy until I can put Mommy in one just like it." And within a week she was gone.

You know, I did everything I could for Patsy, even after she was dead. . . . They didn't play her records at all after she was gone, so I did *I Remember Patsy* [in 1977]. And they started playing her records, and they did a book on her, and they did a movie on her [*Sweet Dreams*]. You know, I never went to see it because I seen little [advance] snips of it, and I think it kind of made her look slutty. And she was everything but slutty. I mean she might tell you where you could go in a New York minute. But she was not like that, and I don't know why they did that.

In her autobiography, Tammy Wynette talked about the sexual harassment women had to deal with in country music. I wonder if you saw the same.

I never noticed it. Probably wouldn't have known the difference [if I was a victim], I married so young. I didn't notice any difference in the way men acted with me. They were all nice to me. But I didn't notice any difference in the way they talked to me or anything.

Disc jockeys wouldn't . . .

No. No. This girl one time that was on Zero took me out on my first little deal to get my record played. She made a date for me and herself in Nashville, and we were supposed to go get bikinis and go swimming with them. Well, I didn't know that was a date. I called my husband and told him what was gonna happen and, oh, he like to died. He said, "Don't you dare do that. She's settin' a date up for you." That's what that was and, boy, I let them know I wasn't goin'. No, I've never had no more trouble.

I think they know who to say somethin' to. They really do. They know what they're dealin' with.

When you were promoting your first record, there were disc jockeys who accepted you. Were there jocks who demanded money for plays?

There was a guy in Oregon when I lived on the West Coast. I said, "Here's the picture that my husband took." It was with this old bedspread hanging up. Well, it was all I had. We made a few pictures up; they were little ones. And I said, "Here's my record. My husband did all of this." He looked at me and said, "How much money do you have?" I said, "I ain't got none. Me and my husband are sleeping in the car and eating bologna and crackers and cheese." "Well, if you can't pay me to play it, I won't play it." I just picked my record up and said, "Well, I can't leave it then because if you ain't goin' to play it, we ain't got enough to give everybody."

When your first began recording with Ernest Tubb ...

Ernest put me on the *Ernest Tubb Show* before I got on the *Opry* and that was over the same 50,000-watt station. He helped me again on the first show on the *Grand Ole Opry*. I don't know how many I did straight *Grand Ole Opry* shows. Seventeen dollars a night and if you did the second show, you got $3. Gosh, I needed it, so I stayed for the second show.

So Tubb gave you a leg up when you needed it.

Let me tell you something about Ernest Tubb: I don't think anybody has ever given Ernest Tubb the credit. Ernest Tubb helped everybody, *everybody*, in country music when they got to Nashville. I do not think that anybody has ever said, "Thank you, Ernest." When Ernest got sick, I went to Texas to do a show for him to help with his medicine and stuff. I couldn't even get his band to go. I couldn't get nobody to go to do this benefit show. That was a sad thing.

Tell me something people don't know about Ernest Tubb?

They probably don't know that he loved to gamble. He played cards with the boys on the bus.... When they told him I was comin' to his bus when we first started workin' together, he'd let on like he never played cards, that he didn't do anything wrong. When I'd go in, he'd cook for me. He'd open up a can of chili, the hotter the better. I'd say, "This is too hot." Then he got to where he was buying little cans that wasn't hot. He would cook for me, but [he would tell the boys], "You tell me if she's fixin' to come." Because every now and then, he'd say a little dirty word. "You watch the windows and let me know if she's comin' in." He wanted me to know that he was perfect, and I thought he was.

Wanda Jackson once said in an interview that when she appeared on Ernest's portion of the Opry, *he demanded she get out of her strapless dress and put on something more conservative.[2] Would that have been in keeping with Ernest's character?*

No. Ernest wouldn't have cared what she wore because I don't think Ernest made it his business to do anything but help you. I really don't.

What was your reaction when MCA finally let him go?

That was the worst thing I ever heard in my life. I went to MCA, and
... I talked to 'em about puttin' out a bunch of albums so we could make
money. I said, "Put 'em out and we'll have enough money so we can buy
the medicine for Ernest." Did you know they didn't even know who Ernest
Tubb was? I said, "You don't know who Ernest Tubb was? He built the
company. He was [one of the] first ones on your label. You don't even
know who Ernest Tubb is?" I said, "You all are fixin' to hit bottom then,
if you don't know where it come from." And I think they pretty well found
out that.

Very sad, and when he died there was no money for a tombstone.

Nope. And I'll tell you what. One of the worst things that hurt me, I sent
a check to help buy his monument thing that they were puttin' up. And the
boy that works at Ernest Tubb Record Shop, sent the check back because I

Loretta Lynn with mother Clara Webb Butcher (left) and sister Crystal Gayle
(right), accepting the Academy of Country Music's Artist of the Decade
Award, May 2, 1980. Author's collection.

had given up my fan club and they were mad, and he got mad at me too [because of that]. I'm pretty sure that's why he sent the check back. He didn't want nothin' to do with me. It broke my heart. Me and Ernest Tubb helped each other, and it's sad that he had to act that way.

Tell me about recording with Conway Twitty.

Everytime somebody would say, "I'd like to record with Loretta." Merle Haggard or anybody. Doo would say, "She has a singing partner." He wouldn't let me record with nobody. Conway Twitty was it. And they were great friends. Me and Conway was great friends. We had our businesses together and never had one fight.

He'd laugh at me every now and then 'cause I called pizza, "pee-za." He said, "Loretta, it's pizza." I said, "It's pee-za. Look at how it's wrote." He always laughed about when he said, "We're gonna have pizza." I'd never had it. Both buses stopped at this little Pizza Hut. And I said, "I don't want it. I'm afraid I won't like it." Well, he finally got me in there and I looked up on the wall and I seen there was all sizes. He said, "Ladies first." All my band and his whole band was in there. My backup singers and all. And, I looked and I looked and I said, "Conway, I may not like it. . . . I think I'll have that nine-inch pecker-roni up there." I looked around and they all left. I was standin' there by myself and they were all outside rollin' on the ground. I was so mad. I didn't get no pizza. I left. I looked at the woman and I said, "Where'd they go?" She said, "They all left, and if I had somebody else here, I'd leave too." I didn't get the pizza neither.

Your duets with Conway really helped establish him as a country artist.

That's the only time he got an award. That's the saddest thing that ever happened. He had [eighty-three solo country] hits. Now why didn't he get an award by himself? You tell me. If you don't think politics is politics.

He wasn't stroking the right people? Or he started out as a rock and roller and people held that against him?

I really don't know what happened. But it was the saddest thing that ever was that the only time he ever got an award was when I was with him. When I was out in L.A. [for an awards ceremony], he wasn't even nominated for an award. . . . I was sittin' there and Conway knew I was fixin' to take four awards home. But I didn't know it. Everybody, just about, was in the same category I was in. It always made me nervous. That's why I won't go to 'em today. . . . But I felt a little tap on my shoulder and I didn't even know

Conway was there. I looked around, and I said, "Well, Conway." He said, "I'm here for you honey." He wasn't nominated, but he was there for me. How could you not love somebody like that? We stayed in business twenty years together, never had a quarrel.

With the duet "As Soon as I Hang Up the Phone" [recorded in 1974] whose idea was it to record Conway's part over a telephone?

Let me tell you how this happened. Conway gave me this song and said, "Take it to Owen Bradley for Crystal Gayle, my sister." Well, Owen said that it was too country for Crystal. Well, I heard the song and I listened to it. I just took the song and done all the talking, and I said, "Conway, you and I are gonna do this song. It's too country for Crystal," Owen said, "She said, "There's no way you and I can do this song. It just wouldn't work. This is not the kind of song that we would want to do." So I showed him what I done. I said, "You do this and I'll do this." It took him out of the singin' part of it, and he didn't like that a doggone bit, but he had to do the talkin'. I loved his talkin'. At the end, I sang, "As soon as I hang up the phone." I was cryin', and then he went bam! [with the receiver]. He was in another room with the phone. He was in the one room, and I was in another room. He called me on my phone. Before I could get what I had to say to him out, he hung up on me. I just walked in right there and said, "You hang up on me like that again, and I'll walk out. I won't sing this song." He thought it was funny. He was rolling.

You did your part holding a phone to your face?

Yeah. And he was in another room talking to me. "Loretta, but there is something I got to tell ya ..." It just made me so mad when he hung up on me like that. I'm very, very funny. If I'm singin' a song I'm livin' it. When I write it or when I'm recordin' it, I'm livin' that person, and I think that probably comes through. We had to do it over then, and Owen said, "Damn, Loretta we had it perfect." Not as far as I was concerned.

What's the duet you like best?

That one. He liked "Feelings" better and "Mississippi Woman."

I always picked a song for me and Conway that had a great beat and a good melody and told a story, but that didn't matter as long as I thought the melody was good and the beat was good. Me and Conway both would pick 'em. They'd be playin' songs for us, and me and Conway both would look at each other when there was a song that we know was a hit. We'd just look at each other. We didn't have to say a word. We'd just look at each other and say, "Yeah. Keep it for us."

With actress Sissy Spacek on Lynn's NBC-TV show in 1981. Author's collection.

him, he'd turn 'em down. I'd up and sing a little ol' song I wrote, and that was fine. "We'll do that one. What else have you wrote?" After a year, he never asked me to ever come in with songs. He just knew that when it was recording time, I would be there with songs. And then I started writing for my sister Crystal. . . . The only time he got mad was when I wrote a song for [sister] Peggy Sue, and it was called "I'm Dynamite." He said, "Loretta, that's a good one for you. You really been needin' a good slow song, and that's a smash." I said, "No. Owen, you said if I could find Peggy a hit, you would record her." He got mad at me for about three months, and then I come up with a couple more hits and he got over it.

He's one of the greatest producers ever to work in Nashville. What accounts for his greatness?

I think you either know or you don't know, you know? I think it was just absolutely plain old common sense. He recorded pop, he recorded rock, he recorded country, and anything he recorded made it.

Once you got into the studio and recorded, did he get involved in much once the recording had started. Did he offer his advice . . .?

And I'd offer mine. On "I'm the Other Woman," I said, "Owen, this [is] how I'm goin' to do it . . ." He said, "Naw, you ain't gonna tell me how you're gonna do it." I said, "Yeah, I am." I said, "I wanna say, *I want to introduce myself. I'm the other woman.*" He said, "That's a hell of an idea."

When you first started recording with him, did he try to get you into a rock sound?

I was on the West Coast. All I listened to was pop. On every album I put a pop song, like "Secret Love," "Blueberry Hill." I was an Elvis Presley fan. I did one on every album. He would leave out of the studio, have him a cigarette or stand outside and talk to somebody, and he'd come back in after I got it done. He did not want me singin' anything but country. He said, "You was born to be country, and that's the way it goes, and I ain't gonna have anything to do with any other thing." And that's the way it went.

Once Jimmy Bowen came to MCA, he wouldn't let you record with Owen. Why was that?

Jimmy Bowen was a great producer, but Jimmy was a controller. I didn't record for [a while] after I lost my son, and then when I went back to cut my album, Jimmy Bowen had come in and he was doin' all the producing for MCA. Owen had left. So, they wanted me to use Bowen, and that's what

I did. He is a good producer, but it was still too ... it took him a month when it shouldn't have took but three hours.

Did Owen have any weaknesses as a producer?

I never heard one time that he was weak on anything that he produced. Nothing.

When Chet Atkins come in, they started lettin' him be the producer at RCA. Chet come over to me and says that he wished he could have got me before Owen did. He said, "You're still the greatest singer in country music. I'm a little jealous, but you got the best producer in the business." I said, "I know that, Chet." He said, "But you do know I produce!" I said, "I know that, Chet." Chet was a great guy. He was funny. He wanted to tell jokes. Him and Owen would get together and they would tell jokes. It was good to see the two together.

Close-up of Lynn, 1970s. Author's collection.

That's something for Chet to say you were the greatest when he had Dottie West and others ...

Well, you brought up a name. She had just walked onstage to do the *Grand Ole Opry* when he told me that. She had just walked onstage to do her song, and he said, "You're still the greatest singer when it comes to country music in Nashville, Tennessee." Of course, she wasn't that country.

When I got to the end of Coal Miner's Daughter, *it seemed to me that you were a woman under seige. You were working hard. The record label was after you. The promoters were after you. The fans were after you. I wonder if you've reached equilibrium in your life?*

I had to. I just had to say, "Hey, I will do this. I won't do that. I'll do this or that." It had to come to that because it was gettin' too hard. Every fan wants five minutes with you. And I can understand where they're comin' from because I'm a fan myself. I know that they don't understand. But if I spent five minutes after every show, I wouldn't get away from there for ten months. . . . It can't be done. It breaks my heart not to be able to, but I can't.

In your second autobiography, you go into great detail about your marriage and how you stayed with your marriage. How did this woman who in her songs didn't take anything tolerate so much in her marriage?

But that's how I didn't take anything . . . was in my songs. I could write one and say, "There! Take that!" He didn't never know which line was his. Every one had a line or two or three or four about him. I think he knew it, but he didn't make no big deal out of it. It was a hit song and he didn't say nothin', and I didn't either. That's how I got him back.

Interviews with Loretta Lynn were conducted on February 13, 2002, and March 29, 2002.

Notes

1. Loretta Lynn, with Patsi Bale Cox, *Still Woman Enough: A Memoir* (New York: Hyperion, 2002).
2. "Rocking the Gender Line," *Country Music Magazine* (March 2002).

Sheb Wooley
Dreams Will Come True

I n their own ways, many of the artists featured in this book indelibly marked the national consciousness. Loretta Lynn, Chet Atkins, Charley Pride, and Eddy Arnold impressed pop music audiences, appeared on the proverbial network variety show circuit, and wrote autobiographies published by New York houses. Ambassadors, they proved that country music was American entertainment. Sheb Wooley, though, held uniquely impressive ambassadorial credentials. He enjoyed a multidimensional career that made his peers in country music seem stuck in a Nashville quagmire.

While many country singers dreamed about Hollywood fame, appearing strictly in B-grade celluloid disasters, Sheb Wooley parlayed his music career into credible motion picture roles. Four years into his recording career, in 1950, he copped a part in *Rocky Mountain High* with Errol Flynn, and for the next fifty years he repeatedly won small roles in film classics such as, *High Noon*, *Giant*, *Seven Brides for Seven Brothers*, and *Hoosiers*. Wooley added television to his c.v. in 1959, when he began a five-year stint as the beloved scout Pete Nolan in CBS's *Rawhide*. Most country music singers would be lucky to host a syndicated television show or make guest spots on network television, but country singer Sheb Wooley was an actor. Ultimately, his was among the most dynamic of careers to emerge in country music.

BORN APRIL 10, 1921, in Erick, Oklahoma, Shelby F. Wooley grew up amid the ravages of Dust Bowl drought. On his father's ranch, he saw crops droop and die and swirling sand and dirt blacken the sky. "It would get so dark they'd have to close down the schools," he told writer Don Cusic. "It was so dark you couldn't even read or see."[1] Many of

Sheb Wooley (left) with Walter Pidgeon (right) in an episode of the 1960s CBS-TV series *Rawhide*. Author's collection.

the Wooleys' fellow Oklahomans found the sun again in California, but Sheb's family stayed put on their land. In the brighter times of his youth, Sheb learned to ride and rope (which served him well in the movies), but Red Foley, Ernest Tubb, and the guitar lassoed him.

In his teens, he picked with the Plainview Melody Boys in Elk City, Oklahoma, and after working in the defense industries during the Second World War, he rambled to Nashville, where the music business was just starting to congeal. When Sheb arrived, there were no major label offices, few music publishers, and business dealings revolved around radio station WSM, home of the *Opry*, where singers, record men, publishers, and con artists hovered about all day.

The new guy in town hitched up with WSM competitor WLAC and signed on with the enterprising Jim Bulleit, who owned Bulleit Records. However, he soon found himself dusting Nashville off his boots, thrown out by an angry musicians union. His trail led to Dallas where he signed with another small label and starred on radio for General Foods' Calumet Baking Powder. In country music, flour and baking powder were gold dust. Milling companies around the nation spent big bucks sponsoring radio performers such as Bob Wills, Flatt and Scruggs, and, then, Wooley. With Calumet behind him, he appeared on an extensive Texas radio network, catching fire like hill country grass. Possibilities, nationwide possibilities, awakened. Buoyed by the response to his radio shows, he sold himself to a major recording outfit, MGM Records, which at the time had Hank Williams in its stall.

In the first years of his MGM contract, he recorded western-oriented material that mingled with his western movie roles, but his releases only sold moderately. However, all that changed later in the 1950s when he recorded the pop-oriented "Are You Satisfied?" (1955) and the rocking novelty "Purple People Eater" (1958), which claimed the number one spot on the pop charts for six weeks. Experimenting with pop and rock, Wooley's sales came to life. "I realized it was a business," he told historian Kevin Coffey. "I loved recording and I loved writing all kinds of different songs, so I thought, you know, if that's what the market is, let's go over there. And I did that little move. I didn't have any feeling about it, except that I had gone long enough without a hit. MGM gave me more freedom—I was with the label twenty-seven years and I don't know why they gave me so much freedom, but I appreciate it."[2] From the late '50s onward, Sheb Wooley peppered his country and western output with pop croonings and outlandish novelties.

In 1962, his thriving novelty pursuits entered a new realm when he acquired the pseudonym Ben Colder and began parodying country hits. An already fabulous career took another shape: Sheb Wooley, comedian. In ten years, Ben Colder, a drunken alter ego, unleashed six country smashes, almost as many as Sheb Wooley.

THERE WAS A SONG THAT CAME ALONG—I was recording for MGM Records— and my producer in Nashville held this song for weeks and weeks. I was on the West Coast, this was while I was doing the *Rawhide* series. I couldn't get away. He said, "You gotta come down and record this song because it's a hit." By the time I came down, Rex Allen had been into town and they finally had given up on me doing it. Rex had cut it and it was out and it was breaking wide open. It was a song called "Son Don't Go Near the Indians." Remember it? He says, "You dummy. You missed a hit." I said, "Don't worry about it. I'll do one called, "Son Don't Go Near the Eskimos." He said, "How does it go?" I said, "Oook-shoook-mooogie-mushy-doggy-oook-shoook-mooogie-ay / Son, don't go near the Eskimos / Please do what I say." Everybody laughed. We were sitting around eating dinner. That was the end of it, I thought. The next day, he says, "I think that might be an idea. If Rex's record sells a million, we can at least do a third of that with a parody." I went on back to California and forgot about it. He called me one day, "You got that song written yet." I said, "What song?" He said, "That oook-shoook-mooogie Eskimo thing." I said, "No." He said, "Well you gotta get down here and record it." I said, "Okay, I'll write it on the plane on the way down." Which is what I did. Everybody was knocked down with it. We went in and recorded it and it was pretty funny.

I had a Sheb Wooley release two weeks before that. He said, "We can't kill your other release right now. We gotta come up with another name. Send me some names." So I sent him Klon Dike, I. Ben Freezin, Ben Colder. The record came out as Ben Colder; nobody knew who it was. It was a hit. Everybody around the [Nashville disc jockey] convention said, "Who is this guy? Who is this Ben Colder that's got a smash?"

Then they said, "This is a hit. We got to do an album now." I said, "Oh Lord. I never thought about that." We just started digging for songs, and I did that album and I did nineteen other albums because that's what was making the money for the record company. It was making me money.

Were you doing it reluctantly?

Not really. I enjoyed it. I did a song that Faron Young had done, "Hello Walls." I did it like a drunk. "Helllooo Wallls . . . I didn't see you standin' therere." Well, Ben started being a drunk. The next one was, "Allllmost Per-rrrrsuaded." I took on this drunken personality. It gave me an excuse to drink. I drank in those days some.

You had recorded novelties before. That wasn't your first stab at humor.

It gave a little more freedom, as a matter of fact, to have this [with a drunken slur] loose personality that don't give a hoot. Ben sold lots of albums, and the jukeboxes loved him because these songs that I [parodied] were major hits, million sellers. I'd do "I Walk the Line No. 2," "Almost Persuaded No. 2," and so on. They had the title and they had the humor.

Sheb Wooley promotional photo. Author's collection.

That was a different approach, so they'd buy a quarter of a million of them, jukebox [operators] would. I don't think that goes on your charts, as far as putting it up the charts. But it sells records.

What were the reactions of the artists and the writers whose songs you parodied?

Most of them just loved it. Most of them cut me in as half writer on my version: Marty Robbins, I did two of his; Johnny Cash, I did some of his. I did anybody's that had hits. One guy who said, "Please don't do it" was the late John Hartford. I got carried away during the war between the Israelites and the Palestinians back in the '60s. I wrote a thing called "Gentile on My

Mind." We went ahead and cut it. John said, "Oh God, please, please, please don't do that." So we didn't put it out.

Another time, Harlan Howard had some song that he wished we wouldn't do, so we didn't do it.

You said some of these artists cut you in on the writing. I guess by all rights they really wouldn't have to do that with a parody?

No they didn't. They really didn't. As a matter of fact, some of them didn't. On some of the biggest hits I had, they didn't cut me in. That was their choice.

Billy Sherrill and Glen Sutton wrote "Almost Persuaded," the original that David Houston did. He sold around 700,000. I did a parody that sold about half of that, around 350,000. They didn't cut me in. That was all right.

That made it a million seller.

It was just about half again as much as they would have gotten out of it.

Once you hit with parodies, did writers begin to bring parodies to you?

No, that didn't happen much. . . . Jack Clement produced some of the records. He produced "Almost Persuaded No. 2" [in 1966]. He produced "Harper Valley P.T.A. (Later that Same Day)" [in 1968]. A guy who's a drunk says [with a drunken slur], "Hi everybody, I saw the sign out there that said P.T.A. Thought that meant Party Time Already. Here I am. I'm ready to go." That sold a lot of records, sold 350,000 records.

When you initially had the success as Ben Colder, did you try to avoid being identified as Ben Colder?

Yeah. Then he started outselling me on records. Half the people were calling me Ben and the other half were calling me Sheb. During that time, I was really living a double life. Most of those years I was in the *Rawhide* series in a straight acting part. I'd do anything to keep away from hard work.

Did you know as a child that you wanted to be an entertainer?

I had no idea about comedy at that time, although I guess I always had a little imp on my shoulder. They used to have country dances back in Oklahoma at somebody's home. Somebody would have a big living room and they had sets. When they'd call your set you'd get out there and dance with your partner and there'd be about six couples. They had a fiddle and a guitar player sittin' over in the corner on cane bottom chairs. When I was seven or eight years old, I used to crawl right in between them and sit back there in the corner. I had stereo. I heard every run that old Bob made. Ed Hill was the fiddle player. I just ate that up. I said, "Oh Lord, that's what I want to be." I'd sit there and dream about that. About that time, Bob Wills was coming in and I heard him on radio in Oklahoma. I used to go around dreaming that I was up onstage, telling this guy to play that part. You gotta be careful what you dream. Dreams want to come true. Dreams try to come true. Dreams will come true, if you follow them.

Everything I ever dreamed has come true. I went to see the movies and I saw Gene Autry and Roy Rogers and other cowboys riding around and I wanted to do that. I did that.

I did it, everything I ever dreamed. It wasn't easy to get to it, but looking back, everyone of them came to pass. I never dreamed any dreams that were unbounded, that I was not able to reach.

Did anybody know about what you wanted to do when you were a child?

No. As a matter of fact, my dad had a little bit of musical talent. He kind of booted me out of the herd. He didn't think I could carry a tune. He'd laugh at me for singing, when my voice was changing. When I finally said, "I'm going to try the music business," he told me, "I don't think you'll ever make it." I said, "We'll see." That was his problem, not mine. It's not the way to raise children. I believe you should encourage children to do anything that's in their scope.

My brother, who was two years older than me, had a son that was mentally a little bit off. He loved music and he would talk about it. My brother would put him down, "Oh Bill, you can't do that." "I wanna be a movie star like Sheb." "You can't do that Bill, you can't do that." The boy came up with cancer when he was in his early twenties. I took him to California with me. I had already taught him how to play. He loved Johnny Cash. I'd give him open tuning on a guitar, and he could play. He played that guitar. They had given him five months or so to live. I talked to some movie friends of mine, and they said they'd like to do a movie on him. I had a ranch up there in California and I had a bunch of horses and we'd go out riding and talking. We had a lake there close by and we'd go up on the lake. In a sense, Bill got to do everything he dreamed. He made a movie, these guys came out and made this movie. Then he was back in Clovis, New Mexico, and all of his buddies from school, we took this movie down there and ran it for him, he was the hero of the day. They all saw the movie. . . . Anyway, it's just sort of, I believe, true that dreams ought to come true.

Sheb Wooley in the 1986 film *Hoosiers*. Author's collection.

You said you had told your father that you were going to go out and make it as a musician, what did that mean? What did you go do to try to become a musician?

I'd been writing a bunch of songs, and I was going to go to Nashville to try to publish my songs. That's as high as my hope went. I didn't place anything, but I got some encouragement from Ernest Tubb. He heard some of my songs and he said, "Hey, you write pretty good. You got one song there I thought about recording, but Red Foley's got something that sounds quite a bit like it right now. I won't do it right now. But that's all I needed right then, somebody to tell me I was a songwriter. I didn't know. From Erick,

Oklahoma, what do you know? Later both Red and Ernest recorded some of my songs.

You went directly to Ernest Tubb to pitch those songs?

It wasn't too difficult to get to stars in those days. I just wandered down here and went up to WSM, it was up on a hill in those days. Most everybody showed up there at some time or another to do *Noontime Neighbors* or another show. And then on Saturdays they had a show from the Ryman Auditorium, they broadcast the *Checkerboard Jamboree* with Eddy Arnold and Ernest Tubb and different ones. So, I'd go down there and hang around and I met Ernest's guitar players, the Short Brothers and they invited me to come out and play the songs for them, which I did. And then they played them for Ernest. Then Ernest, next time I saw him, he said "You'll make it as a songwriter." He gave me some encouragement.

You landed at WLAC in Nashville.

I came to explore the *Grand Ole Opry* and WSM and so on. All I got from WSM was one show a couple of times a week. They put me on this *Noontime Neighbors* show which paid $7.50. I'm staying at a hotel that cost more than that. Things were cheaper, but they weren't that cheap. I saw financially that I wasn't going to make it. So, I went over to WLAC, and I said to the program director, "I won't charge you anything. I don't want any money. I just wanna be on the radio. If you'll let me tell where I'm gonna be playing and I've got a song book that's being published with pictures that I'd like to sell on the air, I'll do it for free." He said, "Well, let's go in here and audition you." They auditioned me and they said, "Okay. Can you start in the morning at 4:45?" I said, "Sure."

The farmers were listening to you.

Yeah.

I fell in with a guy there who had a couple hours as a disc jockey, Herman Grizzard. He did *Daybreak in the Barnyard*. WLAC was 50,000 watts, and I used to get mail from northern California. Most of his show I did.

There was a couple that had a kind of a Christian show, a guy and a girl playing. They built up a little following; they were playing some school houses around the area. They asked me if I'd like to go along. Said they'd pay me $7.50 a day. And I went.

I had a picture printed up with a song on the back of it. I sang that song about everyday, just flogging that picture. And ol' Herman would rave about me. I'd get them quarters [for the pictures] and I'd shake them out of those envelopes, $38 or $40 a week sometimes. I could just about live on that. I was staying at a boarding house at the time.

But the way this boiled down, it was coming up 1946. I thought I had it a little about then. In 1949, it was going to be the anniversary of the 49ers crossing the nation in covered wagons, jumping off in Missouri and crossing the plains. I wanted to take a show on the road across the country. I was hoping to get the Sons of the Pioneers. I needed to get to Chicago to see some advertising agents. I thought the Studebaker Automobile Company oughta be a good fit because they used to make the wagon. I got a chance to sit down with them and tell them my idea, and they said, "It's a good idea, but have you seen our '47 model?" It was streamlined. They said, "We've had a lot of fun poked at us: 'You made a mistake when you took the tongue out of it.' So we want to stay away from wagons. Some of the feed companies might go for it."

I got back to Nashville. I had transcribed my program three days to go to Chicago. I got back and they told me, "They want to see you at the musicians union." I had joined the union here in Nashville when I first came. They never got me a job. That was just foolishness to join the fuckin' union. I went down there and the guy said, "What's this about you making transcriptions?" I said, "Yeah, I was going out of town for a few days, and I transcribed my program." He said, "Somebody has to get paid when you make transcriptions." I said, "You wanna watch me take it out of my left pocket and put it into my right?" Well, anyway we didn't hit it off. He said, "You can't work up there anymore."

You can't work at WLAC anymore?

The shop steward at WLAC had lost some work to me. There was a politician who came to town to try to get elected and I told him, "I got two shows a day. I tell him where you're gonna be, and I'll be there to play for them, and you speak to them." He said, "It sounds good to me. I'll give you $25." He had been using this accordion player who was the shop steward. He had pulled the strings on me there.

Well, it's strange how these things work out. I stuck these transcriptions under my arm and went down to Dallas. Didn't find anything in Dallas, but I went to [radio station WBAP in] Fort Worth. The program director was interested. He said, "There's a big sponsor that's looking for somebody to front a band. The guy we have here now, I don't think he's going to make it. Let me take this into the boss and play it for him." So he took my transcriptions in there and play came back out and said, "We'd like to hire you, but don't have any place for you, no airtime and no budget." The sponsor deal was about six months away.

General Foods had seen what happened with the flour company that sponsored the Light Crust Doughboys. General Foods had lagging sales with their Calumet Baking Powder. They wanted to do the same thing.

I started to leave. I was going to California, and I called back down there just before I left my home in Erick, Oklahoma. I said, "I'm off to California." They said, "Come on down here. We got a little job for you. You can make $30 or $40 a week." So I took it, and got to rolling down there and doing fine, started playing some parties for the rich oil people around the area which I hated, strolling and asking, "What would you like to hear?" It wasn't my style. One night we had a big party out at the Northside Coliseum. They had a horn band playing the dances and I was supposed to do something during the intermission. So I started strolling my tables, strolling around the room. I'd sing, "The Eyes of Texas Are upon You." They'd start singing with me. I said, "You guys are great, come on go with me." Well I got one table going and then I picked up the next table. We wound up with me in the middle of the floor. They got me a chair, and I'm standing out there in the middle of this dance floor, and it's solid-packed people all the way around and we're singing those Texas songs. The guy got a little PO'd because he wanted to start the dancing. The people wouldn't get off the floor; they wouldn't let me off that chair.

I was on the Bobtail Network, on about twelve major stations. [I was based] at WBAP, Fort Worth. We covered five states very well. The idea was that we'd transcribe our program and travel for the sponsor, play rodeos and fairs for free, which is what we did for three years.

Were you signed at that stage to MGM Records?

While I was down there, I made a session over in Dallas. The first session I did for MGM.

Young and Rubicam ad agency gave us credit for increasing sales [of Calumet] by 30 percent. They were overjoyed. So, they flew me and my road manager up to New York, dined us. We saw *Annie Get Your Gun*. While we were there, I had cut these records in Dallas and I had some copies of them with me. That's before I was on MGM. I was on Bluebonnet. I had a little song on there called "Peeking Through the Keyhole Watching Jole Blon." I called up Steve Sholes who was head of RCA-Victor. It was on Saturday, and he said, "My office is not open. I'm just down here cleaning up a little bit." I said, "Sir, I came all the way here from Fort Worth, Texas, to see you." He said, "Well, if you came all the way from Fort Worth, Texas, get yourself over here." So, I went over and played these songs for him, and it was about the time that Petrillo had put the freeze on recording.[3] He said, "I want that song 'Peekin' Through the Keyhole.' I got a guy on the West Coast, I want him to do that." And he liked some of the others. I mentioned that we were going to go by Nashville and visit the *Grand Ole Opry* on our way [back to Texas]. Well, when I walked into the *Grand Ole Opry*, here's Red Foley. He said, "Are you Sheb Wooley?" I had never met him, really. He said, "You got a song I want." I said, "I have?" He said, "My associate in New York called and said you had a song that we needed. I'll give you a $150 advance." I said, "Start writing, I'll take it." He said, "I'll record it." He was hot, you know. In the meantime, this song was released in Texas, Cliffie Stone came into town and he'd go prowl around the record racks and look for things, unusual titles, whatever, and he found "Peeking Through the Keyhole Watching Jole Blon." He took it back to California and recorded it, and it was the only hit he ever had. He sold 400,000 copies of "Peeking Through the Keyhole." Well Red, naturally, said, "I can't record it now that Cliffie's got it."

But Sholes had said he had a guy on the West Coast who would record it.
    When I walked out of [Sholes' office], one of the Aberbach boys[4] was sitting in that outer office. He walked in there and heard that song, and called Red.

Behind Steve's back.
    Well, in a way because Steve had a guy on the West Coast—I forgot his name, even—said he wanted to record him on that. But he didn't get it done.

It's interesting that the Aberbachs would be there in Steve's office even on a Saturday.
    That's right. I started getting calls from the Aberbachs from California, New York. I was in Fort Worth. They said, "Why don't you send us some more songs? My father liked your songs." I sent 'em a bunch of songs. They became my publisher. They put me on retainer of, I think, $25 a month. They published my stuff for quite a little while.

Some people would call them operators, the Aberbachs.
    Yeah, they were. Either one of them would say, "I have to ask my brother about that."
    I had a song that they got me a cut on called "Too Young to Tango" by

Teresa Brewer [in 1953]. It was a hit. That and "Ricochet" were on back to back. And they both were going up the charts together . . . and then "Ricochet" took off. But, anyway, I had a ride the rest of the way.

You were going to tell me how you got to MGM.

When I left Steve Sholes, he said, "I would like to record you after this ban is over. I'll write you a letter on that." He wrote me a letter with the offer to be on RCA. Well, after I started doing business with the Aberbachs, they said, "We know where we can get you a better deal." I think they were going to give me one cent per record at RCA-Victor. So, I signed with MGM Records. They got me with MGM Records.

Frank Walker was running MGM at the time.

Great old man. We all just adored him. I had a song later on, after I had been with MGM for some time, called "Are You Satisfied." It broke out in New York. It broke out all over. It was popular. It went pop. They realized that they didn't have a contract on me. I'd been recording for two or three years, and I had had a contract, but it had played out. Now, they got nervous. Uncle Frank comes out to my house, he and his wife. They spent the night. He said, "I told 'em my boy Sheb would never pull away from us." I had no intentions of leaving, whether he came out there or not because they had been very good to me. I had Jesse Kaye out there on the West Coast, he produced me. He was the liaison between the motion pictures and the records. His offices were at MGM studios, out there. And he's a great guy. I loved him dearly. He just always did things for me. He'd throw things my way. If a part came up to sing over [an actor] on a movie, he'd have me there. He got me a lot of work.

We cut "Purple People Eater" sometime later.

How did that song come to you?

Well, I must say, that Jesse just let me do just about anything I wanted to do.

My friend Don Robertson, the songwriter, we were partying together, and he tells me this joke: He said, "This little boy came home from school. He says, 'Daddy. What has one eye, one horn, and flies and eats people?' Dad says, 'I don't know.' 'A one-eyed, one horned flying people eater.'"

I said to Don, "There might be a song in there. You wanna write something on it?" He said, "No. You go ahead." He's a ballad writer. He said, "It's not my style." Well, I wrote it the next day. I'd write a verse and show it to my wife and she'd laugh. It worked out pretty good. Don had a song called "I Can't Believe You're Mine." It was a slow time for Don. Well, I put that on the back of "Purple People Eater." I saw his first writer's check for $23,000. That was just the start. He thought it might have been worth fooling with after all.

The Aberbachs kept Steve Sholes on retainer in a way, so Steve would give their songs preferential treatment. Do you believe that they did that with MGM?

No. I was getting my own cuts. I picked out what I wanted to cut out of my writings. Or MGM sent me a song every once in a while, and I cut a few of them.

But they weren't paying anybody at MGM to give their songs preference?

I don't believe so. Now they may have been paying for some other artists, but not me because they had the in through my publishing. They didn't need to pay for me.

You were still with MGM when Mike Curb was in charge.

Yeah. I was with them for twenty-seven years. He never bothered us. I remember when my contract came up, I called down there, and said, "I wanna know if Mike wants to pick up my contract." And the guy on the phone says, "Just a minute." He got back on and said, "Hell, yes." That was in the '70s. That was my last contract there. They went out of business, but I was dropped shortly before they went out of business.

Of the actors you worked with—John Wayne, Errol Flynn, Gene Hackman, any of them—which one of them do you think might have made a good country singer?

I'd pick James Dean. He played guitar. I never heard him sing, but I betcha he could. You could get more out of him then you could all them others. He was a very sensitive little guy. Great kid. I thought he was wonderful.

The day before he got killed, he just had gotten that new sports car. I was walking across the lot at Warner Brothers and he said, "Get in. I'll take you for a ride." We whizzed around that lot. That's the last time I saw him.

I had a singing date in El Paso, Texas, with a group of people, like a *Grand Ole Opry* [package show]. And I'm just standin' in the wings, ready to go on. Then some guy comes up and says, "Damn. That's too bad what happened to James Dean, wasn't it?" I said, "Whadda you mean?" "He got killed in a car." And [then the emcee. said], "Here's Sheb

Wooley!" I got out on that stage. Whew! I said, "I gotta take a minute folks. I just got word . . . " It flat destroyed me. But anyway, tighten our belts and go on.

How did you balance what was two full-time jobs, working the songs and acting?

It seemed to work out all right. There was a little bind, like I mention earlier, when I couldn't get away from *Rawhide* to record. But that was about the only time. I might have slacked up on my writing some.

However, I wrote an album [in 1960] called *Rawhide*, a western type thing. Do you remember a motion picture called *How the West Was Won*? Well, MGM asked me to do an album because they didn't think that the album they had was going to be strong. They were wrong. They wanted a backup on it. We reissued it [in 1965] as *It's a Big Land*. It's probably the best album I ever made. I did research on it, dates, places, location . . . where the Donner party reverted to cannibalism.

There's a joke going around town; they tell it on George Jones and myself. On George's bus, we were crossing from Utah over into California, and the bus's brakes got hot up there in the mountains, so the bus driver stopped. George and I got out. I said, "George, right in this area is where the Donner party got snowbound, ate their mules, and some of them ate each other. George said, "Damn. I haven't seen a paper in four or five days. I didn't hear anything about it." . . . They swear it's true. But I'm not gonna tell you either way.

How did you get involved in Hee Haw?

I was the Comedian of the Year for the CMA that year, and they wanted me. . . . *Laugh In* had been a big show, now *Hee Haw*, how far do you have to go, a country *Laugh In*.

So, [producer John Aylesworth] started putting it together, and Jack [McFadden, Buck Owen's manager] brought me down there. I didn't like it too much. I thought it was gonna set country music back thirty years. I always hated when I was doing a show and they brought the old cow and wagon, and bales of hay on the stage. "Shit. Another one of these." It didn't have anything to do with the show.

But it got off the ground, and I wrote the theme song for it. I was recording for MGM while we were down here shooting *Hee Haw*. I had a session and I had about fifteen minutes left. I said to the singers, "Line up, get in there, and do this." "Hee-hee-hee-haw-haw." We put it down, I took it over there, and he said, "That's our theme song." He called all of the so-called

Sheb Wooley promotional photo. Author's collection.

writers together and said, "Write us a theme song." Everybody was writing lyrics, you know. Well, I had been around enough to know that you don't talk over lyrics. You can't say "Here's Buck Owens" over lyrics.

Why don't we see more humor and comedy in country music today?
     I don't know for sure. I think it has something to do . . . it has a lot to do . . . with the programming of the radio stations. Maybe they don't program as much [comedy]. I guess it may be a little more risky getting a

comedy hit. They've fallen into a pattern. To me it all sounds pretty much alike. Nobody varies their sound. Not like we used to. It used to . . . when somebody came on . . . one of the stars, you knew who it was immediately. You knew it was Johnny Cash or Buck Owens. Maybe it's because I don't listen that much, but I have to ask "Who's that? Who's singing." Because [the singer] sounds like four or five other singers. And they're all good. I'm not saying that they're not good, but they're all in [slips into falsetto] one key . . . it's all up there.

And I don't see much heart in it.

Is the industry taking itself too seriously? It can't poke fun at itself anymore or at the people who listen?

I think so. They seem to have taken on an image of themselves—maybe it's the manager [to blame]: they . . . are . . . the . . . star. Now you meet these guys personally and they're just regular. But when they're around the public they come on that way.

And they don't vary on their recordings that much.

You and Hank Williams were on MGM. Did you work much with Hank Williams because of that association?

It never happened for that reason. We did a few shows together. We did the *Louisiana Hayride* in Shreveport. He was on there, and I used to bring my band down there and appear. We got to know each other. Somebody booked us at an International Harvester thing in Shreveport, at a fair, in a tent. Hank and Audrey and Sheb Wooley and the Calumet Indians. He was pretty sober, all that week. He'd say, "What do you thing about this one?," and he'd sing—drivin' along in the car—"how 'bout this one?" He'd go from one to the other. He had a way with a song that boy did.

But he kept it together that whole week?

Yeah. He kept it together. He didn't drink that whole week. I don't think he really got into the booze until a little later. Of course, he wasn't hot then. And, as the heat rises, it gets harder on a country boy. As the crowds get bigger, the ego grows up a little more. I know because I was one.

Did you get a bit too big for your britches?

Oh, I'm sure I did. I drank considerable. I felt bigger than life sometimes. Nobody is. I've certainly gone through some changes. I don't know if you're aware of that I have leukemia. It seems that when a person gets a deadly ailment like this—which can be deadly—they start thinking about a bunch of things they might do different. My favorite channel right now is the Wisdom Channel. It's built on spirituality, not so much religion, very little religion, as a matter of fact. Just spirituality.

I'm off on a kick like that. . . . I started writing some songs. Just yesterday, I wrote a song called "Change Your Thinking, Change Your Life." That's where it's that. It's in your thinking.[4]

The interview with Sheb Wooley was conducted on August 8, 2001.[5]

Notes

1. Don Cusic, *Sheb Wooley: Rawhide/How the West Was Won* (Liner notes), Bear Family Records compact discs, 1995. BCD 15899-AH.
2. Kevin Coffey, Sheb Wooley, *Wild and Wooley, Big Unruly Me* (Liner notes), Bear Family Records compact discs, 1997. BCD 16150–AM.
3. James Caesar Petrillo was president of the American Federation of Musicians. On January 1, 1948, he instituted a recording ban, the second of the decade, seeking improved compensation for musicians.
4. Julian and Jean Aberbach owned and operated the Hill and Range publishing company, which controlled the songs that many country artists—particularly RCA artists—recorded.
5. Sheb Wooley died on September 16, 2003.

Billy Walker
Circumstances

After interviewing Billy Walker for a magazine article, he and his wife, Bettie, asked to take a look at the finished product before it ran. Although I often send subjects copies of articles after they've hit the newsstands, I rarely send them before, and, if I do, I never promise to make changes artists might suggest. But what the heck, Walker—who casts a stern countenance and towers like an SMU linebacker—had sat for hours answering my questions, first in his conversion van, behind a country music park stage in Cortland, New York, and then in the green room of a shopping mall show hall near Nashville. The Tall Texan also had readily obliged in previous years whenever I needed a comment for other stories. So I figured I owed it to him. I e-mailed the story.

In my piece, I reckoned Walker something of a Nashville Forrest Gump, a man who'd witnessed many of country music's main events: Hank Williams's final tour, Elvis's first major appearance in Memphis, Patsy Cline's last show (he gave up a seat on the ill-fated flight that killed her, Cowboy Copas, and Hawkshaw Hawkins), and Red Foley's death backstage in Fort Wayne, Indiana. I was pleased with the Gump metaphor, figuring readers would immediately get it.

One day later, the following note popped up on my computer: "Billy was not happy with the first line[,] being referred to [as] Forrest Gump, who was a retard." Delivered by his wife, it rang like the best answers *he'd* given me in the interviews: colorful and direct. Since I only stood to lose my oh-so-clever metaphor and the in-your-face quotes he'd fired off in our conversations remained intact, I complied and dumped Gump, replacing him with Pug Henry, Herman Wouk's character in *The Winds of War*, who saw up close momentous developments in the Second World War. But, alas, even that metaphor never saw the light of day: my editor chopped it.

Pug or no Pug, Gump or no Gump, Billy Walker may be the most important interview in this collection. His eyewitness accounts undoubtedly give form to country music history, to which the definitive biographers of Hank Williams and Elvis Presley can attest: Colin Escott and Peter Guralnick respectively relied on Walker's recollections to trace a mile or two in their subjects' journeys. More than the proverbial fly on the wall, Walker is a microscope through which artists' views of producers, studio musicians, radio station executives, and life on the road zoom into sharper focus. He traveled abreast of Lefty Frizzell, Marty Robbins, Johnny Horton, and other significant country artists, recording with the same producers, playing the same radio barn dances, making the same gigs. And since many of these men are no longer around to speak for themselves and didn't speak much with reporters and historians before they died, it falls to their peers, men such as Walker, to offer clues about how they might have viewed events in their careers.

Colin Escott sees another dimension in Walker's representativeness, suggesting that the singer turned up on the bends of country music's every twist and turn following World War II. "In a very real sense, the career . . . epitomized the changes that overtook country music over a thirty-year period. Starting out with Texas honky-tonk music, he flirted with rock and roll, then went to Nashville just as the Nashville Sound was a phrase on everybody's lips."[1] Few performers appeared on the crests of country music's various and relatively recent modulations. But Walker did. And he got in return a license to comment on country music's past, present, and future.

BORN JANUARY 14, 1929, in Ralls, Texas, Walker knew the Great Depression's sting early in life. His father darted from job to job and home to home to support eight children. Then, in 1935, Billy's mother died. The elder Walker, with no way to both work and properly supervise his eight children, parceled out Billy and two of his brothers to the Waco Methodist Orphans' Home, where he remained for five years, until his father remarried. Even after leaving the orphanage, Billy's family struggled with the hard knock life. But there was for the Walkers an outlet in music. "My Dad loved gospel music and especially the original Stamps-Baxter Quartet," he recalled in an interview. "The big thing in Texas then was the old fashioned singing conventions and I'd go to those with Dad."[2] Billy mimicked what he heard, crooning in a quartet that also included his father, stepmother, and a family friend.

Walker parlayed his gospel roots and the music of the cowboy actors

1950s promotional photo. Author's collection.

he idolized into spots on radio and local jamborees, and by the age of twenty he was singing in the big time, appearing on KRLD's *Big D Jamboree* in Dallas and recording for Capitol Records. He posted his first top ten hit "Thank You for Calling" in 1954 with Columbia Records, the label he called home for the next eleven years. Over the following three decades, he often climbed high on the country countdown, charting blockbusters such as "Charlie's Shoes," "Cross the Brazos at Waco," "Circumstances," "A Million and One," and "She Goes Walking Through My Mind."

But Walker never achieved the status of the Frizzells and the Hortons nor that of performers featured in this book such as Loretta Lynn or Eddy Arnold, hence his remarks often taste bitter and perhaps a bit overdone. He primarily blames corrupt figures in the music industry when, in fact, want of more dynamism, and better management also played a role. But there's much truth in what Walker reveals: frustration on behalf of aged artists forgotten by the industry they built, the pocked complexions of lionized country figures, such as Don Law, Johnny Cash, and Jim Reeves, and amazement at his career's unshakable allure. "You never get this stuff out of your blood," he told me. "I've tried to keep from wanting to perform. I don't have to make a living. I ain't rich, but I ain't poor. But there's something inside of you that wants to create, and sometimes it gets so aggravating because you can't get rid of it. Sometimes I'd like to be free from it, but I can't."

MY GRANDFATHER WAS NAMED Harley Chambers Walker, and he lived in a little town called Wedowee, Alabama, and he was inducted into the Confederate Army when he was nineteen and shipped off to fight the Battle of Atlanta and got captured by Sherman and taken right across from Louisville, Kentucky, to Jeffersonville, Indiana. After the war was over they let him find his way back to Alabama. In 1905, my grandfather put eleven kids on a wagon train to central Texas, Bell County, which is Temple, Texas. The biggest facility in Bell County is Fort Hood. My grandfather had another four kids when he was there, so he had fifteen in all. My dad married my mother; her name was Baby Ruth Dyess, so that's why I'm a Texan. They moved out to west Texas, and I was born out in west Texas, in Ralls, which is about thirty miles east of Lubbock, Texas.

Were you farmers?

Yes, we farmed. My dad was kind of a jack of all trades. At that stage of life he was a cotton ginner by trade besides being a farmer. He was also a real great carpenter. When I was born in 1929, the crash put the country into a recession; I grew up in the recession. My dad, later on, ran a small dairy over in Portales, New Mexico. Most of the time I was growing up he was a carpenter; he pasteurized milk, he made ice cream, he did all things that a dairy does.

In the meantime, when I was four years old, my mother passed away. There was eight kids in my family, so my dad had to put me and my two brothers in an orphanage in Waco, Texas. From about six to eleven, during my early part of life, I partially grew up in an orphanage down in Waco, Texas. My dad married a woman with four children and then they had one together, so there was thirteen in all. I come from a rather large family.

I had relatives on my mother's side take my three oldest brothers. Me and my two brothers just older than I am went to the home, and then my dad kept the two girls. It was a very difficult time for my father and for all of us really. That's the way life is; it never discriminates.

My dad came and got us out [of the orphanage] when I was about eleven years old; when I was about thirteen, we moved out to Portales, New Mexico, which is about ten miles the other side of the Texas border. At that time, he was operating a small dairy in this small town. We used to have to work in the fields. My dad's salary was $20 a week; so we had to supplement the income, so my stepmother would take all of us kids out in the early spring and we would pick beans. During the summertime, we would harvest tomatoes. In the fall, we would harvest peanuts. We would contract out [on other farms]. We would chop cotton in the springtime, and in the fall, we would pick cotton. So we had something to do all the time. That's primarily how we existed. We all worked. When I was thirteen, I picked 329 pounds of cotton, and my dad gave me twenty-five cents, which was a lot of money in those days. I could buy a hamburger for five cents; I could go to a movie for five cents.

I went to see a Gene Autry movie called *Public Cowboy Number One*, and I said, "That's what I'm going to do. I'm gonna play and sing like that man on the screen." I have the tear sheet that's put out in front of movies framed in my office. So that fall I went up to visit my uncle about eighteen miles away and picked turkeys for two weeks, that's where you would dip 'em in scalding water and pick all the feathers off it. I think we got eight cents a turkey. I picked enough turkeys in the two weeks to make me enough money to buy me a $6.25 guitar with a twenty-five-cent instruction book. I went to a pawn shop in Clovis and bought the thing. It was a little ol' cheapie, but it was all I could afford. It was something I could learn to play on. I proceeded to teach myself to play the guitar and sing. Then we moved over to Whiteface, Texas, which was about forty miles away, fifty miles.

When I was fifteen, Clovis had one of the few radio stations in the area, and they had an amateur contest. By then the air force base there was operating, so they had it out there and so I went out there. They probably had about fifty contestants. I won the little ol' contest, $3 and a chocolate cake. Three bucks was good money. The guy said, "You sing real great. Do you want to be on the radio?" I said, "Sure." He said, "If you come around on Saturday, I'll put you on. Just bring the guitar. I'll be your announcer and you can sing. Get me three or four songs ready." So I did that, and I used to hitchhike from Whiteface to Clovis, which is about seventy-five or eighty miles every weekend to do that program and then back home.

You were paid?

No. No pay. I did it just because I wanted to be in the business. So I did that for quite a long time, until I got out of high school.

What station was that?

It was called KICA. The station is still in existence today. I went back there about a couple of years ago and visited the old station. They even had the old equipment sitting out in a foyer.

Did you get work from that exposure?

A little bit. There wasn't much outside of honky tonks you could play back then. There was a guy named Sled Allen, he had a wrestling arena in Lubbock, and we used to go over there sometimes and he had a little ol' jamboree on Saturday afternoons, just a two-bit jamboree. And I'd go over and sing with that some. Anywhere I could find to sing, I sang, but there wasn't hardly anyplace where you could make any money. I could get $2 or $3 for singing different places then. But primarily it was most all free, gratis stuff. Just trying to learn what to do and how to do it, and just sing for the love of singing.

What songs were you singing then?

Of course, I loved Gene Autry because he's the reason I got in the business. I sang a lot of Gene Autry songs. I sang some Jimmy Wakely songs. I sang some Bob Wills songs. Primarily they were the three, and you would sing other songs as they came up on the hit parade.

Was there anybody who encouraged you at that stage?

Not a lot. I know my dad, when I started on radio, told me that my guitar was going to take me straight to hell. So, I didn't like that too much. I started pursuing my career outside of that area when I got out of high school. I went with several different groups. We entertained a lot of different places until I was twenty, and me and two other guys formed a little ol' trio down in San Angelo and we did live radio everyday down there and played at a honky-tonk called the Wigwam Club. I got married down there the first time, and went up to Waco where my wife was from and got on [KWTX] radio there. Then I went up to Dallas and auditioned for the *Big D Jamboree*. The guy said, "Kid you sing real good, but nobody knows you from a hill of beans. I tell you what we're going to do: We're going to put a mask on you, and we're going to call you the 'Traveling Texan, the Masked Singer of Folk Songs.'" I was supposed to be some rich kid whose family didn't want him singing that dirty country music. But it got to be a really big deal. In fact, I was in *Vogue* magazine. I got two or three pictures in *Vogue* magazine that year. So it was not a cheesy deal. In the meantime, I was back on the radio in Waco. I met Hank Thompson, Hank was still living there then. Hank said, "I'm gonna move up to Dallas and start a daily radio program. Do you wanna come and be my opening act?" The Traveling Texan deal was just gonna end before I moved up there.

Were you booking out as the Traveling Texan?

Oh yeah. I worked personal appearances with Hank Snow. Hank was still down at the *Big D* at that time. I worked out with several people with that masked deal. I won't say there wasn't a few problems, but when you're trying to get ahead you'll take any avenue you can get.

When you say problems what do you mean?

Some ol' drunk cowboy would come up and say, "I'm gonna see who that is." You had a few problems. I was livin' in Waco and I'd ride the Interurban, a one-car train that started at Waco and went through Hillsboro, all the little towns until it got to Dallas. And it would turn and go back to Waco. It was regional transportation. I would ride that up and change clothes in the men's room in the train station, and then I would catch a taxi over to the *Big D* and I was warned never to come into that place without my mask on. A lot of times this cab driver would call the cops and say, "Hey. There's somebody going to rob that *Big D Jamboree*. I just saw him put on a mask."

It got to be a really big deal. In fact, Hank [Thompson] said, "I think I can get you an audition with Capitol Records, since you pulled this Traveling Texan deal." Sure enough I got a record contract with Capitol of off it, through Hank's help.

You were performing with Hank on radio?

I was on radio by myself in Waco. Hank was still doing some radio programs on an opposite station there in Waco. So when he decided to go to Dallas, he wanted to take a full organization with him. Hank had already had "Humpty Dumpty Heart" and a couple of other hits behind him, so he was already an established star. He had gotten a deal on XERF in Ciudad Acuna, Mexico, 250,000 watts. He had gotten a transcription deal for five nights a week. Hank, man, saw a great opportunity, not only in Dallas but also on other horizons. I stayed with Hank for about a year and had four releases on Capitol within the next couple of years.

Would you have been working with Lee Gillette at Capitol?
    Yeah. Lee's the one who signed me.

Would you record out of Jim Beck studio?
    My first record thing was with Lee, and we recorded at WFAA radio studios in Dallas. The next session we did was in Hank's home. Lee drove out from California and he brought two great big Magnacorders, that was the latest tape equipment they had. Our first deal was direct to disc. My first deal was in July '49, and this was January or February of 1950. He set up the stuff in Hank's home, and we just recorded in Hank's home.

You stayed with Capitol for . . .
    I only stayed with Capitol during the course of '49 and '50. Lee Gillette turned over the reins of the country music part of it to "D" Kilpatrick. I had met him. We had worked a tour in Atlanta. "D" had the distributorship in Atlanta. Atlanta had a lot of country artists in its area then that were doing things. So, "D" called me up one time and said, "I'm coming to Dallas. I need a hotel room, I need a bottle of whiskey, and I need a girl. This is what I want you to do." I said, "Well, we can probably make the reservations and get the bottle of whiskey, but you're going to have to get your own girl." He said, "Well, you're no longer on Capitol Records." Click.
    So I went to Jim Beck. I used to play pretty good rhythm guitar, and I played rhythm on some sessions over there. We all hung around Beck's because Beck was what was happening in those days. Me and Lefty and Ray were working the *Big D Jamboree* together then. We couldn't pool enough money to buy a beer or a Coca-Cola. So the happening place was Beck's place. In early '51, Beck got me a deal with Don Law with Columbia. I started recording with Columbia in February of '51.

So Jim Beck did more than just run his studio . . .
    Oh yeah. Beck is the reason that Lefty Frizzell got a recording contract. He's got his name on a few of those early Lefty songs, like "If You Got

the Money I Got the Time" 'cause he kind of helped put those songs together. He could recognize talent, and if Beck had not died when he did, the recording industry would have been big in Dallas, because Beck was an innovator: he knew sounds, he knew studios, and his was fastly becoming a great place to record.

Can you describe Beck as an individual?

He was about six feet tall. Weighed probably about 250 pounds, a little thick around the tummy. Nice looking. At that time, I'd say Beck was probably forty-five or forty-six years old. I recorded with him '51 through '55. I think he died in '56 of carbon tetrachloride poisoning. Not only did he get Lefty a contract, but he got Ray Price a contract with Columbia. He got me a contract with Columbia. He cut Marty Robbins's first hit in there, "I'll Go on Alone." Carl Smith cut some hits there. Decca started coming and cuttin' there; Paul Cohen began to cut a lot of stuff there. He was really beginning to happen, and he was getting a good sound out of that studio.

To make ends meet you played on some sessions?

Well, I played on a lot of Hank's Capitol stuff back then. I played rhythm guitar on some other Columbia sessions and some other sessions that people did there whenever I could get it.

In January of '51, I got a call to audition for a thing up in Wichita Falls, Texas, for a station up there called KWFT. They had a barn dance. Bill Mack was up there then; Bill Mack was the Midnight Cowboy out of Fort Worth and Dallas for thirty years, a disc jockey. But before that he was up in Wichita Falls. Bill wrote songs, had a little band, sang some himself, made a few records. The station had about four or five live acts; they probably did fourteen or fifteen live radio programs a day. I did four shows a day for them. Then they had a jamboree on Saturday night called the *KWFT Western Barn Dance*. My contract said that I would do these four shows everyday, but one of them was sold to a product called Hadacol. I did a sixteen-station hookup for Hadacol for a year and a half. There were two or three 50,000-watt stations that carried that show to Texas, Oklahoma, part of Arkansas, part of Kansas, New Mexico. My first record for Columbia came out in early '51. During '51 I was building up a following off of these broadcasts. In early '52 I had a song called "Anything Your Heart Desires," which I cut at Beck's. It bubbled under the top ten that year. It was a big hit record for me. It just didn't show it chart-wise, but sales-wise it was. I knew nothing about promotion in those days. It just did it on its own. In

July of '52, Hadacol went out of business 'cause the government said it had too much alcohol in it. It was a big-time product, because in '51 they had the Hadacol train with Bob Hope, Hank Williams, and Milton Berle. Anybody that was anybody was on that Hadacol entertainment train, so it was a big deal. Whenever my deal with Hadacol was coming to an end, I came to Nashville to make records, and Webb Pierce, he and Faron Young were over here in town cutting some of those Gannaway films.[3] We were at the Clarkston Hotel, which was an old hotel that's not there anymore downtown. I was recording at the Tulane Hotel, Castle Studios. Webb and Faron come over and say, "When are you going to come down on the *Hayride?*" I said, "My deal is ending with Hadacol, up there in Wichita Falls. Do you think ol' Horace Logan would want me down there?" Webb picked up the phone in my room and called Horace and said, "We need Billy Walker down on the *Louisiana Hayride.*" And so Horace said, "When can we get him?" This is about the first of July '52. I said, "How about an appearance on July the 15th?" So we set it up, and when I got over there Horace gave me a contract for the *Hayride.* I had a big hit and when you got a hit they want you. I stayed there from July of '52 to about November of '55.

So Don Law was not only recording you out of Jim Beck's, he was bringing you up to Nashville as well.

Yes.

Did you have any management at that stage?

No. I was just running by the seat of my britches. No management at all. I was just raised on farming and ranching, I didn't know anything. I just had to learn by trial and error. Sometimes that's not a very wise way to go because you get very distrustful of people. When you see other managers doing [artists] under, and when you get done under yourself two or three times you learn you can't trust anybody because they don't look out for you, they look out for themselves.

In retrospect, in those early days with Capitol and Columbia, do you think you got a fair deal? Do you think you were getting paid what you were owed?

I really never gave it a lot of thought simply because I knew that if I was going to get popular [I had to record]. When I went into it, I didn't go into it for the money; I got into it because of the love of performing, the love of trying to create things. Only later on do you figure out you're getting shafted by these people. It was just an avenue to try to earn a living by performing. The records were nothing more than a vehicle. I got a penny a record.

As long as those records were helping you get work performing, you were happy.

Yes. In '52, old Don had said something about me recording "Mexican Joe" when Jim Reeves had just cut it on a small label. I covered "Mexican Joe," so Jim and Fabor Robison outpromoted me in the charts. I had over 100,000 sales, I think 130,000 sales, and 130,000 sales then was pretty big money. From early on, I made these companies money.

Jim was announcing on the Louisiana Hayride, *but was not allowed to sing on the* Hayride.

They wouldn't let him sing until "Mexican Joe" come out, and then they let him sing.

Why didn't Horace Logan let Jim sing?

I don't know. Jim had a way of irritating people. He was not the gentleman, [the term] they hung on him, "Gentleman Jim Reeves." We had a lot of flare-ups, Jim and I did because he never forgave me for covering "Mexican Joe." He always held a grudge and later on we worked a lot of shows together and we came into—not actual physical conflict—but pretty close to it. That does not diminish his stature as a great artist. Our personalities just didn't click.

It strikes me that Horace Logan may have been a difficult man to work for.

Horace really wasn't all that difficult. It's just that he got something in his mind, and that's the way it was going to be 'cause he was the boss. So I don't know what the difficulty between him and Jim was because Jim came there sometime in early '53.

Did you get most of your work from the Hayride *exposure in Texas? Is that where the* Hayride *propelled you?*

I had come from Texas, so I was pretty well established in Texas before I started on the *Hayride* 'cause of that sixteen-station network and being on the radio four times a day at KWFT, which was a 50,000-watt station at 620 on the dial. They picked it up in Dallas like a local station. I was more of an advantage to the *Hayride* than they were to me, but it was an identification place to work out of, just like the *Grand Ole Opry.* You don't make a lot of money, but it's an identification for you.

It's well known that the Opry *kept a very close eye on the* Hayride *and hired people away from the* Hayride. *Were you aware of that at the time?*

Oh yeah. Right after I came there, Webb was already flirting with the Opry. I think "Wondering" was out at that time, which was a very big record for Webb. Just a few months later on, Webb left the *Hayride* and came to Nashville and so did Faron. So I knew. In fact, if "D" Kilpatrick had not inherited the job that Jim Denny gave up, I would have come sooner. Hank Williams wanted to bring me. It was one of the deals, Hank was going to come back and he was going to bring me with him. Hank and I got to be friends on the *Hayride* down there. In fact, I sang at his second wedding down there. I was his opening act the very last tour he ever made. When we where in Dallas on a tour, he made the deal to come back to the *Grand Ole Opry* starting in February of '53. He had said to them, "I'm going to bring Billy Walker back with me, and I want him to be a featured part of the *Grand Ole Opry.*" Whenever Hank died and "D" Kilpatrick was the manager, it was a lost cause for me.

You sang at his wedding in New Orleans . . .

He had the Jambayla wedding in New Orleans [on October 19, 1952]. He got married two or three times on that trip. He got married that Saturday night. Then he got married on the stage in New Orleans twice. So he got married that weekend three times.

He called me up one night at about 2:00 in the morning, and he said, "Billy, I want you to sing at my wedding." I knew he was thinking about getting married again, and I said, "Well, okay. Let me know when it is and I'll do it." "You don't understand. It's tomorrow." I said, "Tomorrow? When is it going to be? So I can write it down." Well, he said, "It's going to be in New Orleans." Here we are in Shreveport. That's 320 miles from New Orleans. I said, "Well how am I going to get there?" He said, "Well, you're going to fly with me and Billie Jean." I said, "I am?" He said, "Yeah." I said, "When are we going to leave?" and he said, "Seven o'clock in the morning." By then, it's 2:30. I said, "I sure am glad that you decided you wanted to call me." So I flew down there and sang at their wedding and enjoyed it and then he booked me on a tour with him as his opening act, that last tour he did from December 11th through December the 21st.

Was Hank that hard-up for cash that he had to exploit his marriage?

Well, I have an idea he was, but the thing about it was ol' Oscar Davis run off with all the money, stole him blind.

He was the promoter of the shows.

We had two crowds of 5,000 each that day, and Oscar ran off with all the money from both crowds. We got there at about 9:30 or 10:00 in the morning and the first show was at 2:00. We checked into the Jung Hotel, which was only a block from the auditorium, and in between 10:00 and 2:00, Hank got drunk. God, it was embarrassing. Oscar was a good promoter, but you had to keep your eye on him all the time. If you didn't, he'd run off with all the proceeds. You wouldn't see him again for months.

Certainly he would have had a reputation by that stage and people would have stayed away from him; Hank would have stayed away from him.

That's the first time I ever met Oscar Davis; I didn't know him from the hill. Oscar promoted shows here in Nashville. In fact, he wound up to be a pretty good friend of mine. I used to go by and take him stuff later on, before he died, tried to help him do certain things. But he wasn't too honest.

So he left you and Hank and everybody else holding the bag.

I never did get paid for the show.

Was anybody else on it?

Yes, Tommy and Goldie Hill . . . and a big disc jockey down there. . . . Oscar just didn't do nothing for nobody. He just took the money and left town.

My hit song, which came out in February '52, was still in the top ten in New Orleans at the time [of the wedding]. It was called "Anything Your Heart Desires." Hank come out right in the middle of my hit song, drunk. "Well when ol' Hank comes to get married, he wants to get married." He just stopped everybody, and the crowd just goes ape because it's Hank Williams's wedding. He knew I was pissed at him, so the next time he saw me, he said, "Oh Walker, tell you what I'm goin' to do, I got a tour comin' up in Texas. You gonna be my opening act." Well that soothed my feathers a little bit because Hank Williams was a big deal back then.

On that tour his death was near.

But he was still performing. He was still doing a good job. What killed Hank Williams was that he stopped in Knoxville and he got a pain shot for his back and he went on down the road and he started drinking on top of it and it killed him.

The last show was in Austin.
Yeah. At the Skyline Club in Austin. I have a picture of me and him and Floyd Cramer at Snook, Texas, December the 18th.

Could you see what was going to happen to Hank at that stage?
He rode with me all the time. Me and him and that quack doctor he had, Toby Marshall. Hank knew he was getting messed up. He told me that after his New Year's date that he was gonna take some time off, and he planned on going somewhere to get rehabilitated. This Toby Marshall had him on some kind of drugs that he didn't like. He was having real back pains because of an operation he had on his back wasn't working out too well. He intimated like it was going to be in the Carribbean somewhere. I really don't know 'cause he never told me exactly where it was. I was supposed to come to the *Grand Ole Opry* with him because he had made a deal to come back to the *Opry* on February the 1st. Cause I was with him when he was talking to these people. He wanted me to come and be part of his troupe. He said, "You're not going to be a part of my act" 'cause I already had a hit record then. "I want to take you to the *Grand Ole Opry* and help you." But it never worked out. It took me another eight years to get there.

Did you glimpse the genius of Hank Williams?
He wasn't a great singer, but he had a charisma, a different kind of charisma than Elvis Presley had, a different kind of charisma than Garth Brooks, a different kind of charisma than Jim Reeves. He just had his own way of approaching people and they loved him.
We had a $5 bet on "Kaw-Liga" and "Your Cheatin' Heart." He told me "Kaw-Liga" was going to be the biggest song he ever cut and I said, "You're crazy. 'Your Cheatin' Heart' will be.'" Of course, "Kaw-Liga" stayed a couple more weeks than "Your Cheatin' Heart" cause it was on the same record. But "Your Cheatin' Heart's" been cut by probably 200 people.

Were you surprised when you learned of his death?
I really was.

I would think if you see this man drinking so much and taking drugs that when you learn of his death, you wouldn't be surprised.

He knew he was messed up, and he intimated to me like he had somewhere to go for rehabilitation after New Year's. He said he had two dates he had to work. He had to be somewhere at Christmastime. I learned that he went down to see the ol' boy he kinda started out with who had a big band down in Panama City. I called that ol' boy, this has been about five years ago, and he said, "Yeah, Hank spent Christmas Eve with me, and he went to the Blue and Gray game in Montgomery, the football game Christmas Day." I was just trying to retrace his steps. December the 21st was our last job together.

It really caught me by surprise. I knew he was hooked on drugs; I didn't know exactly what kind because, man, I was twenty-three years old. I didn't know what drugs were. I knew kinda what marijuana was, but I never really was around it. I really didn't know what he was taking.

My New Year's Eve thing, I was out in Carlsbad, New Mexico, at the *Eddy County Barn Dance*. The next day I was driving over to Andrews, Texas, about 150 miles away because a gal who was recording on RCA then, Charline Arthur, she was out there and we had a show date booked there together. She was on the radio talking about Hank Williams's death. That's how I learned about it. It hit me like a ton of bricks. I really wasn't expecting it, really wasn't, 'cause I didn't think he was that bad off.

Had Hank lived what would he be doing?

I think he would have weathered the storm had he taken care of himself, like Bill Monroe, like Roy Acuff, like Red Foley, like Ernest Tubb. I think he would have been in that stature. He would have been still thought of as a great star, but not as great as he was because you have that epitome and then you're gonna start coming down. He would have had a lot more hits in his life. He didn't sing good, but he had the ability to communicate, therein lies it all.

What about the industry brought so many people to abuse drugs and alcohol?

Lefty drank beer and whiskey, but I don't think he abused anything else. Ray Price drank a little. I never drank a beer until after I was twenty-one years old. But you know beer and whiskey's been around since the Garden of Eden, probably, but drugs, they were something foreign to us back in the '50s. About the only thing that we ever took was some of those Benzedrine tablets to keep us going. We'd work a date and we'd have 500 miles to drive before we got to another town at 10:00 and we had a 7:00 show that night, so we'd sleep all day, we'd sleep the best we could and then we'd do the show and drive another 500 miles. But that's the only thing that we ever took, just something to stay awake.

But, of course, there were people like Johnny Cash whose drugs got the best of them.

In the early '60s, I worked a lot of shows with Cash. He embarrassed the heck out of us on a lot of those shows. I didn't know what he was on. I wasn't interested in being like that. I guess it's my upbringing even though I knew better than to fool with that kind of stuff.

Could you give me an example of a show on which Cash embarrassed you?

I could give you a lot of 'em. Whether he was drinking with some kind of drugs, sometimes he wouldn't show up or be an hour late and everybody would have to pad until he got there. We'd go out between shows to get something to eat and he'd just act crazy. He used to get crazy. I remember a tour way back there where him and Luther and Marshall bought 500 baby chickens, and at this hotel in Omaha, Nebraska, they let 100 baby chickens out on each floor of the hotel.[4] There was another time when we were working this long tour together and we stayed in one location [and traveled short distances to shows] and they took this hotel room and chopped all the furniture down to Japanese style and painted it black. We was on one trip and they bought fifty or sixty of them cherry bombs and they'd flush the toilet and light the cherry bomb—which will go off underwater—and blow the pipe out underneath. It got to where we wouldn't stay where they were staying.

You talked about being on the road and long drives. There were times when you had to rush back to the Opry for a Saturday night. You must have thought at some point, "Is this all worth it?"

Whenever you begin to make a good living at something, you have to do what is the accepted thing to do in order to keep that money coming in. So, it was just something we knew we had to do. I've flown back from California—caught one of those red eye specials—fly in here do the *Grand Ole Opry* and the next day fly back to California and I got $15 for doing the show.

When I was running buses one time in the early '70s, we was going out west. I was without a driver; I had a couple of guys in the band who were driving. I stopped at this truck stop and I can't remember the name of the town we were going to out in Wyoming. It was going to be about three or four hours longer unless I took this road straight over the mountains. I asked, "What kind of road is this?" They said, "You won't have any problems." I got up this mountain and this road kept getting smaller and smaller. By then, there wasn't nothing to do but put this thing in grandma at the top of the hill, and I made my band get out and walk the mile and a half down at the end of all these winding turns. I was praying each time that I could make the next curve. I've got a 40,000-pound bus running down this hills and I'm not going to risk anybody's life but my own.

I can tell you a thousand stories about traveling in automobiles, but one night Ferlin Husky was riding with me and Ferlin was drinking a lot and Ferlin and Simon got to fighting back and forth, with his alter ego [Simon Crum].[5] He said, "Stop this thing. I'm going to whip Simon's ass." And so I stopped and got out and he started fighting himself. I thought, "Golly." But a lot has changed since those days.

Your first national hit was "Thank You for Calling" [in 1954]. I think that song is unique because you didn't hear very many country songs with sound effects and it was a precursor of the telephone song "He'll Have to Go." Whose idea was the ringing telephone?

I'll tell you the story about how the song came into being. I played a honky tonk outside Mexia, Texas. This was in December of '53 and I knew that I was going to record in January, so I called Cindy Walker [who lives in Mexia]. I'd known Cindy for three or four years. I met her when I was working the *Big D Jamboree*. I said, "I got to record in January, and I thought I'd call to see if you have anything." She said, "I don't have anything, but I thank you for calling." I said, "Okay, you write that." The next morning, real early, she called the hotel and said, "Honey, I got your song." I went out to her house and she had a verse and a chorus. She made me a little ol' demo on what she had, and I got back home and made a demo myself and sent it back to her. And just as soon as she got it, something clicked inside of her, so she sent me the rest of the lyrics to finish up the song. So I went in and cut the thing, and it come out smokin'.

All my career I've been hawked by song sharks. Before my record come out, Columbia cut Jo Stafford on "Thank You for Calling," and her record was out three days before mine was. I find the songs, and they cut 'em on somebody else. I did get played on a New York station by a guy named Martin Denny. He had a radio program in New York City that he played my record on instead of her's.

I cut a song called "I'm a Fool to Care" in '55 and about four weeks later, Les Paul and Mary Ford come out with it.

In '57, I split a record session with Buddy Holly out there in Clovis. Norman Petty's wife and I were in the same grade when I was going to school some in Clovis. I cut a song called "I've Got You on My Mind Again," that Slim Willet gave me [who wrote] "Don't Let the Stars Get in Your Eyes." I called Norman and said, "Norman, I don't have a lot of money, but I got to cut this and send it into Columbia because I think it's a hit." He said, "Come on over. I'm doing Buddy Holly on a Monday. I'll split the session with you. You got anything I can publish and put on the other side?" I wrote some silly song called "Viva la Matador"; I cut that and let Norman publish it. We cut this thing and he sent into Columbia. Don Law accepted it, and paid them the session money on it, so that got me off the hook. It wound up to be in the top ten and started getting hot. Well, who cut it but Gale Storm. That just killed me 'cause I was getting pop play in Cleveland, Ohio, and other places. It really started building.

Then "Funny How Time Slips Away" comes along in '61, and everybody covered that. When "Charlie's Shoes" got hot, Guy Mitchell covered that. Then in 1966, I had a song called "A Million in One" that Dean Martin and Matt Monro both got in the pop charts on when my record started hitting in the pop field, so man it's just been one thing after another.

People don't remember that you were the first person to have a hit with "Funny How Time Slips Away" [in 1961].

The thing about it is, I was hitting in the pop field. Columbia wouldn't touch my record. I was working a record hop up in Grand Rapids, Michigan, for a pop deejay. Me and Bobby Bare was out on the same trail with the same guy plugging our records all over Michigan, Ohio, and everywhere else. Here's a hillbilly from Texas with a song that everybody was playing. Columbia wouldn't support me. RCA cut a record on it by a white guy who sounded like a black woman and took the pop play.[6] Took my song that should have been my hit, all over hit. I did get a hit in the country charts, but it wasn't as big as it could have been had they got behind me.

You first saw Elvis Presley in Memphis.

When "Thank You for Calling" was big, me and Slim Whitman played the Overton band shell in Memphis, and Charlie and Ira Louvin was on that show, too; Charlie had just gotten out of the service that week. Bob Neal asked that night if it was all right to put this kid on the show for a couple or three numbers. I had met Bob before and I knew his reputation as a disc jockey. In fact, we had hired him to promote the show. Slim said, "Bob is he pretty good?" Bob said, "Yeah. He just put a record out here and it's playing pretty good in town." I said, "Well let's put him on." I watched him and what he did with the audience, and I went back to Horace Logan and I said, "I don't know what this guy's got but he's got something."

What did you see that night?

He played guitar. He had this kid playing kind of a Chet Atkins guitar and he had this big ol' boy plucking the bass. He was kind of shaking and he had long hair. He just had something different. I had never seen nothing like it. I talked to his mother that night and they were living over in the projects. They didn't have a phone. It was a neighbor's phone [they used]. I got his phone number and I gave it to Horace. I said, "You get him over and give him a shot on the *Hayride* because he's got something different." He did and the rest is kind of history. I took him on a tour with me in January '55 out to west Texas. Elvis Presley got popular in west Texas quicker than anywhere else because that *Hayride* signal hit west Texas like a local station. It just knocked the dials off out there, 600 miles away.

Did they go as wild for him in west Texas as they did back in Memphis?

Me and Tillman Franks was promoting the shows together. Tillman had an act called Jimmy and Johnny and they had a song that had been real big called "If You Don't Somebody Else Will." I was still riding off of "Thank You for Calling." I'd had "Anything Your Heart Desires," "Thank You for Calling." So I asked Elvis, "What do you charge me to go out on this tour with me?" He said, "$150 a day plus $10 car expenses." Midland-Odessa was our first date, and I took him over to Roy Orbison's television show at about 4:00 in the afternoon. We plugged it from there, so we had a big crowd there at that Hector County Coliseum show. The next night was Lubbock and half of those people who saw the show [in Midland-Odessa] drove to Lubbock the next night. Then we played San Angelo and we had to do two shows in San Angelo. Instead of paying him $150, we just split it three ways, me and Tillman and Elvis.

Would that have been a lot to ask for in those days, $150 a show plus $10?

No! It was dirt cheap. . . . I let him close the show [after the first one]. I've been around anybody whose anybody in this business and he's the only phenomenon I've ever been around.

More so than Hank Williams?

I could understand Hank Williams, but Elvis Presley was such a good lookin' guy and he had something so radically different. He was a good lookin' white guy singing halfway black music. It was just like wildfire.

Did part of the audience not know what to make of him and therefore not respond to him?

You had two sets of audiences just like you got nowadays. It's the same syndrome as back in those days. You've got these kids who sing this new music, and the older audience don't like it. We got the same division as we had back then. When he started on the *Hayride* in about the first of September of '54 and he left there about March of '55, he changed half of that crowd.[7] Half of it was mostly women and that auditorium seated 5,000 people. When he left, they left. It literally devastated the *Louisiana Hayride* and they never did actually recover from what happened.

Did you think he was a flash in the pan, a fad?

About two years before he died, we rode on a plane together, and we were laughing. I said, "Man, I knew you had something different. I just didn't know it was going to last this long." Everybody else thought he was a flash in the pan, too. In fact, RCA did not want to buy his contract. Julian and Jean Aberbach guaranteed RCA the money to buy Elvis's contract. Julian and Jean were a couple of Jewish boys that owned Hill and Range songs, and they knew what was exploding. These guys who sit in these big offices, they never know what's happening until it hits them so hard that they can't [ignore it]. That's what's going on nowadays. This business is crumbling around these guys' feet because they never get out of these ivory towers over here and find out what the real public is wanting. For five years Elvis only recorded Julian and Jean's Hill and Range songs. They were pretty good guys; you knew where you stood with them. I just wish that I could have had the same kind of deal, but I didn't know how to work anything like that. You're from west Texas, you grew up on a farm. Half of the time you didn't know what to think because you'd never been involved. You got out of high school and that was all. I didn't know how to put things together.

Elvis had Tom Parker.

I was sitting as close as you are whenever they shook hands at the ol' Texas Café, right around the corner, when they shook hands and made a deal, in Shreveport. Tom Parker and Tom Diskin flew in and made the deal with him.

What was your impression of Elvis as a person?

I thought he was a very well-mannered young man, always did. He always had compassion for people. He treated people with respect. The restraining force of his life—his mother—died when he was twenty-one years old. He's already a millionaire. He could snap his finger and get anything he wanted, so where is your restraining force going to be? That's what happened in his life. Had his mother lived longer, he probably would have settled down and not done some of the things he did.

Were you on the Hayride *and the* Ozark Jubilee *at the same time?*

I started going up there to Springfield, Missouri, with Si Siman and those guys, guesting on the *Ozark Jubilee*. It was a network radio show then on ABC. Then when they went to television, I agreed to quit the *Hayride* and be a part of that up there. I started November of '55 up there, and I stayed up there until about February of '59, something like that.

Did you believe that Missouri was going to be a capital of country music, that this was going to be a good place to work out of?

Having gone up there several times and seeing what they were doing, I knew that television was going to be the new medium. I'd already done a bunch of television myself. In fact, I had a television show there in Shreveport a couple of days a week. I wanted to get more exposure by way of television. I wanted to be in on the new medium.

Si Siman, tell me what he was like.

That whole bunch over there was a bunch of rip-off artists. The old man that owned KWTO was a controlling ol' fart. They get you in a position and they change the deal on you. ABC was paying them a lot of money to do that show, and my deal was that I would get $125 a show. When I moved there and started to do some work for the radio station and the *Ozark Jubilee* on the weekend and booking out, they changed the deal to $25 a show. I don't have much respect for Si Siman or his methods of operation or John Richardson who was his partner. . . .

I quit the *Ozark Jubilee* because I was in worse shape than when I was on the *Louisiana Hayride* financially because they were double contracting you. In other words, they would have a master contract to produce this show for several thousand dollars, and they'd issue you a personal contract with Top Talent, their booking agency. You might get $200 for the show, but they was getting $500 for you in a package.

So they were selling Billy Walker for $500, but giving you $200?

Yeah. So they're controlling your life. You got no way of bargaining. So, I said, "I'll go back to Texas. I know what I can do in Texas." All this time, Randy Hughes would come over with different people as a road manager and a musician. He said, "Billy, you need to come to the *Grand Ole Opry*. There ain't nobody making any money in the country music business, except people out of Nashville." Finally, I had a lot of dates booked with a dance band out of Texas, and I knew if I was ever going to get on a concert stage, what I really [needed] to do. . . . What I really wanted to do when I went to the *Ozark Jubilee* was to be a major concert artist. So, their fair-haired guy was Red Foley and then there next fair-haired guy was Porter Wagoner. I knew I was sucking hind tit all the way. If you ain't gonna be somebody's fair-haired boy then get the heck out and get your own thing. I had really gotten sick of playing all the dance halls, honky tonks. A honky tonk is really nothing but a smaller dance hall, that's all it is.

In November of '59, Hughes called me again. He called me periodically all the time. He had just gotten Patsy Cline on the *Grand Ole Opry*, I think in August of '59. In November, he said, "If I can get you a spot on the network show and we'll pay for you to fly over here, will you come over here and talk to these people?" I said, "You betcha." So we was out in El Paso, Texas, me and my band. We were playing a big honky tonk that night, and I said, "Get what you can. I'm flying to Nashville and doing the network *Prince Albert Show*. By then Ott Devine was the guy that was running the *Grand Ole Opry*. I made a deal to come to the *Opry* on the first day of 1960.

You eventually relocated to Nashville.

Yeah. I moved from Fort Worth, the first of February.

When you came to Nashville you then began recording with the Nashville session people who were there.

"Thank You for Calling." I took my own band that I had at the time. Those earlier records you used mostly your own musicians, or you used some of them and supplemented some of the studio guys. [After the introduction] of the Nashville Sound, you could come into town and record and go back and teach your band what you cut up here, rather than drag them all the way, you got to pay all their expenses to come over here and do this. It got to be where it was the ideal thing to do.

Were you satisfied that the session singers and instrumentalists would be fresh sounding enough? They were recording for everybody else in town.

You really didn't have too much of an option. There wasn't any money in the music business in the '50s, there wasn't any money at all. When I got a nationwide hit, I was getting $100 or $150 at the most for me and my guitar. With a band I could get $300 a night.

Did you have any favorite session people?

They were more or less chosen for me. I enjoyed the guys who I had a rapport with. Tommy Jackson was a great fiddle player, I loved his fiddle playing. There was some people I didn't enjoy as much I did others. Once I got here I had more of an opportunity to help choose who I wanted. But Grady Martin was the leader on most all of the Columbia sessions. He was just a really good arranger. Producer Don Law really never done much; he sat in there and timed the songs. In those days, we sat around and we'd sing a little bit and somebody would hit a lick and say, "Ooohh I like that." So they'd work that up. It was kind of a mish-mash of a bunch of people hitting different notes and saying, "Do you like this?"

As the leader, what would Grady Martin do?

I would sing the song through once, and he would try to help figure out an intro that would help set up the song, whatever kind it was. Then we would just run through it two or three times and everybody'd get a feel for it. Then we'd try to put it down in a take and if it didn't kind of jell, we'd do another one and maybe do it a little bit different. It was kind of a trial and error thing.

You have a striking vibrato. Is that something that came naturally to you?

I guess it did. There's a lot of people who think Marty Robbins and I sound alike and I say, "I was making records before he was." But with the advent of "El Paso" [the comparisons increased], and I said, "Hey, we're both vaccinated by the Sons of the Pioneers, Gene Autry and Roy Rogers." Autry influenced Robbins too. I met him right after he cut "I'll Go on Alone" in '52. We did sound similar on certain songs, especially on western songs because our voices were primarily in the same timbre. I didn't think we sounded that much alike. On "Cross the Brazos at Waco," Grady Martin led the session and he played guitar and he played on "El Paso": you're gonna sound similar.

By 1960, you were regularly hitting high on the country charts and you were doing it with crooning style.

I'm a ballad singer, whether it be an uptempo ballad or a slow ballad.

Why weren't you crossing over as much as an Eddy Arnold or Jim Reeves, rival ballad singers?

I come from west Texas, and I grew up with fiddles and steel guitars, playing dance music. I just like to sing songs. I wasn't what they call an insider, trying to weave my way into different organizations to help my career. I just tried to do it on my talent. A lot of these guys played political games better than I did. Maybe they had more talent than me. I don't know.

1960s promotional photo. Author's collection.

What was the politics of recording in Nashville in the 1960s?

There really wasn't any politics going.

You didn't have to record songs that you didn't want to record or record songs that were in the publishing company of the A&R director or the label?

That's always been around. I cut a few songs because the A&R man said he believed it would be a good song. I don't think Don Law ever took a nickel. He was a very honorable man. He was Owen Bradley's contemporary; he was Chet Atkins's contemporary. He made as many hit records as Owen or Chet, he just didn't play the politics game, so you don't hear his name like you hear the others. And Don, he was an Englishman, and all he could play was a radio. Owen, of course, was a musician. Chet Atkins was a musician. So they had a little bit different agenda than Don Law did. But Don Law knew how to go out and find talent and he knew how to record it. Me and Ray Price and Lefty Frizzell were working the *Big D Jamboree* and eventually he recorded all of us and eventually we all hit with Columbia Records. You know what Lefty and Ray did, I still have to be judged by what I did. He found Carl Smith. He could hear talent and he would go out and he would catch you when you didn't know he was there. He would find out what people like about you and he would come back and apply that to a record.

What was it like recording with him in a studio. What would he be doing? What role did he have?

He had certain people who led the record sessions, like Grady Martin. Grady led most of my record sessions. However, the first hits I had, I brought my own band. We arranged our own records. Then times began to change, and the expertise of recording began to change. So your musicians that you had in your band didn't have that recording expertise. It took longer to do it, and it took more money to do it. Finally it got to where it was unfeasible to bring your own band into record because these bands here in Nashville could do it better and faster and more creatively.

All Don would do was sit back and punch stop watch, and he would make a few suggestions every now and then, but the musicians and the artists mingled together with their creative abilities to make these records. It wasn't like nowadays where the genius producer goes in there and he calls all the shots. He tells you what songs to sing. He tells you how to sing them. And he don't know nothing. What he is is a frustrated artist.

He couldn't make it himself, so he's going to be genius to somebody else. It wasn't like that in Don Law's and Owen Bradley's and Chet Atkins' day.

So Don Law's talent would be in signing the artist, finding songs, and then letting the artists do what they want to do.

He cut "He'll Have to Go" with Billy Brown, and all Jim Reeves did was copy Billy Brown's record. But Don would call the sales department of Columbia Records and say, "This is a hit. We've got to have more help on it." After about nine months of Billy Brown's record being out and it not coming up and making a smash, Jim Reeves knew what the song was going to be. So Jim cut it and it exploded.

Do you think the brass at Columbia valued country music?

No. Because we were a stepchild. You see, country music was about 10 percent of the overall business of a record company. They had big bands; they had classical, they had jazz, they had different styles of rhythm and blues, so we were just "a minority part" of music. I've seen many a record lost not because the artist wasn't a hit, not because the record didn't have it in the groove, [but because of] lack of promotion, lack of interest. The old phrase money talks. Some guy comes along and starts peeling off $100 bills in the palm of a promotion man and he's going to start promoting what's greased his palm. If you didn't have it, you didn't get it. I know at one time the guy that run *Billboard* . . . I couldn't get him to make "Cross the Rio at Brazos" number one because I couldn't afford to buy a $25,000 ad. He said, "Billy, when you come across with $25,000, I'll make you number one." He said, "Sonny James buys ads all the time." I said, "I got four kids in school and Sonny don't have no children."

You couldn't go to Don Law at that stage and say, "Can you make this happen?"

There wasn't no record support then. You did it on your own or you didn't do it. You could get maybe the publishers to do so much, but after that it was paying them but two cents back then.

But the labels would pay for ads.

Yes. But the squeaky wheel got the grease. The New York boys called the shots then. If I had been a little bit more political, who knows?

I quit Columbia because Don Law got hooked up with an ol' gal called Irene Stanton. Don was drinking a lot back then. I would find hits songs and I would bring them to Don, and he'd want to screen everything. I'd come and sing these songs to Don, and he'd say, "What do you think about that Irene?" "Oh Don. I don't think so." She was wanting to get her name on them, and she did. When my contract was up in '66, I wouldn't re-sign with Columbia. And Don Law said, "Billy, you'll never have another hit." And I said, "You just watch me." So I went out and had twelve straight with Monument. When you said, political things, when a guy gets to drinking and he's got a woman on the string, there ain't nothing that's got any integrity to it.

On Monument, you were one of the people who ...
   ... gave it a resurgence.

You were with MGM in the early 1970s.
    Fred [Foster] had some partners, so when my contract ran out with Fred he was inactive.[8] He wasn't doing nothing. The partners had him in court, wanting their money out of the company. I waited around for three months, then I told Fred, "I gotta do something." He said, "Well, I can't do anything." Buddy Lee was booking me then, and Buddy said, "Hey I think I can get you a guarantee with MGM." Shoot, I'd never had a guarantee at all. Well, I'm sorry, I had a guarantee with Fred, and I liked that guarantee, so much a month because if they got something invested with you, they'll wanna get the money out. So, yeah, I'll take a guarantee. So I signed with Buddy Lee who negotiated a deal with Mike Curb, and as long as Mike was president of the company, I was having hits, "A Million and One" made number one in two magazines and number three in *Billboard*; I didn't buy enough ads. Then I had "I'm Going to Keep on Loving You" made number three. I had "She Goes Walking Through My Mind." As long as Mike Curb was president, I was getting looked after. Whenever Jimmy Bowen took over the presidency right after Mike Curb, man, he tried to kill everything that Mike Curb did, so all my stuff went right down the tube. I never did lose a contract for not being able to sell records, it's political. It's just like RCA, the last company I was with. I had hits with RCA. What happened was the guy I was assigned to, Ray Pennington, they had a big feud and so I got the ax because it was a political move. Our first record was a top ten that ran a long time, "Word Games."

Did Mike Curb produce your sessions at MGM?
    No. Jim Viveneau produced most of the stuff I did. Mike came in and put his singers [the Mike Curb Congregation] on a couple. One album Mike sent over Don Costas. We did one album together. Me and Darrell Glenn had

written a song that could have been a gigantic smash called "Gone Our End-less Love" that Mike put the singers on. I said, "If you want to use my track for a Don Costas instrumental go ahead and do that." If they had gotten behind it, it would have been a gigantic record. It was kind of a singing instrumental.

Some of the MGM material of the 1970s seems produced on the cheap?

They were bad records wasn't they? . . . Some of that was Jimmy Bowen's stuff. It ain't about creating music, it's about how much you can make. Jimmy Bowen, he gathers all the money he can make in life, and he's dying of cancer. Where is the big deal for that? I've never seen a guy going with a Brink's armored car to the graveyard. It's all going to become somebody else's. You ain't gonna take a thing with you except the influence for the kingdom of heaven. That's all you're gonna get. That's why the last twenty-five years I've tried to devote myself to the kingdom of heaven. I really love the Lord, and I really try to live my life in a manner pleasing to him. And try to get other people involved in the Lord. On my tombstone: "He loved the Lord and he loved his music."

You never get this stuff out of your blood. I've tried to keep from want-ing to perform. I don't have to to make a living. I ain't rich, but I ain't poor. But there's just something in you that wants to create and sometimes it gets so aggravating because you can't get rid of it. Sometimes I'd like to be free from it, but I can't. It's just part of me, from the time I said, "I'm gonna do what that guy does right there" at thirteen years old. I've done that all my life. I don't know what else to do; I guess I'll die doing it. But I enjoy it. I really do. I've worked with about everybody who's ever had any kind of name in the country music business and a lot of people in the pop field.

You've been on the Opry *since 1960. What's your opinion about the status of the* Opry *and where it's going?*

It's really difficult to say. You'd like to think that there will be some people who sacrificed like we sacrificed to keep the *Grand Ole Opry* going. I sacrificed a lot of weekends to come and keep the tradition alive. It cost me money. I'd work tours to California, wind up doing a Friday night show and catch a midnight special back to Nashville. Get in there sleep three or four hours, do the *Grand Ole Opry* and catch a plane back out that night and fly back to California. Hey, you know what it paid me in those days? Fifteen dollars. I probably spent $250 coming back and forth. So it cost me money to work the *Grand Ole Opry*.

I can tell you several artists who have used the *Grand Ole Opry* as a stepping-stone to their career, and they say how much they've enjoyed it and how much it means to them. They get all that publicity and all that hype and then you don't see 'em for three or four years. They might come back when the network wants them. But they don't care anything about the music, and they don't care anything about the show. They're just users. They use the name. They use the association; it's not like they had to have it to make their career, but they chose to. They chose to be a part of it, but they don't have any loyalty to it. Vince Gill does. Garth Brooks does. Outside of that, there's not many others who do.

After your generation of Opry *performers retires, who's going to carry that torch?*

I don't really know because it was different when we were working. We were owned by an insurance company, and the *Grand Ole Opry* was never designed to be a big money maker. It was designed to entertain people and help sell insurance by the identification. It never was designed to be a "ticket item" like it's having to become now. They say, "The *Grand Ole Opry* ain't makin' as much money as we want it to make." Well, hey that whole complex would not be there unless we paid the price for keeping it alive. But they don't see it that way because they didn't have to make it, they just bought it. You can buy the name but you can't buy the show. The show ain't for sale.

So are you saying that we could be seeing the end of the Opry?

I'm not going to say because I don't know what kind of a music trend may happen. But if it keeps on like this, the average life of an artist nowadays ain't but about four or five years. I've been doing this since I was fifteen years old. I've been making music forty something years, fifty years.

So I'm not really sure exactly how the *Grand Ole Opry* is going to fare. You have people who know nothing about the history of it. You can give somebody a book to read or a program to fill but if they didn't live this particular show for any length of time, then they don't know what it really means to be an historical entity. And that's what's happened. They have no earthly idea of what went on before because it's something that happened before their time and they could care less.

You're talking about the management?

Yeah.

Is alternative country the next generation or is the country-pop or down-right pop of Faith Hill?

Faith Hill is a good singer. She's a beautiful woman. The first time I introduced her on the *Opry*, the first time she was ever there, she was delighted to be there. But they use country music as a stepping-stone. The real ambition is to be a pop artist. They can't get started in the pop field so they come on and say, "I love country music. I love country music." Then they get a hit and when they can do something for the business, they don't do it. It shows their hypocrisy. I'm not talking about Faith. She's a lovely lady with a lot of talent. You can't knock talent; it's success. Tim McGraw I don't know very well. I don't think I'd walk across the street to pay to see him. But as I said, you can't knock success.

There's been an album that's been the number one album from the soundtrack of *O Brother Where Are Thou?* And it shows that people are hungry for some type of music other than this pop-rock stuff that they call country nowadays, something real, something substantial. It's all a money game, and I've heard the guys who are in charge of Warner Brothers, and the guys who were in charge of Sony, the guys who are in charge of MCA get up and make statements: "We're going to get rid of that country crap. We're going to put out what we want to. We like the Eagles." That's what you got. You got rock 'n' roll artists who can't get a job no more and so they come and they infiltrate Nashville and try to tell everybody this is country music. And that's what I resent. I resent California and New York taking over a business that we created and calling it their own and making it something else.

We weren't platinum album people, but we sold enough to make these companies big money. We didn't have to spend $100,000 to make a singer. We could do it on $250 when I first started. I never had an album that cost more that $4,000 or $5,000 to make. Now it's $150,000 to $200,000. There's so much graft and greed going on the poor ol' artist don't know what he's doing. Graft and greed is what caused this business to change. I guess that I'm telling you a lot of things that are probably detrimental to me. Well, what are they going to do to my career? Kill it?

Interviews with Billy Walker were conducted on June 9, 2001, and August 6, 2001.

Notes

1. Colin Escott, "Billy Walker: Cross the Brazos at Waco" (liner notes), Bear Family Records compact discs, 1993. BCD 15657 FI.
2. Buddy Lee Attractions publicity material. Undated.
3. In the 1950s, Al Gannaway produced programs for television syndication featuring *Grand Ole Opry* performers.
4. Luther Perkins and Marshall Grant were the Tennessee Two, Johnny Cash's band.
5. Husky recorded humorous records in the 1950s under the name Simon Crum.
6. Walker is referring to Jimmy Elledge's version of "Funny How Time Slips Away." It was produced by Chet Atkins and reached number twenty-two on the *Billboard* pop charts in 1962.
7. Presley's last appearance on a regularly scheduled *Louisiana Hayride* broadcast was March 31, 1956.
8. Fred Foster founded Monument Records in 1958.

BIBLIOGRAPHY

Arnold, Eddy. *It's a Long Way from Chester County.* Old Tappan, N.J.: Hewitt House, 1969.

Cusic, Don. *Sheb Wooley: Rawhide/How the West Was Won* (Liner notes). Bear Family Records compact discs, 1995. BCD 15899-AH.

Dawidoff, Nicholas. *In the Country of Country: A Journey to the Roots of American Music.* New York: Vintage, 1998.

Escott, Colin. *Billy Walker: Cross the Brazos at Waco* (liner notes). Bear Family Records compact discs, 1993. BCD 15657 FI.

Escott, Colin, with George Merritt and William MacEwen. *Hank Williams: The Biography.* Boston: Little Brown, 1994.

Franks, Tillman, with Robert Gentry. *Tillman Franks: I Was There When It Happened.* Many, La.: Sweet Dreams Publishing Company, 2000.

Guralnick, Peter. *Last Train to Memphis: The Rise of Elvis Presley.* Boston: Little, Brown, 1994.

Guralnick, Peter. *Lost Highway: Journeys and Arrivals of American Musicians.* Boston: D. R. Godine, 1979.

Guralnick, Peter, and Ernest Jorgensen. *Elvis Day by Day: The Definitive Record of His Life and Music.* New York: Ballantine, 1999.

Kingsbury, Paul, ed. *The Encyclopedia of Country Music.* New York: Oxford University Press, 1998.

Lynn, Loretta, with George Vecsey. *Coal Miner's Daughter.* New York: Warner Books, 1976.

Lynn, Loretta, with Patsi Bale Cox. *Still Woman Enough: A Memoir.* New York: Hyperion, 2002.

Malone, Bill C. *Country Music USA.* Austin: University of Texas Press, 1985.

Malone, Bill C. *Don't Get Above Your Raisin': Country Music and the Southern Working Class.* Urbana: University of Illinois Press, 2002.

Malone, Bill C., and Judith McCulloh, eds. *Stars of Country Music: Uncle Dave Macon to Johnny Rodriguez.* Urbana: University of Illinois Press, 1975.

Nash, Alanna. *Behind Closed Doors: Talking with the Legends of Country Music*. New York: Knopf, 1988.

Pride, Charley, with Jim Henderson. *Pride: The Charley Pride Story*. New York: Morrow, 1994.

Whitburn, Joel. *Top Country Singles, 1944–1993*. Menomonee Falls, Wisc.: Record Research, 1994.

Whitburn, Joel. *Top Pop Singles, 1955–1993*. Meonomonee Falls, Wisc.: Record Research, 1994.

INDEX